Changing Japanese Business, Economy and Society

Also by Masao Nakamura

JAPAN IN THE GLOBAL AGE: Cultural, Historical and Political Issues on Asia, Environment, Households and International Communication (*editor*)

THE JAPANESE BUSINESS AND ECONOMIC SYSTEM: History and Prospects for the 21st Century (*editor*)

THE SECOND PAYCHECK: A Socio-Economic Analysis of Earnings (*with Alice Nakamura*)

Changing Japanese Business, Economy and Society

Globalization of Post-Bubble Japan

Edited by

Masao Nakamura

Konwakai Japan Research Chair and Professor
Institute of Asian Research and Sauder School of Business
University of British Columbia
Vancouver, Canada

First published 2004 by
PALGRAVE MACMILLAN
Houndmills, Basingstoke, Hampshire RG21 6XS and
175 Fifth Avenue, New York, N.Y. 10010
Companies and representatives throughout the world

PALGRAVE MACMILLAN is the global academic imprint of the Palgrave
Macmillan division of St. Martin's Press, LLC and of Palgrave Macmillan Ltd.
Macmillan® is a registered trademark in the United States, United Kingdom
and other countries. Palgrave is a registered trademark in the European
Union and other countries.

ISBN 1–4039–4134–3

This book is printed on paper suitable for recycling and made from fully
managed and sustained forest sources.

A catalogue record for this book is available from the British Library.

Library of Congress Cataloging-in-Publication Data
Changing Japanese business, economy, and society: globalization
    of post-bubble Japan / edited by Masao Nakamura.
        p.   cm.
    Includes bibliographical references and index.
    ISBN 1–4039–4134–3
    1. Organizational change.   2. Globalization.   3. Social change—Japan.
    4. Japan—Economic conditions—1989–   I. Nakamura, Masao, Ph. D.
    HD58.8.C4626 2004
    306.3'0952—dc22   2004041582

10   9   8   7   6   5   4   3   2   1
13   12   11   10   09   08   07   06   05   04

Printed and bound in Great Britain by
Antony Rowe Ltd, Chippenham and Eastbourne

Contents

Foreword by Pitman Potter   vii

Notes on the Contributors   xiv

1   Introduction   1
   Masao Nakamura

Part I   Japanese Views on Globalization

2   Ryotaro Shiba (1923–96) and the Call for Meiji Values
   in a Global Age   17
   Sinh Vinh

3   Surviving a Globalized World: Lessons to be Learned
   from Japan's Problem-Solving Incapability   40
   Yoshihiko Wada

4   The Mind Roaming above the Ocean: Mental Health
   of Young Japanese Sojourners in Vancouver   55
   Etsuko Kato

5   Okinawa after the Cold War and the Return
   of American Military Bases   77
   Keisuke Enokido

**Part II   A Changing Business Environment: Individual
         Rights and Globalization**

6   Aging, Female and Foreign Workers, and Japanese
   Labor Markets: An International Perspective   107
   Alice Nakamura, Masao Nakamura and Atsushi Seike

7   *Gaijin* (Foreign) Sumo Wrestlers Help Japanese
   Tradition to March On: A Case Study of Foreigners
   in a Japanese Labor Market   144
   Takanobu Nakajima and Kazuhiro Harakawa

8 Gender as Intersectionality: Multiple Discrimination
   against Minority Women in Japan   158
   Jennifer Chan-Tiberghien

Part III   Post-Bubble Japanese Business: Adjusting
           to the New Era

9 Why Does Japan Receive So Little Direct Investment
   from Abroad?   185
   Shujiro Urata

10 Japanese Society under Marketization and
    Globalization   203
    Takanobu Nakajima

11 The Post-Bubble Japanese Business System and
    Globalization: Implications for Japanese Society   220
    Masao Nakamura and Kozo Horiuchi

Index   261

Foreword

This volume presents research findings concerning the effects of globalization on social cohesion in Japan. The research was conducted in connection with a project at the Institute of Asian Research at the University of British Columbia entitled 'Comparative International Studies of Social Cohesion and Globalization'. Supported by a strategic grant from the Social Sciences and Humanities Research Council of Canada, the project focused on research and knowledge-building on issues of globalization and social cohesion in five countries in Asia – China, Indonesia, Japan, Korea and Sri Lanka. This volume on Japan has been prepared under the direction of Professor Masao Nakamura of the University of British Columbia. The context for this important work can be understood by reference to the broader dimensions of studies of globalization and social cohesion.

Perspectives on globalization

Globalization has been a feature of the human condition for several centuries. In recent years, particularly in the aftermath of the Cold War, globalization conditions have accelerated with increasingly permeable national borders easily penetrated by flows of capital, people and information. To a large extent, this process has been justified by ideologies of liberalism and concomitant support for free markets, free trade and freedom of ideas. Globalization is not the same as internationalization, which presupposes cooperation and interaction among autonomous nation-states, but rather is a process by which the state itself is challenged.[1]

The phenomenon of globalization may be addressed in terms of material and ideological dimensions, recognizing that these are at once intersecting and yet possessed of distinct features. Material aspects of globalization extend to changing content and processes of print and electronic media; diet and dress; economic, business and financial structures and processes; relationships between labor and capital; knowledge and technology; and many other operational elements of globalization. These material dimensions create new opportunities and expectations for exchange and communication. In addition, the material dimensions of globalization encourage a self-supporting value system that privileges some and marginalizes others, based on their access, familiarity and facility with these material dimensions. Material dimensions also contribute to and derive from ideological dimensions.

Ideological dimensions include official and popular attitudes and rhetoric on social, political and economic organization and behavior, and other expressions of norms, values and beliefs that both inform and derive from material elements. In particular, the discourse of globalization also describes the spread of liberal ideals of individualism, autonomy and capitalism around the world.[2] Globalization of private law, for example, is often juxtaposed with public law regimes aimed at a collectivist approach to social welfare,[3] and it is also proposed as an antidote to 'crony capitalism' and other perceived ills in the economies of East and South East Asia.[4] While the capacity of the liberal industrial economies to promote visions of globalization derives as much from political and economic power as from the inherent wisdom of the ideas themselves,[5] there is little doubt that the influence of liberal ideals of private property have spread dramatically since the 1990s. The circumstances of the United Nations Convention on Contracts for the International Sale of Goods (CISG) and the World Trade Organization (WTO) agreements on intellectual property rights ('TRIPs Agreement'), trade related investment measures ('TRIMs Agreement'), trade in services ('GATS Agreement'), and dispute resolution (the 'Dispute Resolution Understanding') are particularly noteworthy examples of the globalization of private law and private property regimes.[6] The CISG Convention establishes uniform default rules for international sales contracts that impose norms drawn from the liberal market systems. The WTO reflects *inter alia* the export of liberal notions of private property rights particularly in the areas of intellectual property rights enforcement and protection of investment rights. The WTO's Dispute Resolution Understanding, particularly its provisions for binding decisions by dispute resolution panels, reflects liberal norms of legal institutionalism. The liberal legal norms associated with globalization constitute a belief system driven by changing historical conditions of socio-economic and political relations in Europe and North America. The essentially one-way direction by which these norms are disseminated around the world reflects imbalances in political and economic power between developed and developing economies that characterize the current dynamic of globalization.

In the face of these trends, state governments are challenged to devise policies to ensure protection of public good within their jurisdictions, despite their weakening level of control. Protection of labor and environmental conditions is threatened by the prospect of capital flight in the face of regulatory initiatives. The state's capacity to prevent the introduction of pornography and hate literature is undermined by the prospect of trade sanctions aimed at securing market access for media industries. Policies aimed at capital accumulation and development of indigenous technologies are challenged by a combination of private capital mobility and state action in pursuit of the free trade objectives of the private sector. While globalization has been linked to these and other issues of the political economy of markets, the linkage between globalization and local social cohesion is less well understood.

Dimensions of social cohesion

Although the prerequisites and conditions for social cohesion are not well understood, its absence can be identified by reference to dimensions of conformity and diversity in political and socio-economic conditions, and by instances of social disorder.

Conformity and diversity

If the process of building social cohesion can be analyzed in light of the dimensions of belonging, inclusion, participation, recognition and legitimacy these dimensions in turn can be assessed in light of the interplay between conformity and diversity. Conditions of conformity and diversity may be examined by reference to data on the extent of differentiation in patterns of social, economic and political relations.[7] Conformity and diversity in economic relations would be measured by reference data on differentiation in patterns of income, employment, consumption, housing, transportation and so on. In the area of social relations, conformity and diversity would be examined by reference to data on differentiation in patterns of religion, belief and ideology, norms of family relations, socio-economic dualism and pluralism, privilege and marginalization with respect to class and gender, ethnicity and so on. In the political area, the conformity and diversity would be examined by reference to data on differentiation in patterns of political participation, institutions and their operation and effect, political-legal culture, and other variables.

Social disorder

While all states and their governments have a strong interest in maintaining social cohesion for the purpose of social welfare and good governance, the mechanisms by which social cohesion is achieved remain obscure. If social cohesion is taken to mean 'the ongoing process of developing a community of shared values, shared challenges and equal opportunity based on a sense of trust, hope and reciprocity',[8] then it falls to the state and the society to create the conditions by which this process can be achieved. Although the prerequisites and conditions for social cohesion are not well understood, its absence can be identified by reference to data on breakdowns in social order. Data on social disorder extend to conditions attendant on riots, political disturbances and so on in the selected countries prior to and during the globalization era. The analysis extends beyond simply the recording of events to include content analysis of published reporting, to achieve understanding of the contexts, origins, responses and aftermath of the reported breakdowns in social order.

By comparing conditions of conformity and diversity in social, political and economic relations with conditions of the breakdown of social order, the research builds on the work of Chandler, Sigelman and Tsai,[9] who looked strictly at the division of labor. Division of labor in economic relations is one (but by no means the only) measure of conformity and diversity. By separating social, economic and political relations, the study can examine the ways in which these relationships (which admittedly overlapped to some degree) reflect conditions of conformity and diversity. This then permits the policy consequences to be seen in broader terms than simply issues of economic performance.[10] The multifaceted approach would permit linkages to be drawn between conditions of social, economic or political conformity, and diversity and instances of the breakdown of social cohesion, thus going beyond the existing work, which examines social diversity in the context of economic growth.[11] By examining the combined factors of social, economic and political relations and the extent to which conformity and diversity exists within this, the project addresses the more comprehensive issue of social capital. This in turn may be linked with conditions of cohesion, economic diversity and economic growth.[12]

By relying on various dimensions of social cohesion, the project builds on existing literature addressing social cohesion generally. However, rather than assume that diversity has a potential for social conflict or contributing factors to social cohesion,[13] the project hopes to identify how complementarity between conformity and diversity can contribute to social cohesion under different conditions.[14] The complementary relationship between conformity and diversity may contribute to localized perceptions of, and resolutions of, issues of social cohesion by reference to the importance of building social capital.[15] Approaches to complementarity may also help to resolve the issue of perception, which is seen as a critical component in the feeling of belonging that is an important dynamic of cohesion.[16] This project examines these various factors in cross-national context to generate an understanding of the global dimensions of social cohesion.

Study of Japan

Understanding the relationships between globalization and social cohesion requires an international comparative approach that generates data and analysis of conditions in a diverse array of countries and societies. The experience of Western liberal states with globalization is mediated and eased significantly by the commonality of legal and political institutions. In Asia, by contrast, governing legal and political institutions are either indigenous and relatively alien to the liberal tradition, or imposed through a process of colonialism and neo-colonialism, and thus also in conflict with the notion of the supremacy of liberalism. In addition, Asian states and societies embrace a wide variety of economic, social and political conditions. Also, in part as a result of their increased participation in the globalization process and the phenomenon of rapid economic growth, the conditions of specialization of labor that Durkheim identified as an important factor in social cohesion are evident as conditions of transition.

This volume on globalization and social cohesion in Japan includes reports on local perspectives on globalization, individual rights and changing business practices. Specific topics include such issues as challenges in Japanese problem-solving, mental health among Japanese migrants, labour and gender relations, foreign direct investment and market change. The volume illustrates the ways in which the impact of globalization depends heavily on local material and ideological conditions. Japanese historical perspectives on the world, as well as material features such as outward migration and accommodation of foreign military bases in Japan, provide an important context for Japan's engagement with the world. And differing perspectives and conditions on labour, gender and tradition have a significant impact on the ways that Japan's business environment engages with global forces. Adjustment of Japanese business to the challenges of globalization in turn reflects a complex range of local ideological and material factors. The Japan study suggests that while globalization poses challenges for pre-existing values and material relations, local norms and power relations also determine much about the process and outcomes of interaction with globalization.

As a major component in the Institute of Asian Research's interdisciplinary project on 'Globalization and Social Cohesion in Asia', the Japan study complements our other country studies on China, Indonesia, Korea and Sri Lanka. We hope also that the Japan volume will stand alone as an important contribution to knowledge about this important economy and as further testimony to the ways that the Asian experience with globalization remains intersected with local conditions.

PITMAN POTTER

Notes

1 Noam Chomsky, *World Orders Old and New* (New York: Columbia University Press, 1994); David Held *et al.*, *Global Transformations: Politics, Economics and Culture* (Stanford, Calif.: Stanford University Press, 1999); Saskia Sassen, *Losing Control? Sovereignty in an Age of Globalization* (New York: Columbia University Press, 1993).
2 See, generally, K. Jayasuriya (ed.) *Law, Capitalism and Power in Asia* (London, Routledge, 1999); A. Woodiwiss, *Globalization, Human Rights and Labour Law in Pacific Asia* (Cambridge University Press, 1998); T. Ginsburg, 'Does Law Matter for Economic Development?', *Law and Society Review* (2000), vol. 34, no. 3, pp. 829–56; D. Trubek *et al.*, 'Global Restructuring and the Law: The Internationalization of Legal Fields and the Creation of Transnational Arenas', *Case Western Reserve Law Review* (1994), vol. 44, no. 2, pp. 407–98; P. B. Potter, 'Property: Questioning Efficiency, Liberty and Imperialism', in N. Mercuro and W. J. Samuels (eds), *The Fundamental Interrelationships Between Government and Property* (Stamford, Conn., JAI Press, 1999), pp. 177–90; D. Barry and R. C. Keith, *Regionalism, Multilateralism and the Politics of Global Trade* (Vancouver, University of British Columbia Press, 1999); F. Jameson and M. Miyoshi (eds) *The Cultures of Globalization* (Durham, North Carolina, Duke University Press, 1998); F. J. Lechner and J. Boli (eds) *The Globalization Reader* (Malden, Mass., Blackwell, 2000); F. Rajaee, *Globalization on Trial: The Human Condition and the Information Civilization* (Ottawa, International Development Research Centre, 2000); J. Tomlinson, *Globalization and Culture* (Chicago, University of Chicago Press, 1999).
3 David Kennedy, 'Receiving the International', *Connecticut Journal of International Law* (1994), vol., 10, no. 1, p. 1.
4 See, generally, G. W. Noble and J. Ravenhill (eds) *The Asian Financial Crisis and the Architecture of Global Finance* (Cambridge University Press, 2000); G. Segal and D. S. G. Goodman (eds) *Towards Recovery in Pacific Asia* (London: Routledge, 2000). For discussion of the applicability of liberal models of financial regulation to developing economies, see S. Haggard and C. H. Lee, *Financial Systems and Economic Policy in Developing Countries* (Ithaca, NY, Cornell University Press, 1995); and S. Haggard, C. H. Lee and S. Maxfield (eds) *The Politics of Finance in Developing Countries*, (Ithaca, NY, Cornell University Press, 1993).
5 R. H. Wagner, 'Economic Interdependence, Bargaining Power and Political Influence,' *International Organization* (1988), vol. 42, no. 3, p. 461.

6   Citations for all laws, regulations and treaties are provided in www.wto.org and www.un.org.
7   Emile Durkheim, *The Division of Labour in Society* (Trans. W. D. Halls) (London: Macmillan, 1984).
8   Jane Jenson, *Mapping Social Cohesion: The State of Canadian Research*, Canadian Policy Research Networks Study No. F03 (Ottawa: Renouf Publishing, 1998).
9   Charles Chandler, Lee Sigelman and Yung-Mei Tsai, 'The Division of Labour and Social Disorder: A Cross-National Test of a Durkheimian Interpretation', *International Journal of Comparative Sociology* (1986), vol. 27 nos 3–4, pp. 161–71.
10 Dominique M. A. Haughton and Swati Mukerjee (1995) 'The Economic Measurement and Determinants of Diversity', *Social Indicators Research*, vol. 36, pp. 201–25.
11 Ajit Bhalla and Frédéric Lapeyre, 'Social Exclusion: Towards an Analytical and Operational Framework', *Development and Change* (1997), vol. 28, pp. 413–33.
12 John W. Wagner and Steven C. Deller, 'Measuring the Effects of Economic Diversity on Growth and Stability', *Land Economics* (1998), vol. 74, no. 4, pp. 541–57.
13 Albert O. Hirschman, 'Social Conflicts as Pillars of Democratic Market Society', *Political Theory* (1994), vol. 22, no. 2, pp. 203–18.
14 Bert Useem, 'Solidarity Model, Breakdown Model, and the Boston Anti-Busing Movement', *American Sociological Review* (1980), vol. 45, no. 3, pp. 357–69.
15 Roger Blakeley, 'Social Capital and Public Policy', Abstract (n.d.). Social Capital Database.
16 Kenneth A. Bollen and Rick H. Hoyle, 'Perceived Cohesion: A Conceptual and Empirical Examination', *Social Forces* (1990), vol. 69, no. 2, pp. 479–504; J. C. Buckner, 'The Development of an Instrument and Procedure to Assess the Cohesiveness of Neighbourhoods', *Dissertation Abstracts International* (1986), vol. 47, 2669B–2670B (University Microfilms No. 86–20. 752).

Notes on the Contributors

Jennifer Chan-Tiberghien is Assistant Professor in the Faculty of Education, and a Faculty Associate of the Center for Research in Women's Studies and Gender Relations, University of British Columbia, Vancouver, Canada.

Keisuke Enokido is a PhD student in the School of Community and Regional Planning, University of British Columbia, Vancouver, Canada.

Kazuhiro Harakawa is an undergraduate student in the Faculty of Business and Commerce, Keio University, Tokyo, Japan.

Kozo Horiuchi is Professor and former Dean of the Faculty of Humanity and Environment, Hosei University, Tokyo, Japan.

Etsuko Kato is Assistant Professor of Anthropology, International Christian University, Tokyo, Japan.

Takanobu Nakajima is a Professor in the Faculty of Business and Commerce, Keio University, Tokyo, Japan.

Alice Nakamura is Professor in the School of Business, University of Alberta, Edmonton, Canada.

Masao Nakamura is Professor and Konwakai Chair of Japanese Research at the Sauder School of Business, Institute of Asian Research and Faculty of Applied Science, University of British Columbia, Vancouver, Canada.

Pitman Potter is Director of the Institute of Asian Research, and a Professor in the Faculty of Law, University of British Columbia, Vancouver, Canada.

Atsushi Seike is Professor in the Faculty of Business and Commerce, Keio University, Tokyo, Japan.

Shujiro Urata is Professor in the School of Social Sciences, Waseda University, Tokyo, Japan.

Sinh Vinh is Professor in the Department of History, University of Alberta, Edmonton, Canada.

Yoshihiko Wada is Associate Professor in the Faculty of Economics, Doshisha University, Kyoto, Japan.

1
Introduction*

Masao Nakamura

In recent decades, Japan has pursued policies of internationalization and globalization in many aspects of both private- and public-sector affairs. For example, in the 1980s and 1990s, many Japanese universities added an 'international department', and generous budgets were allocated for these. Also, many Japanese firms began investing more heavily overseas. Nevertheless, internationalization as a concept, and interest in this, in Japan substantially pre-dates the 1980s. The Meiji Restoration in 1868 opened up Japan to foreign countries,[1] and internationalization in the sense of learning from the West was of the utmost importance to the Meiji government. The Meiji view was that Japan needed to catch up with the West in order to avoid being colonized. Another wave of internationalization initiatives swept the nation after Japan's defeat in the Second World War. Japan was gripped by an urgent national urge to learn about Western perspectives and standards, and about institutions such as democracy and competitive markets. In addition, increased interest in internationalization accompanied successive attempts within Japan to liberalize the nation's trade rules.[2] All along, however, some Japanese feared internationalization; they worried that some of the new ways brought in from abroad might harm Japanese society.

The strong negative feelings of some Japanese towards internationalization have tended to go hand in hand with an inward-looking and isolationist way of thinking.[3] These reactions hamper the implementation of changes that are needed to enable Japan to achieve the internationalization goals set out by the country's leaders and for the nation to maintain its standing in the world community.

In this book, different aspects of Japan's globalization are discussed from a variety of points of view. The discussions illustrate factors that

1

could shape, or be useful for predicting, developments in Japan's markets for labor and goods. Many of the issues are familiar to Western firms. Indeed, foreign firms that faced, and solved, some of these problems elsewhere in previous years may find new business opportunities through selling solutions to Japan!

The issues dealt with in this book range from business and economics to social and government relations practices and policies. The issues discussed are interrelated, all linked to Japan's globalization and the influence and roles of government and businesses.

In Chapter 2, Sinh Vinh discusses contemporary thinking about globalization espoused by the Japanese historian Ryotaro Shiba – a way of thinking that has been embraced by large numbers of Japanese. Ryotaro Shiba[4] is regarded by many in Japan as the most influential historian of the latter half of the twentieth century. Many Japanese, including four of Japan's recent prime ministers,[5] have publicly declared their support for his views concerning the historical course Japan has taken in recent decades. In his writings, Shiba has asserted repeatedly that Japan cannot ignore globalization and must internationalize. What convinced him of this is his recognition that freedom and human rights marked the standard of civilization in the late twentieth century. In his view, Japan was (and is) isolated, and has tended to take civilization for granted. Shiba asserts that Japan has adopted bits and pieces of what civilization means, but not civilization in its essential whole. At the same time, Vinh notes that Shiba has raised grave concerns about the effects of internationalization on Japan, and has suggested a number of philosophical dimensions in which he feels that Japan might take leadership with respect to the evolving nature of internationalization.

Isolation from the rest of the world has shaped much of Japan's history. Alliances with other countries have not been part of the Japanese way. In Shiba's view, embracing freedom and human rights at home, and taking leadership in a world where freedom and human rights are the guiding principles, would require Japan to accept alliances. Yet Japan lacks the experience and skills to form alliances. This is part of the basis of Shiba's concerns about internationalizing Japan. In Chapter 2, Vinh elaborates on Shiba's thinking about formative events in Japan's modern history. Vinh also discusses Shiba's suggestions regarding how Japan might cope with internationalization and alliances.

Throughout the rest of this book, the types of problems raised by Shiba, that Vinh outlines, concerning Japan's internationalization are discussed in various contexts and from various perspectives, with an emphasis on what they mean for Japanese society.

In Chapter 3, Yoshihiko Wada discusses the ineptness of public decision-making in Japanese society. In the West, disclosure of accurate information to the public is deemed to be essential for the proper functioning of a democratic society. For example, disclosure by public corporations of correct accounting information is absolutely expected in the USA, and this presumption is embodied in US accounting regulations. Public disclosure of accurate information is seen in the USA as a precondition for the efficient functioning of securities markets and essential for protecting investors from fraud. The USA also has strict product liability rules and anti-trust laws to protect consumers, and compliance is encouraged through the expenditure of substantial amounts of public resources for monitoring and enforcement. Violators are often severely punished. Japan has lagged behind both the USA and the European Union (EU) in this regard. Nevertheless, Wada feels that globalization has been forcing Japan to move forward in this area, especially with regard to the interests of the public when these are visibly threatened.

Wada discusses a number of recent situations in Japan when accurate information was withheld intentionally from the public. In some of these situations, events subsequently proved that the failure to provide accurate information had been contrary to the public interest. For example, Wada cites the suppression of legally required auto recalls, the failure to properly inform the public concerning fatal side effects of government-approved drugs, and the omission of certain operational steps that were legally required for running nuclear power plants and nuclear fuel processing facilities. Often no penalties were imposed on violators who were caught, or the penalties handed down were so light they could not have been expected to discourage effectively future fraudulent reporting.

In Japan, close relationships between Japanese businesses and government bureaucrats have been commonplace. While these relationships may facilitate national economic planning,[6] it seems clear that they also encourage companies to find ways of influencing the government monitoring authority. The predictable consequence is that government monitoring does not function effectively. Wada argues that the negative aspects of relationships of this sort were a drag on the Japanese economy throughout the late 1980s and the 1990s. Many bribery cases have emerged involving Japanese government bureaucrats at all levels, and most of the guilty parties received light sentences.[7] Wada forecasts that, if the current lack of adequate protection of the public interest continues, this will inhibit Japan in trying to develop a sustainable society in the twenty-first century, a century when countries with liberal democracies are expected to prevail globally. He suggests that, in order to develop a sustainable society – one consistent with the globalizing world – Japan must build tangible, high-profile negative feedback mechanisms that have teeth and muscle, backed by a credible will to force corporations and government offices to disclose accurate information.

The next two chapters describe the experiences of some special groups of Japanese citizens. These experiences point to further problems associated with globalization that Japanese society has not been responding to adequately. In Chapter 4, Etsuko Kato describes the overseas experiences of increasing numbers of disenchanted young people. Japan's education system is not structured to respond to students' personal tastes and preferences, and increasing numbers of young people cannot, or choose not to, find regular work in Japan. In these circumstances, Kato argues it is not surprising that some choose to drop out of Japanese society and take their chances overseas: chances that have been opened up by globalization.[8] Being unable to find 'the right places' for themselves in Japan, these young people have left Japan for various overseas locations, often with little in the way of well-defined objectives for study, work or personal development, and have become temporary sojourners in locations around the world. As described in subsequent chapters (for example, Chapters 6 and 11), Japanese labor markets primarily serve the needs of new graduates; they are not set up to facilitate matching between available jobs and job-seekers who are beyond the new-graduate stage. Japanese people who spend their young adult years abroad trying to find themselves, and then return subsequently to seek work in Japan may find it even harder to find suitable work. Kato sees Japan as a society unprepared for coping with people who do not fit into the established system.

In Chapter 5, Keisuke Enokido describes how globalization is affecting the people of Okinawa. Okinawa is both an island and the southern-most prefecture of Japan. It is located strategically in Pacific Asia and was a major battlefield in the Second World War, where many Japanese and US soldiers died. After the war ended in 1945, the USA occupied Okinawa and it became the site of one of the largest US military bases in the region. Unlike the situation in the rest of Japan, however, the US occupation of Okinawa did not end in 1952: it was twenty years later, in 1972, when the USA returned Okinawa to Japan.[9] However, even then, the USA retained all its military installations there. This continuing American presence in Okinawa, with a very large number of US soldiers based there, has been a source of social problems and concerns for the local population.[10]

In his chapter, Enokido documents and discusses a number of these social problems, focusing on them from the perspective of the perceptions of the residents of Okinawa. The most pressing of these problems are crimes committed by US military personnel. Okinawa's historical role as an important provider of military bases, first to the Japanese military until the end of the Second World War, and then to the US military after the war, makes this prefecture unique in Japan. Okinawa's experiences are not well understood by other Japanese. The life and fate of the people of Okinawa are, in many ways, dictated by Japan's global policies and are greatly affected by the Japan–USA Security Treaty. This treaty obliges Japan to maintain the massive US military installations in Okinawa (as well as elsewhere in Japan). Enokido argues that Okinawa mirrors global geopolitics and the position of Japan within this political milieu. In the main, the Japanese government's policies towards Okinawa have been limited to economic development planning.[11] In most practical respects, the Japanese government has continued to support US military policies in Japan and in the Pacific region, including the continuation of the Japan–US security treaty. Enokido explains that the residents of Okinawa would like to achieve a breakthrough in their relationship with the outside world, but feel that so far they have made little progress. He states that the prime concern of the people of Okinawa, the issue of the US military bases, is not even on the agenda at higher levels of government, either within or outside Japan. Enokido feels that the people of Okinawa must actively pursue alliances with stakeholders. Enokido suggests, in particular, that one way to overcome the current impasse is for the people of Okinawa to develop stronger and wider connections with external non-governmental organizations (NGOs) that are willing and able to play active roles in both forcing other Japanese and the Americans to treat local Okinawan concerns and preferences more seriously.

Institutional, economic and cultural factors reflecting deeply-rooted social values are believed partially to explain the low level of labour force participation and the very limited upward mobility in the work-place of Japanese women. These factors could affect both the demand for, and the supply of, female labor. For example, if Japanese culture is perceived as being responsible for the observed low level of career commitment on the part of the majority of married women in Japan, especially after they have children, this could lead employers to decide against investing in the human capital of their female employees, or to avoid hiring women altogether. No single employer, in isolation, can change the culture or social norms of a nation. In these circumstances, employers would be expected to be reluctant to invest in the human capital of their female workers because of their short anticipated job tenure.[12]

In Chapter 6, Alice Nakamura, Masao Nakamura and Atsushi Seike discuss employers' hiring practices and other employment decision processes. They argue that these practices discourage women from working, and are part of the explanation of why so many female workers choose to give up work after marriage or childbirth. Japanese culture is also believed to be one reason for the slow and indecisive way in which the labor market for foreign workers in Japan has been developing. The tiny population in Japan of legal immigrants reflects Japan's official immigration policies. At the same time, the number of illegal foreign workers has continued to increase, and employers in many sectors of the Japanese economy need these illegal workers.

Another demographic issue facing Japan is the rapid aging of the population. Japan's total population is expected to begin shrinking in a few years' time, both absolutely and proportionately, and the older age groups will grow relative to the younger and working-age ones. The public policy issues Japan faces in this area are fraught with conflicting views as to what is happening and what should be done. Few practical solutions have been put forward for dealing with the looming labour shortage. Solutions could include enforcing equal employment opportunities for women and relaxing immigration rules. Yet suggested measures such as these have met with vocal disapproval from some quarters and apathy from others. For example, the authors note that the majority of Japanese still believe that bringing in more immigrant workers is not an acceptable option to cope with the relative decline in the younger cohorts of workers.[13]

Sumo wrestling[14] for the Japanese is not just a popular spectator sport. It also represents Japan's tradition and culture. Sumo, like judo and some other traditional Japanese sports, is a formal part of many physical education programs in schools. Many schools also offer sumo as a regular extra-curricular activity for their students. In Chapter 7, Takanobu Nakajima and Kazuhiro Harakawa discuss the economics underlying the management of the Japan Sumo Association (Nihon Sumo Kyokai) which runs Japanese sumo as a spectator sport, and focus on the role of foreign sumo wrestlers. The behavior of foreign sumo wrestlers is of particular interest, Nakajima and Harakawa explain, because the Japan Sumo Association is managed on the basis of what many regard as Japanese management methods. Therefore, an understanding how the Association (employer) and foreign wrestlers (workers) cope with each other can deepen our insight into Japanese practices and how these hold up when foreign workers are involved.

Professional sumo enjoys government endorsement as an important sports activity reflecting authentic Japanese culture. The Japanese public television system broadcasts all the tournaments of the professional sumo tournaments (Grand Sumo) held six times a year (fifteen days for each). Despite all of the privileges accorded to sumo, to run the professional sumo organization as a business while discharging its mission to maintain sumo as a national sport representing Japan's traditional culture is financially an increasingly daunting task.

In the last few decades of the twentieth century, Japan's popular spectator sports increased in number significantly.[15] The proliferation of alternatives has contributed somewhat to a decline in the number of sumo fans as well as a decline in the supply of young Japanese who aspire to become professional sumo wrestlers. Increasingly, many competent foreign sumo wrestlers have been allowed to join the Association as a result of the decline in the number of domestic applicants wrestlers.

Nakajima and Harakawa discuss the economic reasons why the Sumo Association uses a seniority-based wage system and guarantees lifelong employment for all sumo wrestlers who achieve certain levels of professional success, and explain how Sumo wrestlers' careers after their retirement from active participation (which could happen as early as in their early thirties or even late twenties) are set up for them. The types of problems facing foreign sumo wrestlers are similar to those faced by many foreign workers employed by Japanese corporations. Nakajima and Harakawa analyze the reasons why professional sumo became less popular among Japan's young people, and suggest certain changes in the Sumo Association's industrial relations practices that could improve the attractiveness of sumo as a professional career choice for young people.

The discrepancies between Japanese and Western ways of dealing with individual rights continue to puzzle foreign observers. We are living in the twenty-first century, a hallmark of which is a strong commitment to individual rights and liberalism. These are believed by many to be the bedrock on which national competitive strength and prosperity can be built in a globalizing world, with standards that are increasingly global in nature.[16]

And yet, in comparison with the USA and the EU, Japan has far fewer laws, regulations, policies and enforcement mechanisms to help protect individual rights. For example, the country has little in the way of laws or policies to help ensure equal employment opportunities for women and immigrants. Issues to do with individual rights are the focus of Chapters 8 and 11.

In Chapter 8, Jennifer Chan-Tiberghien argues that, despite Japan's relatively slow adoption of Western-style anti-discrimination measures, the recent global developments at the United Nations (UN) and in grassroots non-governmental organizations (NGOs) elsewhere have prompted some Japanese NGOs also to put anti-discrimination issues on their agendas. Chan-Tiberghien focuses on the activities, for example, of the Japan NGO named the Network for the Convention on the Elimination of All Forms of Discrimination Against Women (CEDAW) to promote anti-discrimination against women. (Japan ratified the UN's CEDAW Convention in 1985.) She argues that, while the spread of human rights norms for women and the implementation of these norms within Japan brought about marked improvements in gender equality in the late 1990s, women in certain minority groups continue to suffer from racial and other types of discrimination. Chan-Tiberghien discusses a number of new legal measures that have been adopted in Japan, including the Equal Employment Opportunity Law,[17] the Child Abuse Prevention Law and the Anti-Domestic Violence Law.

Chan-Tiberghien argues that, from the 1990s onwards, the human rights movement brought the issue of discrimination against ethnic, racial and sexual workforce minorities into the open. The pressures to import foreign labor on the one hand and the human rights movement in Japan on the other have opened up questions such as whether Japan will experiment with some model of postnational citizenship based on universal human rights rather than *jus sanguinis*, as has long been accepted in most Western nations. At the same time, the question of why most Japanese women have not chosen to accept Western-style feminism has been left unanswered. Without understanding this, it seems likely that the impact in this area of the NGOs will continue to be limited. Nevertheless, the types of public policies Japan develops for dealing with worker groups such as women and immigrants will have a significant impact on the evolution of the Japanese business and economic system, and on Japanese society as a whole.[18]

Japan is known for massive government regulation of business and other activities. Some feel that this regulation culture has been sapping the potential of the Japanese economy, and a number of these critics believe that one of the most pressing policy issues for Japan is to devise ways of creating space for creative activities via a reduction in regulations. They maintain that one of the main engines for global economic growth has been the deregulation of business activities in many developed and developing countries. In fact, deregulation began in the 1990s and seems to be continuing.

In Chapter 9, Shujiro Urata discusses why Japan continues to attract so little foreign direct investment (FDI) from abroad. Massive increases in the amounts of FDI in the last few decades of the twentieth century are thought to have contributed significantly to the globalization of the world economy.[19] Many developed countries, as well as developing ones, have tried to get foreign firms to set up in their countries. These countries recognize the potential for acquiring the human and physical capital and technology that come with FDI, in addition to direct job creation. Virtually all developed countries have reasonably balanced amounts of inward and outward FDI, the main exception being Japan. In 1999, the Japanese share of world outward FDI was 6.2 per cent while the corresponding figure for inward FDI was a mere 0.8 per cent. In his chapter, Urata argues that excessive regulation and anti-competitive behavior explain some of Japan's low level of inward FDI. He feels that another important reason is the inadequate level of internationalization of Japanese society, thus enabling and fostering the retention of outdated practices. In order to expand FDI in Japan, he feels it is necessary for the Japanese to acknowledge the contributions of foreigners and foreign firms to the country's economy and society. In this regard, Japan's policies since the Meiji Restoration in 1868 have generally pushed the nation in the opposite direction, with an emphasis on exports and outward FDI and a marginalization of imports and inward FDI.[20] Urata argues that, if this isolationist orientation is not reversed from within Japanese society, Japan is unlikely to become fully internationalized and cannot expect to enjoy substantial increases in FDI.

In Chapter 10, Takanobu Nakajima discusses the mechanisms the Japanese government has used historically to maintain a highly regulated society, and mentions that many of these must change. Many Japanese government regulations involve licenses that must be obtained for substantial fees, which must be paid in advance. There is some awareness within Japan that these licensing requirements impose a burden on firms and individuals that may be inhibiting economic activity and innovation. Indeed, the government has attempted to reduce the costs of licensing. However, one of the main approaches to lowering these costs has been the reduction of the selection of options from which applicants are able to choose. Licensing requirements pervade every aspect of Japanese life. Traditionally, all this red tape has helped to make it easier for the government to plan and administer the economy and public services, and to shape society. Also, standardization of the options available to potential licensees is an effective cost-cutting measure, but not one that necessarily deals effectively with the main perceived effects of regulation on the economy. In his chapter, Nakajima also points out that historically it has been the case that, when licensees caused problems (for example, things such as bank fraud, accidents and the fatal side effects of some government-approved medicines), relatively little in the way of *ex-post* responsibilities were imposed on either the licensees or the licensors – the government offices that award the licenses. He argues that the system worked better in the days when the government was involved more directly in the economy and had access to large amounts of accurate information about the Japanese business sector and many other components of society. Nevertheless, Nakajima makes the case that, while Japan's regulatory system worked fairly well back in the high-growth era prior to the mid-1970s, it always had important drawbacks.

Nakajima argues that, if Japan is to succeed in its current reform efforts, the current system of licenses must change, and that Japan must move to an *ex-post-facto* system that permits most firms and individuals to engage in their activities without invasive or expensive government regulation. Under the envisioned model, markets would become the main judge of acceptable activities and would be allowed to play a greater role in determining the success or failure of both businesses and individuals. It is envisioned that, when problems arise – such as when an approved commercial product turns out to be defective and causes customer injuries or other problems – then the licensor and licensee could be held accountable. Where fraud is found to have been involved, Nakajima argues, those responsible must be punished severely for their acts. As he sees it, this envisioned system would better accommodate choices based on individuals' tastes and preferences while keeping licensing costs to a minimum. This system is also pictured as being more consistent with practical realities. For example, the licensee may have key information that is not known to the licensor (the asymmetric information problem). Nakajima explains that this is essentially the US system, and that the reforms (deregulation) currently being undertaken in Japan by Prime Minister Junichiro Koizumi are aimed at achieving this transformation.

As part of this deregulation process, the Koizumi Cabinet has initiated processes aimed at increasing significantly the numbers of professionals such as lawyers and accountants certified by the Japanese government. New US-style law and other professional schools are being created. However, unlike the US situation, the organizational structures, curriculums and personnel of these new professional schools are coming under strict regulation and require approval by the Ministry of Education, Culture, Sports, Science and Technology. At the time of writing, Japan's deregulation process itself appears to be mired in regulations, with its longer-term success in transforming Japanese society into a more Western-style society with less regulation still in question.

In Chapter 11, Masao Nakamura and Kozo Horiuchi discuss Japan's attempts to reform certain long-standing business practices.[21] Many agree that Japan requires significant restructuring to enable the Japanese economy to recover. However, any significant change will probably be costly, partly because it will require readjustments of the existing equilibrium and the distribution of power among people, firms, government and other actors in Japanese society.

Nakamura and Horiuchi describe certain changes that took place in Japan in the 1990s and early 2000s, and discuss the relationships of these to the globalization of Japanese society. They ask which of the many Japanese business practices are more compatible with the US and Western European models. They also consider how Japanese society might cope with internal challenges to reforms in areas such as labor management, supplier management and corporate governance. Reforms in areas including these are needed so that Japanese corporations can acquire needed management skills and prepare to cope with global competition. They also note that significant global pressure is being placed on Japan to introduce new environmental management practices.

Nakamura and Horiuchi argue that one policy problem the Japanese public and private sectors must now face is the formulation of a logical basis (a conceptual framework) for developing practical methods to deal with the diverse needs and interests of various constituents, including taxpayers, workers, shareholders and debt holders. As discussed in Chapter 10, these days the demands of Japanese society are more diverse than ever before with regard to things such as educational, employment and investment opportunities. However, the existing Japanese government and corporate institutions keep trying to provide similar menus of services to those developed during the 1960s–80s. Revised Japanese corporate governance practices must be compatible with diverse public interests. Unfortunately, the hard work of developing and implementing this conceptual framework has not yet moved very far forward; indeed, there are those who argue that it has only just begun.

It is believed that the Japanese business and economic system was in equilibrium in the 1980s, prior to the bursting of the 'bubble' economy. The current ongoing reform must bring the Japanese business and economic system to a new and better equilibrium: one in which most of the stakeholders of Japanese society will feel better off than before. To achieve this goal, it is not sufficient simply to undertake marginal or unidimensional adjustments of specific practices. Comprehensive changes are required and these will become possible only when the Japanese business and economic system as a whole is motivated to change. The way in which Japan achieves this goal will affect not only the Japanese but also the rest of the world. For this reason Japan will certainly continue to be a source of global intellectual curiosity for decades to come.

Notes

* Early versions of the studies for some of the chapters in this book were presented in draft form at a research conference entitled 'Comparative International Studies of Social Cohesion and Globalization', held at the Shanghai Academy of Social Sciences on 26–27 November 2001. The conference was sponsored by the Institute of Asian Research of the University of British Columbia and funded in part by a Social Sciences and Humanities Research Council of Canada (SSHRC) Strategic Grant. The initial research and further development of some of the papers in this volume was also partially supported by funding from that same SSHRC Strategic Grant. We are grateful to this support. In addition, the editor of this volume acknowledges separate research support for completing this volume from SSHRC and from the University of British Columbia Hampton Fund research grants.

1   A few countries (for example, China, the Netherlands), however, had access to commerce with Japan before the Meiji Restoration via the port of Nagasaki.
2   For example, liberalizing the Japanese computer market in the 1970s so that US competitors could sell their products on a more equal footing with Japanese firms, and relaxing the Japanese law prohibiting imports of foreign rice in the 1990s both generated Japanese interest in learning about their foreign competitors.
3   These characteristics were not always present in Japan's history but became very visible from the seventeenth century (the Edo era) onwards.
4   This is Taiichi Fukuda's pen name.
5   This includes the prime minister at the time of writing, Junichiro Koizumi.
6   This is the source of the well-known term 'Japan, Inc'.
7   These bribery cases involved virtually all government agencies including the Ministry of Finance, the Ministry of International Trade and Industry, and the Ministry of Foreign Affairs.
8   Many of these young people take advantage of the no visa entry and working holiday visa arrangements offered to them by some of the countries in North America (for example, Canada), Oceania and Europe.
9   It is generally believed that Eisaku Sato, then Japan's prime minister, was awarded a Nobel peace price for his successful efforts to have Okinawa returned peacefully to Japan.
10 Of the 50,000 US soldiers stationed in Japan at the time of writing, about 30,000 are in Okinawa.

11 Okinawa, along with Hokkaido, has lagged behind the rest of Japan in terms of economic development.
12 In economics terms, this would imply a situation where the reasons for a depressed level of Japanese women's career success include statistical discrimination by Japanese employers (the demand-side problem).
13 This is so despite some rising but minor support in the private sector for more relaxed rules of immigration (for example, Nippon Keidanren (2003)).
14 In Japan sumo is called a sports activity, its spectator sport version being 'Grand Sumo'.
15 In Japan, most of the world's spectator sports have their Japanese counterparts. Particularly popular sports include baseball, soccer, golf and tennis.
16 See, for example, Fukuyama (1991).
17 This revised Equal Employment Opportunities Law still lacks an enforcement clause, the existence of which has been viewed as essential for ensuring equal employment opportunities for women in Canada, the USA and the EU.
18 We should also note that many foreign firms and some Japanese firms operating in Japan have taken advantage of highly educated and trained female labor, which is the yet highly untapped and underutilized human resources in Japan, to their advantage (for example, Morgan and Morgan, 1991).
19 For example, FDI grew at an annual rate of more than 20 per cent throughout the 1980s.
20 One strong argument that has bolstered support within Japan for the promotion of exports while blocking imports is that Japan lacks natural resources and hence must earn foreign exchange to be able to import necessary natural resources from abroad.
21 As was the case with the Meiji Restoration and subsequent internationalization movements, the Japanese government is responding to current pressure to meet the challenges of globalization in terms of the joint Japanese government and business sector policy initiatives. Many joint government–private-sector committees have been set up for this purpose.

References

Fukuyama, Francis (1991) *The End of History and the Last Man* (New York: Free Press).

Morgan, James C. and Morgan, J. Jeffrey (1991) *Cracking the Japanese Market: Strategies for Success in the New Global Economy* (New York: Free Press).

Nippon Keidanren (2003) *JAPAN 2025: Envisioning a Vibrant, Attractive Nation in the Twenty-First Century* (Tokyo). (See also: http://www.keidanren.or.jp/english/policy/vision2025.pdf.)

Part I
Japanese Views on Globalization

2
Ryotaro Shiba (1923–96) and the Call for Meiji Values in a Global Age

Sinh Vinh

'Globalization' generally refers to the development that took place after the end of the Cold War in the early 1990s as more countries embraced free trade economics, leading to greater flows on a global scale of people, goods and money. Even before Japan was caught up in the wave of globalization, an internationalization program had been initiated from the early 1980s by the Japanese government in an attempt to 'internationalize' many aspects of Japan's domestic systems, including rules and regulations, to reduce the 'trade friction' the country experienced with the USA and European countries following the 'economic miracle'. Although there are authors who make a distinction between 'internationalization' and 'globalization' – the former is to be encouraged and the latter to be avoided[1] – the two terms are often used interchangeably. Such is the case in the Japanese language as well, in spite of the fact that the formal translation of 'internationalization' is *kokusaika* and that of globalization is *gurobarizeshon*. In the literature discussed in this chapter, the terms have been interchanged unconsciously; when translating them into English, therefore, I have tried to follow the nuance of the terms as they were originally used in the Japanese language.

Even before Japan experienced the sybaritic period of a 'bubble economy' in the late 1980s, Ryotaro Shiba (1923–96) was among the first in Japan to express his apprehension about his country's fortunes. His immediate concern was the current state of the inflated real estate market in Japan and the investment fever gripping the nation. To him, this alarming situation was more an ethical issue than an economic one (BS, 1996, p. 110). Prior to Shiba's death in 1996, the bubble burst and Japan's economy stagnated, a situation that had been incurred, in the words of one writer, 'by her own affluence' (ibid., p. 60). Even more concerned about Japan's bleak prospects in this new economic atmosphere, Shiba called for the restoration of Meiji values to deal with the myriad problems facing his country in a globalizing world. It is significant to note that a number of incumbent politicians, along with prominent cultural and economic leaders, expressed their profound regret at Shiba's untimely death, and shared his concern for Japan's future prospects. Particularly noteworthy is the fact that four of Japan's prime ministers revealed that not only were they avid readers of Shiba's works, but also that they had been inspired by the ideals imbued in them.

Why did Shiba consider that Japan had no choice but to assume an active leading role in the international community? What was Shiba's view of Japan's current problems? What were the Meiji values that Shiba believed were necessary for Japan's reinvigoration in the global era? Before answering these questions, as background, a biographical sketch of Shiba is in order.

A brief biography of Ryotaro Shiba

Ryotaro Shiba, Teiichi Fukuda's pen name, is generally regarded as the most influential novelist-cum-historian in Japan in the latter half of the twentieth century. Many of the issues in Shiba's works and his inspirational ideas for addressing them can be traced back to his wartime experiences.

While attending Osaka Gaigo Gakko (now Osaka University of Foreign Studies), Shiba was drafted into military service in 1943 and after a brief period of training was sent to a tank regiment in Kwantung in northeastern China. Six months prior to Japan's surrender in August 1945, his tank regiment was transferred back to the Kanto region to defend Tokyo in anticipation of an American landing. During the war years, Shiba was disturbed consistently by the fact that in spite of 'their magnificent appearance', the medium-sized tanks deployed by his regiment 'had neither defensive nor offensive power' (SB, 1996, p. 230). Their steel plate was extraordinarily thin, and their 57 mm gun barrel was too short to produce significant piercing power. Shiba believed that if these tanks were to be engaged against any other country's tanks at that time, they stood no chance of winning (Murai, 1997, p. 44). They were simply unfit for action. He was thus angry at the thought that he and other youths were being sent to the battlefronts simply to die. The questions in the young Shiba's mind during the war became all the more acute at the time of Japan's defeat: 'What had prompted a country to embark upon such a war of absurdity?', 'What was Japan?', and 'Who were the

Japanese?' (Shiba, 1998, pp. 4–5). The works Shiba wrote later were, according to him, also letters addressed to himself, as a means of providing answers to the questions that had disturbed him during the war years.

In 1948, Shiba joined the *Sankei Shinbun* as a reporter. From the mid-1950s, he began to write popular historical novels which were received with enthusiasm by the reading public. In 1960, he was awarded the prestigious Naoki Prize for his *Fukuro no shiro* (*The Citadel at Night*). To follow up his early successes, Shiba decided to leave his job with the newspaper in 1961 in order to devote himself to writing historical novels.

Many of Shiba's works were concerned with those who lived to the best of their ability during turbulent times in Japanese history. He focused in particular on the late Tokugawa and Meiji years, during which Japan transformed itself, to the world's amazement, from being a feudal state of some 260 domains in self-imposed isolation into a unified and modern nation. Through Shiba's works, some figures, who until then had barely been mentioned in Japanese historical textbooks, were rescued and placed at the front of the stage of history and became idols to many readers. Typical of these was Ryoma Sakamoto (1835–67). Before Shiba's masterpiece *Ryoma ga yuku* (*Ryoma Goes*) appeared between 1963 and 1966, few people in Japan were aware of the role this 'man of high purpose' (*shishi*) from the Tosa domain on Shikoku island had played in the political movement that culminated in the Meiji Restoration. Shiba (1963) argues: whereas most *shishi* in the anti-*bakufu* faction took it for granted that bullets were the only means by which the *bakufu* could be overthrown, Ryoma conceived that if one were able to see things from a vantage point a meter higher than ordinary people, then there would be nothing in this life that could only be resolved in one way; as from that vantage point one would be able to find, from different perspectives several solutions to the problem. Ryoma later played a crucial role as an intermediary in the eventual restoration of imperial rule, commonly known as the Meiji Restoration, of 1868. Yet, when the Meiji government was created, he adamantly refused to serve in the new government, saying: 'It was not because I wanted to become an official that I overthrew the *Bakufu* . . . I only wished to open the door of history so that Japan might be able to advance in the future.' Shortly afterwards, he was assassinated by an extremist group in Kyoto. Because of the influence of *Ryoma ga yuku*, Ryoma's name and his role as a *shishi* who had selflessly sacrificed his life for Japan's rejuvenation are referred to with respect whenever people talk about the eventful years prior to the Meiji Restoration.

In 1967, Shiba was given the Mainichi Art Award for *Junshi* (*Following My Lord in Death*), a novel dealing with the life of General Maresuke Nogi (1849–1912), a hero of the Japanese army in the Russo-Japanese War, who committed *seppuku* (self-immolation) following Emperor Meiji's death. Ten years later, in 1976, Japan's Art Academy honored Shiba with the Emperor Prize for his two-volume, non-fictional novel *Kukai no fukei* (*The Landscape of Kukai*). During this period, Shiba also produced other masterpieces such as *Saka no ue no kumo* (*Clouds Over the Hills*), depicting the lives of three young men (Shiki Masaoka and the Akiyama brothers) from Iyo (present-day Ehime prefecture) on Shikoku island, who worked tirelessly during the difficult early Meiji years, and *Tobi ga gotoku* (*As if He Was Flying*; 1975–6) that reconstructs in a lively way the tempestuous political climate of the first ten years of the Meiji era, focusing on its main protagonist, Takamori Saigo (1827–77). In 1982, Shiba received the Yomiuri Literary Prize for *Hitobito no ashiato* (*People's Footprints*), a moving two-volume novel portraying the lives of those growing up under the influences of Shiki Masaoka's poetry. In 1983, he was awarded the Asahi Prize. In 1991, he was honored by the Japanese government as a Person of Cultural Merits (*Bunka korosha*), and two years later was presented with an Order of Culture (*Bunka kunsho*). When Shiba died in March 1996, he was greatly missed by many of his compatriots. He is remembered as a national writer (*kokumin sakka*) and as a cultured man of great erudition, who had written many masterpieces full of historical insights. His contribution to Japan's postwar culture has been compared to that of André Gide, Jean-Paul Sartre and Albert Camus to twentieth-century France.

Japan and internationalization

Why should Japan assume a more active role in the international community? Shiba addressed this question in a lecture, formally entitled 'How to Construct the New Japan' (*Atarashii Nihon o do tsukuru ka*), which he delivered at a forum commemorating the founding of 'The Twenty-first Century Japan Committee' on 10 May 1991. Considering the original title to be somewhat pretentious, when the lecture was revised for publication Shiba changed it to 'Should We Make a Commitment?' (*Fumidashimasu ka?*).[2]

Prior to this lecture, Shiba joined the famous writer Yasushi Inoue in a table-talk (*taidan*) that was arranged by a newspaper company at the request of the latter. Inoue died shortly afterwards, at the age of 83. When the discussion touched on the issue of the 'international environment' surrounding Japan, Inoue said to Shiba tersely and without any elaboration: '[It is now time that] Japan should enter into a partnership, don't you think?' (*Nihon mo kumiai ni hairanakereba narimasen ne?*). The Japanese term for partnership that Inoue used was '*kumiai*', which in Shiba's opinion, was 'typical of Inoue's language' as 'it poetically refers to [that is, 'intuitively invokes' – like a brief *haiku* poem] the essence of the issue of [Japan's] alliance (*yoriai*) in the contemporary world.' According to Shiba, since the Nara period (710–84) and even after the Meiji Restoration (1868), Japan had not entered into an alliance with other countries. Indeed, he felt that Inoue had captured succinctly the nature of the challenges Japan faced at the end of the twentieth century in an increasingly globalized world. In addressing the questions raised by Inoue, Shiba focused on historical background and current realities to provide an answer to why Japan should be prepared to adopt an active leading role in the international community, the gist of which is described below.

He began by defining the terms 'civilization' and 'culture'. 'Civilization' (*bunmei*) is 'an ambiguous term, designating a value system; or to emphasize the point, it is a set of standards which all people like to cross their national border to share'. Civilization ought to be something that everyone can share, and in sharing, feel its universal values (*fuhen-teki kachi*) and obtain a sense of comfort (*benrisa*) and security (*heiwa*). The rules of a civilization should be simple; to take as an example the world of aviation, at take-off and landing, one has to fasten one's seat belt.

In contrast to the universality of civilization, culture (*bunka*) is peculiar (*tokushu*), irrational (*fugori*), and only relevant to particular individuals or groups. For example, when opening a sliding door (*fusuma*) in a Japanese room, it is possible to open it when standing or to open it simply with one's foot; in Japanese culture the etiquette is to kneel down first, then use both hands to slide the door. Though this practice is 'awfully irrational and peculiar, for those who share that culture it gives a favorable impression'.

Shiba argued that, from ancient times, Japan has not – like most other countries – generated its own civilization, and has taken for granted that civilization would be something that existed only outside Japan. In adopting civilization, Japan would not adopt it wholesale, but rather selectively. She did so by sending scholars to China in the early seventh century, and again by dispatching students to Western countries in the second half of the nineteenth century. From Chinese civilization, Japan adopted the *ritsuryo* system (penal laws and administrative institutions), and from the West, its legal system, science and technology, and military science.

The *ritsuryo* system, to the Japanese of the time, was a kind of 'one-country socialism' (*ikkoku shakaishugi*), as reflected in practices borrowed from T'ang China such as *kochi komin* (nationalization of all the land and all the people), *kindenho* (system of equally divided rice fields), and *handen shujuho* (system of allotment). These practices, in short, brought all agricultural lands into the public domain, distributing them equally among the peasants, and collecting tax from production. In this way, elements of Chinese civilization were grafted on to that of Japan. As grafts, however, these foreign elements would necessarily cause 'antibody reactions' after their adoption. This was the reason why, following the cancellation of the sending of ambassadors to T'ang China, a uniquely native culture (Heian culture) evolved in Japan. It appeared that, being an island country, Japan would return to its natural isolation as soon as the sending of ambassadors was suspended. Thus, by the time that Japan resumed the dispatch of ambassadors to China under the Ming dynasty in the fourteenth century, there had emerged in Japan a military government led by the *samurai* that departed from East Asian norms and had a resemblance to European feudalism.

With the advent of the Tokugawa Shogunate in early seventeenth century, Japan was closed off politically for more than two hundred years, and it was only with the Meiji Restoration that the country entered the international community for the first time in its history. It is worth noting that this was a self-defence measure implemented out of concern that unless Japan adopted modern Western civilization, the country risked losing its sovereignty and becoming a Western colony like most other Asian countries. Because Japan's natural state was isolation, when the country was opened up during the early years of the Meiji era, there was a craze for all things foreign as Japan attempted to rid itself of most of the elements of the old civilization in order to absorb those of the new civilization.

Shimpei Eto (1834–74), Minister of Justice in the new Meiji government, was correct in identifying the legal system as the basis of modern Western civilization. To Eto, everyone would be equal under a reformed legal system, and the legal system in fact was the modern state itself. He thus worked to replace the old legal system, which was based on the concept of rule-by-status, with a new one from the West based on the notion of rule-by-law. Eto did so by inviting foreign legal experts – most notably the French jurist, Gustave Boissonade – to provide advice, and by sending students to study in Western countries. The services of foreign experts were terminated in the early 1880s, as soon as the Japanese felt they could manage by themselves. After many twists and turns, the Meiji legal system was consolidated in the imperial constitution of 1889.

Considering the time in which it was drafted, the Meiji constitution was a modern document, yet at the same time it perpetuated a particular form of government in which the emperor was the locus of sovereignty and held supreme command over the armed forces (*tosuiken*). Worth noting was the fact that, in the constitution, the army and navy ministers were independent of the civilian government. Because the emperor remained a symbolic figure, the constitution was ambiguous as it was not clear who should exercise the imperial prerogatives. During the 1930s, it was the military who took advantage of this defect to wield power, but at the time of its drafting this defect was not foreseen.

Having outlined the historical perspective as described above, Shiba maintained that this past and Japan's continued inclination to isolation were still affecting the country's attitude towards participation in the wider international community. During the late twentieth century, freedom and human rights had become the standards of civilization. When the government of a country became oppressive towards its people, other countries lodged protests, an intrusion that would have been seen in the context of the nineteenth century as interference in the domestic affairs of that country. For example, when the Chinese government used armed forces to suppress the student demonstrations at Tiananmen Square, many countries, including eventually Japan, protested. By following the lead of other nations in matters such as this, Shiba argued that Japan was repeating the pattern of international relations the country had followed in the past. Though freedom and human rights had been improved to a satisfactory level in postwar Japan, 'she nonetheless does not have the confidence to make the first move in complaining', or perhaps 'she does not take pride in assuming the role of a country that shoulders civilization at this stage' as is the case in the USA, UK or France. He believed the reason for this reservation was brought about by the historical background (*rekishi e no enryo*) that has been described above.

In the meantime, Japan's economic power had increased dramatically, 'even mightier than the UK, which once set civilization standards'. That Japan became an economic giant was, of course, a result of the USA's open-door principle, on the basis of which Japan was able to sell goods on the American market. In addition to freedom and human rights, Shiba identified the open-door principle as another important standard of twentieth-century civilization. He pointed to the USA's vigorous implementation of the open-door principle in its foreign policy as a sign of confidence in its own economy.

Shiba questioned why the open-door principle had become of intrinsic value to the USA, and the open market economy a basic American position. His answer was found in the fact that the USA was thoroughly confident in agriculture and manufacturing, where it was a world leader. In the postwar period, Japan came to recognize the benefits that the open market system would bring to its population; none the less, since the Meiji era, this was the only civilization standard that Japan had not adopted. Instead, while nurturing its manufacturing industry, Japan had developed an intricate protectionism. At the time, this practice was not seen by Japan as unfair, as the country was too weak to envisage that one day it would strike a blow at the US domestic market.

After the Vietnam War, there had been an expectation in the USA that its economy would recover in a few years, with a domestic market even more vigorous than in the past. This expectation, however, was not fulfilled. Instead, industrial products from Japan entered the shrinking American domestic market in large quantities. Perceiving itself to be weak, Japan continued to play down her own economic power in comparison, and did not come to terms with the adjustments required by a maturing economic power. She conceived that only a powerful country such as the USA could afford to uphold the open market principle.

Labor is an important aspect of an open market but, as Shiba noted, it was generally believed in Japan that the country was not equipped to welcome foreign workers. In contrast, American society was seen as being more thoroughly prepared for an open labor market. Being a melting pot, apart from a small number of native American people, the US population was made up of continuous waves of settlers from overseas, and their descendants were mutually governed by law.

Shiba understood the reluctance to reform Japan's immigration policies. Although freedom was no longer a concern in postwar Japan, and the level of freedom in Japanese society had reached almost the same level (*kinjichi*) as that of other leading industrialized countries, he believed that at this stage Japan was not ready to be a torch-bearer of modern civilization. For example, with respect to the free labor market system, Japan should be ready to implement it: to welcome foreign workers; to invite them to live in Japan as permanent residents; and to apply lenient criteria to allow them to become Japanese citizens. But Japan simply had not yet reached that level.

Nevertheless, as Japan's success had been achieved by tying itself closely to the USA's open market economy, it was only natural to assume that Japan should open her market up to a level comparable to that of the USA. Shiba saw that if Japan's economic growth was to be maintained, the country had no choice but to open the labor market on a far larger scale. Paying lip service to 'internationalization' (*kokusaika*) was not enough. Given the choice, the Japanese people would prefer their country to stay intact, but time was running out for Japan to remain a closed society. Shiba warned that avoiding these issues was not an option because it would require effort to reduce Japan's economic power to that of a medium-sized economy. Such an approach would not be popular with the Japanese populace and would have been perceived as running away – a shameful response, according to *samurai* values since the rise of the *samurai* class in the late twelfth century – and it was also a situation that no one in Japan wished to see.

But internationalization meant new challenges. In the process of removing trade and immigration barriers, would Japanese society lose its unique character? In other words, would diversity cause Japan to become a spineless entity and eventually cease to exist? Or would Japan be able to draw on its unique intellectual and moral characteristics, as the USA had done early in its history, using Protestantism to nurture a unifying strength in the face of diversity? Shiba saw this as the only feasible alternative for Japan. The task was thus to reclaim the nation's past unique ethical elements that could be used as a foundation to instill pride in the Japanese populace so that Japan might be able to stand up to the internalizing effects of diversity. According to Shiba, the backbone Japan should rely on in its internationalization was be found nowhere but in what might be understood as *bushido* (the way of the *samurai*) and/or as the spirit of the Edoites (*Edokko kokoroiki*), that emerged as a commonly shared set of values from those who moved to Edo (presently Tokyo) from other parts of the country during the Tokugawa period. The spirit of receptivity inherent in these values eventually fueleed the drive for the adoption of Western values during the Meiji period.

Above is Shiba's response, 'after much reluctance', to Yasushi Inoue's question, '[It is now time that] Japan should enter into a partnership, don't you think?' mentioned at the start of this section. To qualify his response, Shiba admonished his audience with the following comments. If Japan seriously considered entering into a world partnership, it had no choice but to adopt a leading role (*shuyaku*) in contemporary civilization, of which freedom, human rights and the open-door economic principle had become a standard since around the late 1940s. Since Japan's emergence into a modern state, it had not as yet assumed this role.

To illustrate his points metaphorically, Shiba argued that, in the Meiji era, Japan entered the world with a 'children's ticket'. In the Taisho era (1912–25), Japan was 'half ready to back out' from the League of Nations. From the early Showa era (late 1920s and 1930s) to 1945, Japan was 'anti-alliance' (*han-kumiai* – that is, against the Allied powers). The country began the postwar era as 'occupied Japan'. As a former enemy of the Allied powers, in the United Nations Japan was still not a permanent member of its Security Council. In other words, she had not joined the 'alliance' with 'a full-grown spirit' (*otona no seishin*). Whether to become a permanent member of the UN Security Council was not an important question for Japan, but as a 'full-grown member of the world community', the question was, would it be able to share in looking after (*mendo ga mirareru*) the international community? In other words, would Japan be able to set the standards for contemporary civilization?

To accomplish this goal, Shiba suggested that the philosophical underpinning for Japan could be found in the philosophy of the Kegon school (in Chinese, *Hua-yen*; Sanskrit, *Avatarsake*), which was introduced to Japan from China in the Nara period (710–84) and since then had been integrated into the life of the Japanese people as their 'everyday wisdom' (*zoku-tetsugaku*). In the Kegon philosophy, according to Shiba (2002), there is no notion that there are absolute beings like in Christianity. It views the world in relative terms, in which all is harmonized in the essence of the Light. Apart from paying respect to the Light, it conceives all beings as interdependent and everything is interconnected; from the tiny level of an atom or a molecule to the boundlessness of the universe, all beings are reciprocally and mutually dependent on one another for their existence. This spirit of interdependency is reflected in the overseas development activities undertaken by the Seinen Kaigai Kyoryokutai (Japan Overseas Cooperation Volunteers). (See Japan International Cooperation Agency (2004).)

At the present time, however, Shiba maintained that Japan was not ready to undertake this task, as being a carrier of civilization was a role for which Japan had no experience. The Japanese people first had to educate themselves to be ready for it.

Land and Japan's industrialization

That Shiba was regarded as a 'national writer' by his compatriots was because of his utmost concern for Japan's future fortunes (Bungei Shunju, 1996, p. 10). As mentioned in the introduction to this chapter, during the last two decades of his life the question that preoccupied

Shiba constantly was the alarming state of the real estate market in Japan, and having diagnosed this as the root of Japan's problems, he went to search for intrinsic values from the past that would help the country to meet the challenges of globalization.

Writing in 1990, Shiba predicted that future historians would necessarily see soaring land prices in the previous two decades not as an economic phenomenon, but in an acutely gloomy vein, a betrayal against human beings or an anti-social act (Shiba, 1994a, p. 287). To Shiba, it was a psychological phenomenon that was converted to economic activities. The land price manipulators and the manipulated were both bolstered by a 'land price psychology' (*chika shinri*), as if they were captivated by an evil spirit (*mononoke*) (ibid., pp. 287–8).

According to Shiba, in the period around 1970, many manufacturing companies borrowed money from banks to buy land in remote locations on which to build their new factories. Following this, the price of neighbouring farmland and forests began to soar and, effortlessly, the companies' latent property value suddenly escalated. Many then sold parts of their land and made huge profits. 'If this was an economic act', Shiba argued, 'then fraudulence (*sagi*) also became an economic act' (ibid., pp. 287–8). He believed that it was around this time that the sense of dignity about labor (ibid., p. 288) and land (ibid., p. 223) began to waver.

As an illustration, Shiba discussed the case of an old farmer who cultivated his piece of land of about 200 *tsubo*, next to his house in Higashi Osaka City, to grow green onions. 'It looked as if, to the old man, growing green onions was merely a measure to wait until his land turns into a housing lot', Shiba observed, so that he could sell it at a high price. The man was concerned neither about the labor he expended growing the green onions nor the economic questions pertaining to the profit he would realize in selling the onions in the market. Watching the old man working on his field, Shiba wondered if this signaled 'the end of the value of labor', and felt that 'the old man's heart might have become dissolute' (Shiba *et al.*, 1997, pp. 7–8).

To drive home his point, Shiba suggested that his readers think of the moving painting *Semeur* (*Sower*, dated 1850) by the renowned nineteenth-century French painter, Jean François Millet. Supposing the field in this painting was on the outskirts of one of Japan's cities, Shiba wrote, that, if the peasant was merely sowing the seeds to wait until his land turned into a housing lot so that he could make a huge profit, then 'what a degenerated scene that would be!' (Shiba, 1994a, p. 288). In an alarming note, Shiba warned: 'If the value of labor was driven away and the joy of producing things ceased to exist, then the ethics that had been nurtured over the past millennium would fall to pieces' (Shiba, 1997, pp. 7–8).

Shiba thus asserted that it was precisely because of land speculation that 'Japan's economy and spirit had been contaminated' (ibid., p. 92), and it was the 'psychological effect of the land price that had shattered Japan'. 'Not only did it take away the faith in labor from the Japanese people', he maintained, 'but it also compromised the love that they had for their country. It was indeed the greatest detriment to Japan's economy' (Shiba, 1994a, p. 290). If the land question was not resolved, he believed that, for various reasons, 'Japan would become an extremely uneasy country in which to live' (Shiba, 1997, p. 88). If a glass of juice in a first-class hotel in Tokyo cost as much as ¥1,000, Shiba explained, it was simply because the enormous land cost of the hotel was built into this price (ibid., p. 66). In the expensive Ginza district in Tokyo, according to Shiba, the land price was ¥4,500,000 per *tsubo* in the 1960s, so even by then it would not have been easy to pay back a loan if one were to buy 50 *tsubo* to build a restaurant there. In 1987, the midst of the bubble, the land price for the same location jumped to ¥150,000,000 per *tsubo*. 'With this horrendous land price, no matter what kind of shop one was to build', Shiba said, 'one's business simply would not work' (ibid., p. 12).

As a solution to the land question in Japan, Shiba believed that all land should be under public ownership (*koyu*). By 'public', he did not necessarily imply that it should be owned by the state, as in the Netherlands or Singapore – two non-socialist countries. While he admired the land policies of these two countries, the history of land-ownership in Japan meant the country would have to find its own solution. 'Public', Shiba explained, should be understood in a broad sense – that is, the land is to be owned by the Japanese people at large (ibid., p. 25).

According to Shiba, the feeling that land does not belong to any particular individual but rather to the public had existed in Japan for a long time. In illustration, he mentioned the *Taiheiki* (The Record of the Great Peace; fourteenth century) from *The Book of Odes* which stated that 'There is no territory under Heaven which is not the Emperor's'. During the Tokugawa period, 'among the samurai – from the *daimyo* (feudal lords) on the top to the *ashigaru* (foot soldiers) at the bottom – even if they had enough money to spare, none of them would ever think of acquiring land and asking the farmers to do tenant farming on their behalf'. In the same manner, in addition to their own residences, when the major *daimyo* needed land to build as many as seven or eight villas (*nakayashiki* and *shimoyashiki*) to house their retainers who attended in Edo, they always rented land from the *chonin* (townspeople). 'The *daimyo* were conscious that they should not use building their villas as an excuse to acquire lands for themselves' (ibid., pp. 13–14).

The history of privately-owned land in Japan, in Shiba's view, might be traced back to the French Revolution, during which land was privatized and private property began to be sanctified. In the process of adopting the French legal system in the Meiji era, this notion was incorporated into the Meiji Constitution. Shiba held that in Japan, now that there was growing recognition that land had become a cause for economic and cultural malaise, it was only natural that certain limits should be applied to the right of private property. 'Without ethics, capitalism would lose everything', he asserted, citing the correlation between interest and success in early capitalist ventures and the influence of Protestant values that had been shown by Max Weber in his book *The Protestant Ethic and the Spirit of Capitalism* (ibid., p. 13; Shiba, 1994a, p. 289). Shiba wondered why Japanese bankers had forgotten the ethical legacy from the Meiji era that cautions against speculative pursuits, which they should have acquired through their training as well as through their practical work (Shiba, 1994a, p. 289).

Because Japan's industrialization had been achieved over a comparatively short period, the country did not have sufficient time to adjust to the shift of land use from agriculture to industrial use. Also, because only just over 20 per cent of Japan's total area was flat land, Shiba noted that this land had been so heavily urbanized, particularly over the previous thirty years or so, that 'Japan herself had almost become a city' (ibid., p. 100). It was around this time that, 'some sort of a land trick (*maho*) was applied and Japanese capitalism was transformed' (Shiba *et al.*, 1997, p. 66). Shiba did not think that politicians of the time did so on purpose, but believed that they 'simply had mistakenly pressed a wrong button in the process of capitalist evolution in Japan' (Shiba, 1994a, p. 101). In more specific terms, he explained the reasons for the anomalous land situation in Japan: 'In the Japanese case, curiously the land is not immovable property (*fudosan*) but movable property (*dosan*). To borrow money from the banks, the most desirable pledge for them was land (a curious custom indeed), and the landowner might, depending on circumstances, use this cash as working funds to purchase another piece of land. In the meantime, through all sorts of manipulation, the land price soared. The country became like a heated frying pan, and the people were like the ducks flapping on it' (ibid., p. 100). Just before the 'bubble' burst, the value of land lost its economic foundation.

To prove that it would be feasible to keep land in public hands, Shiba cited examples from other countries. In both Singapore, 'a non-socialist city-state', and Hong Kong (before its return to China), the land belonged to the state and to the British Queen, respectively, and the people had only a right of use (*shiyoken*). Similarly, in Switzerland, people had a right of use, but it was believed that land did not belong to anyone in particular, but was providential (Shiba *et al.*, 1997, p. 66). The Netherlands, in particular, was a country that Shiba admired for its effective and innovative land policy; land in this country was in public hands and rented out. A good part of the land area had been reclaimed from the sea during the previous millennium or more. As a world-class industrial power that was able to put in place policies to protect the environment and thus provide a balance between industry and environment, factories in the Netherlands were hidden among woods. The Netherlands was also a leading exporter of dairy and agricultural products. Marking a sharp contrast to 'the garbage and old tire dumps that scattered here and there along the highways in Japan', the Netherlands was, to Shiba, a refreshing country full of excellent grazing land. Because of the 'mishandling (*ibitsu*) of the land problem', Shiba believed that 'the Japanese had lost interest in keeping their country's natural beauty.' (Shiba, 1994a, p. 224). Also of great relevance to Shiba was the fact that in the Netherlands, 'while the market principles were observed, there was no such a thing as land speculation'. His main point was that the mismanagement of land in Japan was a widespread psychological blow that caused the Japanese to lose their attachment to, and respect for, the land and the environment.

Among the industrialized countries, according to Shiba, Japan was practically the only country still faced with a serious land problem (ibid., 101). His contention was that the Japanese should learn from the experiences of the Netherlands, as they had done so previously and gained much benefit through the 'School of Dutch Learning' (*Rangaku*) during the Tokugawa period (ibid., pp. 222–6).

Shiba was also a leading advocate for removing Japan's capital from Tokyo as a means of easing its land problem. Though normally not showing much inclination to be an activist, for this particular cause he was involved as a member of the removal study committee. At its first meeting, Shiba justified his position earnestly: 'Capital removal throughout Japanese history has always been successful. Heijokyo [Nara] was a magnificent capital – quite disproportionate to Japan's national power at the time. Even though it had cost an enormous amount to build it, when the power of the Buddhist priests became excessive in Heijokyo, the capital was moved to Heiankyo [Kyoto], giving rise to what is known as Japanese beauty. Now land prices have reached a horrendous level and have left ill effects on the people's mind. If the land problem is dealt with effectively and the capital is moved, this time, too, Japan will come out better with the change of her capital' (cited in BS, 1996, p. 125). In late 1995, shortly before Shiba's death, the removal study committee recommended that the capital be removed from Tokyo by 2110.

Globalization and Changing Values of Japanese Society

In order to meet the challenge of a global world, Shiba believed Japan needed to restore the *samurai* ethos (*samurai kishitsu*, on other occasions he also used other terms such as *bushido, shikon*, or 'the spirit of the Edoites') which had wavered in present-day Japan (Shiba, 1994b, p. 73). To him, it was the *samurai* ethos, found not only among the *samurai* but also among the townspeople and farmers in the Tokugawa period, that had sustained those who dedicated their lives to Japan's emergence as a modern state during the late Tokugawa and early Meiji years. Shiba thus summarized succinctly the relationship between the Tokugawa culture and the Meiji Restoration: 'It is difficult to describe the *samurai* (*bushi*) in a single word. During those [late Tokugawa] years, their self-discipline (*jiritsu*) and aesthetic sense (*biishiki*) were infused with spirit and vigor. It seems to me that the Meiji Restoration bore no resemblance to any of the revolutions that took place in France, Italy and Russia. The striking difference being it was a revolution undertaken by the *samurai*, who should be seen as the greatest cultural asset of the Tokugawa three-hundred years' (Tanizawa, 1994, p. 133). Just as *samurai* values had sustained Meiji leaders during the Restoration, Shiba believed that they would also uphold the contemporary Japanese in their efforts to address issues arising from globalization.

What exactly were the 'self-discipline' and 'aesthetic sense' of the *samurai* that Shiba singled out in the above statement? With respect to self-discipline, citing the classic dictum from the *Great Learning* of 'being watchful of oneself when alone', Shiba explained that during the Tokugawa period, the *samurai* took this dictum as praxis. The *samurai* insistence on constant self-discipline, in Shiba's opinion, could be compared to the spirit of moral and religious earnestness of the English Puritans in the late sixteenth and seventeenth centuries (Shiba, 1992, pp. 246–7).

As far as the 'aesthetic sense' of the *samurai* was concerned, its most extreme expression was to be observed in the ritual of *seppuku* (self-immolation). Shiba described the meaning of this grisly practice: 'The samurai's vanity was to be found in the last moment of his life: *seppuku*. How beautifully a *seppuku* was performed was viewed as the most eloquent manifestation of the man he had been. For that reason, before a *samurai* son was to celebrate his coming of age (*gempuku*), he was meticulously taught about the etiquette of *seppuku*. I do not imply that there was a tradition in Japan that made death light, but by controlling at will the most difficult thing to overcome for humankind, i.e. the fear of death, the *samurai* attempted to bring forth a psychological tension, aesthetics, and real freedom' (ibid., p. 133).

On a more general level, the *samurai* sense of aesthetics was manifested in Shiba's works through numerous heroes, most notably Ryoma Sakamoto, Shinsaku Takasugi, Toshizo Tsuchikata, Masujiro Omura, Takamori Saigo, and Tsugunosuke Kawai. All these men lived their lives to the fullest during the eventful years before and after the Meiji Restoration. In both life and in the face of death, they could all be called *isagiyoi*, a term that included several connotations underlying the quality of a *samurai*: (i) pure (*kiyoi*), refreshing (*sugasugashii*) [in their actions and thoughts]; (ii) integrity, incorruptible (*seiren keppaku*; abbreviated *renketsu*); (iii) no regrets (*miren ga nai*), composed (*warubirenai*) and brave (*isamashii*) [in adversity and even in the face of death]. The heroes in Shiba's historical novels have been idolized by his readers precisely because they were seen to have led exemplary lives and lived them true to these criteria.

While the *samurai* ethos was still alive in the Meiji era (1868–1910), a new set of values was being adopted from the West. They were seen as parts of a whole that epitomized universal values; to excel in them was to be civilized. Since self-defence was the principal drive behind Japan's adoption of Western civilization, 'to be civilized' in the Western sense was viewed as being an effective measure for the preservation of Japan's sovereignty. It is significant that Shiba extolled not only the *samurai* ethos but also these newly-adopted values. Let us look at a few typical ones to discern the reasons for Shiba's call for their reinvigoration.

Shojiki (honesty)

If 'one has to single out one quality that would bring happiness to daily life', to Shiba, 'it must be none other than *shojiki*.' As the saying '*Shojiki wa Hotoke no moto*' (literally, 'Honesty is the first step to become enlightened')[3] had been used by the Buddhist practitioners in the

Kamakura period (1192–1333), Shiba held that the Japanese word *'shojiki'* must have existed for over 700 years. In Tokugawa Japan, the *samurai* officials had been required 'to have integrity and to be upright (*renchoku*)' but not necessarily to be *'shojiki'*, since their principal governing guideline had been the Confucian maxim 'it is possible to make the people follow the teaching of the sovereign, but it is impossible to explain its details to each of them'. None the less, *'shojiki'* had been regarded as a virtue among merchants, artisans and servants. As its concept already existed in Japan, *'shojiki'* became a perfect translation for 'honesty' when this term was introduced in the Meiji era. Together with the flow of Western ideas into Japan, 'honesty' gained prominence. 'In practice, until the Russo-Japanese War (1904–1905)', in Shiba's view, 'those in charge of governing the country displayed a considerably high level of honesty, without which it would have been impossible for them to produce a glorious era known as the Meiji miracle.' Shiba explained that during the 1930s, however, as the Japanese state became 'dishonest' (*fushojiki*) to the people, this 'dishonesty' had quickly led the nation towards a catastrophe. In contrast to the Meiji Constitution that had given birth to Japan as a modern state, argued Shiba, the postwar Constitution gave rise to individuality and depended totally on the awareness of every individual. 'Without the honesty of every individual', and 'if those who represented government and the politicians were dishonest', he asserted, 'Japan would be at stake' (Shiba, 1994a, pp. 22–6).

Jijo (self-help) and *dokuritsu* (independence)

'Self-help' and 'independence' were the two popular catchwords in Meiji Japan. Most instrumental in the dissemination of the idea of independence was undoubtedly Yukichi Fukuzawa (1835–1901), who has generally been seen as the *philosopher* and the 'founder' of modern Japan. Fukuzawa was crystal clear about the necessity of adopting modern Western civilization: 'The way in which to preserve [Japan's] independence cannot be sought anywhere except in civilization. The only reason for making the people in our country today advance toward civilization is to preserve our country's independence' (Fukuzawa, 1973, p. 193). In Fukuzawa's view, national independence could not be achieved without independent individuals (*isshin dokuritsu shite, ikkoku doritsu*). Previously, *'dokuritsu'* had been used in a negative sense, implying 'isolation'. The term was given a new life when it was used to translate the English word 'independence', which was defined by Fukuzawa as: 'Referring to the spirit of governing oneself, without thinking of relying on others'. Fukuzawa discussed the need for Japan to adopt the spirit of independence in his book *Gakumon no susume* (An Encouragement of Learning), published in 1872.

Masanao Nakamura (1832–91) also played an important role in the dissemination of the spirit of independence in Japan through his translation of Samuel Smiles' *Self-help* (published in 1870). According to Shiba, the spirit of independence and self-help in Fukuzawa's *Gakumon no susume* and Nakamura's translation captured the imagination of Meiji youth and the books were longtime best-sellers. To illustrate this, Shiba cited the case of Kawaji Toshiyoshi, a man from Satsuma (presently Kagoshima prefecture), who had gone to France to study the police system and on his return was entrusted with the task of organizing a new police system for Meiji Japan. When the Satsuma Rebellion broke out in his home province in 1877, Kawaji was put in a most difficult position, as he was required to take part in putting down the rebellion. To encourage those from his home province fighting on his side, Kawaji said: 'Born as a human being, but without having the right of self-help and independence and thus entrusting one's life and one's interest to others, would that be any different from the fastened cows and horses?' (Shiba, 1994a, pp. 176–7).

Gimu (duty)

Newly coined in early Meiji Japan to convey the English concept of duty, *gimu* was, in Shiba's opinion, indeed a brilliant translation. The Chinese character *'gi'* in this translated term 'denotes the sense of righteousness, or that which goes beyond calculation', embedded in the original term. In prewar Japan, *gimu* had been used, however, 'with an emphasis on the restraints with which individuals were bound by the state' as seen in the 'Three major duties of the citizens' (*Kokumin no sandai gimu*): liability to taxation (*nozei no gimu*), military service (*heieki no gimu*), and compulsory education (*kyoiku no gimu*). In other words, Shiba saw that in practice, *gimu* did not convey the rich, invigorated and spontaneous nuance of the English 'duty' found in Horatio Nelson's reputed last words at Trafalgar: 'I have done my duty.' Shiba contended that it was time for Japan to reconsider the meaning of *gimu* in its search for ideas to break away from the country's reluctance to join 'the global village' (*chikyumura*) as a full member (ibid., pp. 221–66).

Seeing these Meiji virtues (*bitoku*) weakening among the younger generation and the unhealthy tight connection between policians and their constituents in present-day Japan, Shiba asked: 'Is it not necessary to go back to the pioneer spirit of the Meiji era?'

Toward the end of the 1980s, in a Japanese-language textbook for sixth-grade students, Shiba wrote an essay entitled '*Nijuisseiki ni ikiru kimitachi e*' (To Those of You Who Live in the Twenty-first Century). It must have required a lot of thought to complete this brief, two-page essay, as he disclosed elsewhere that it had taken him longer to write it than it would have done to finish a novel. Evidently he had anticipated that the end of his life was approaching, as he wrote at the outset 'certainly I will not be able to see the twenty-first century'. He offered several pieces of advice to the students. With respect to nature, 'as human beings are part of nature', he wished them 'to adopt a receptive approach' – that would be his hope for the twenty-first century and also his expectation of them. So far as the students were concerned, he wished them to nurture an independent spirit, practising self-discipline yet being considerate (*yasashii*) to others. If this disposition were firmly engrained in them, it would be apparent when they came into contact with other nations. Just as 'the *samurai* during the Kamakura period had been trained to be dependable (*tanomoshii*)', he urged the students to cultivate themselves to become dependable. This essay represents a succinct summary of the essential ideas he had developed in his career, providing a blueprint for the younger generation to equip themselves with the values necessary for them to meet what he saw as the relentless challenges stemming from an increasingly globalized world.

Conclusion

In conclusion, the following remarks can be made. First, it is significant to note the enormous influence that Shiba's works had on his readers, including a good number of incumbent politicians and prominent cultural and economic leaders. The late Prime Minister Keizo Obuchi, for example, said that *Ryoma ga yuku* (Ryoma Goes) was the first novel by Shiba that he had read. Obuchi recalled: 'It was in 1963, when I was first elected to the Lower House. I was high-spirited, ready to dedicate myself to Japanese politics. Probably I was inspired to be like Ryoma, who escaped from his domain to exert himself in the interests of the country. I was just fascinated by Ryoma . . . who, as [the writer] Hisashi Inoue observes, was "brave and pure, utterly honest, and not crafty or complicated". These traits, which ought to be called typically Japanese, are fading among contemporary Japanese. For this reason Shiba's works gave me boundless nostalgia' (Bungei Shunju, 1996, p. 110). Obuchi (Bungei Shunju, 1996) also concurred with Shiba's concern for the land question: 'In *Fujinsho* (Vignettes of Life), a posthumous manuscript,

Shiba touched upon the bubble economy issue and stated: "The land in Japan is what the people are to rely on. To engage in pursuits such as land speculation to create a frantic climate is unquestionably an ethical issue rather than an economic one." His perception was penetrating indeed.' (Bungei Shunju, 1996, p. 110). Echoing Shiba's vision for Japan's future generations, in his policy speech to the 145th Session of the Diet on 19 January 1999, Obuchi said: 'It is clear to all that the future will be borne by the younger generation. What we as adults can do for the younger generation who will bear our society forward in the future, is no less than to do our utmost to build various bridges to the 21st century, while at the same time, as novelist Ryotaro Shiba once said, we must foster an environment in which the bearers of the future will be of jovial spirit, stern with themselves and thoughtful of others.'[4]

The Prime Minister at the time of writing, Jun'ichiro Koizumi, writing in 1996, reminisced that he began reading Shiba's works in his university years. 'The first book by Shiba that I read', wrote Koizumi, 'was *Kunitori monogatari* [The Tale of the Warring States] which, in a way, really changed the course of my life.' Koizumi indicated that he remained an avid reader of Shiba's writings, through which he began to see parallels between present-day Japan and circumstances in the late Tokugawa and early Meiji eras during the latter half of the nineteenth century. As he wrote: 'Even now, I still read over Shiba's works from time to time. The work that I have re-read most recently was *"Yo ni sumu hibi"'* [literally 'Daily life', a short novel Shiba wrote in the early 1970s dealing with Shoin Yoshida and Shinsaku Takasugi – two prominent pioneers of the movement that led to the Meiji Restoration]. As compared to my previous reading, this time I feel that I acquired a more profound appreciation. On second thoughts, the present day is not dissimilar from the late Tokugawa–Meiji Restoration eras. The Satsuma and Choshu domains, which were hostile [to the contemporary Tokugawa Shogunate government], decided to unite in the Satcho coalition, just like the coalition government of the Liberal, Socialist and Sakigake parties [of the present day]. In much the same way, [at present] a great reform is being called for. Against that background, when I read and ponder over every word by Shiba-*sensei*, naturally, I can see richer nuances in his work.' (Bungei Shunju, 1996, p. 115)

After becoming prime minister, Koizumi drew on an episode from the early Meiji era that exemplified Meiji values in order to provide a motif for his own reform policies. In his policy speech delivered on 7 May 2001, he referred to the story of '*Kome hyappyo*' (One hundred *hyo* of rice) in Nagaoka domain, the home domain of Tsugunosuke Kawai – the hero in Shiba's novel *Toge* (Mountain Pass). During the early years of the Meiji era, the Nagaoka domain suffered straitened circumstances. When it received a donation of 100 *hyo* (approximately equivalent to 7,200 litres) of rice, people were so pleased. Had this amount of rice been consumed, however, it would have lasted only a few days. Torasaburo Kobayashi, the domainal leader at the time, decided to use it as a endowment for schools. As a result, Nagaoka produced many talented people in later years. 'To bear today's ordeal for the betterment of the future was the spirit of *Kome hyappyo*', said Koizumi in his policy speech, 'and this is precisely what we need in carrying out the reform.'

Eisuke Sasakibara,[5] chief of the International Finance Department in the Ministry of Finance, recalled that when he was teaching Japanese Economics at Harvard University as a visiting professor, he spent most of his spare time reading Shiba's works. He acknowledged that Shiba's writings helped him to see the tumultuous events in Japan in perspective and guided him in charting his future path. In the face of 'the rough wave of globalization', the solution provided in Shiba's article 'Should We Make a Commitment?' appeared to him as the only feasible course of action. (Bungei Shunju, 1996, p. 117).

Second, Shiba was able to offer a coherent interpretation of the issues facing Japan in a global age and set them within historical and comparative perspectives. He was also able to suggest sensitive measures to deal with them. Shiba once stated: 'I love postwar Japan so much that if I should have to defend it, I would risk my life to do so' (Shiba, 1998b, p. 239). It must have been because of his frustration during his wartime experience and this love for postwar Japan that in the last ten years of his life, Shiba focused on writing essays, coalescing the insights he had acquired during his writing career. These essays were later published in volumes such as *Meiji to iu kokka* (Meiji as a State), *Showa to iu kokka* (Showa as a State), *Kono kuni no katachi* (The Forms of this Country), *Fujinsho* (Vignettes of Life) and so on, which enjoyed enormous popularity.

Realizing the possible dangers of globalization and the necessity of cultivating relevant values and ethics, he proposed a course of action that recognized that Japan had no choice but to play a greater role in the international community if it was to survive as a significant power. But at the same time, he was keenly aware of the negative aspects of globalization and thus his vision for Japan was a realistic type of internationalization tailored to Japan's cultural and economic realities. Consequently, he called for the restoration of Meiji values to provide an intellectual and ethical underpinning to Japanese society and, eventually, to export as a universally acceptable standard. For all his wisdom and insights as an historian, writer and educator, it is no surprise that Shiba was referred to as the *philosopher* or a compass of Japan (Yoshida, 1996, p. 120).

Notes

1   See, for example, Daly (1999).
2   Discussion in this section is mainly based on this article, included in Ryotaro Shiba (1992, pp. 191–220).
3   In practice, its meaning is close to the English saying 'Honesty is the best policy'.
4   Provisional translation provided by the Ministry of Foreign Affairs of Japan. see http://www.mofa.go.jp/announce/announce/1999/1/119-2.html.
5   At the time of writing, a Professor of Keio University, where he is the director of the Keio Global Security Research Center.

References

BS (*Bungei Shunju*) (ed.) (1996) *Shiba Ryotaro no sekai* (The World of Shiba Ryotaro) (Tokyo: Bungei Shunju).

Daly, Herman E. (1999) 'Globalization Versus Internationalization: Some Implications'. See http://www.globalpolicy.org/globaliz/econ/herman2.hm.

Fukuzawa, Yukichi (1960) *An Encouragement of Learning*, trans. David A. Dilworth and Umeyo Hirano (Tokyo: Sophia University).

Fukuzawa, Yukichi (1973) *An Outline of a Theory of Civilization*, trans. David A. Dilworth and G. Cameron Hurst (Tokyo: Sophia University).

Iriye, Akira (1997) *Japan and the Wider World* (London: Longman).

Itoh, Mayumi (1990) *Globalization of Japan* (New York: St. Martin's Press).

Japan International Cooperation Agency (2004) *Japan Overseas Cooperation Volunteers*. See http://www.jica.go.jp.

Murai, Hideo (1997) *Nihon o shiru: Shiba Ryotaro* (Understanding Japan: Shiba Ryotaro), (Tokyo: Daikosha).

Obuchi, Keizo (1999) *Prime Minister's Policy Speech* (Tokyo: 145th Session of the Japanese Diet).

Ozaki, Hotsuki (1975) *Rekishi no naka no chizu: Shiba Ryotaro no sekai* (Maps and History: The World of Shiba Ryotaro) (Tokyo: Bungei Shunju).

Shiba, Ryotaro (1963) *Ryoma ga yuku* (Ryoma Goes) (Tokyo: Bungei Shunju).

Shiba, Ryotaro (1990) *Rekishi to shosetsu* (History and Novels) (Tokyo: Shueisha).

Shiba, Ryotaro (1992) *Shuncho zakki* (Random Narratives Recorded in Spring Time) (Tokyo: Asahi Shimbunsha).

Shiba, Ryotaro (1994a) *Fujinsho* (Vignettes of Life) (Tokyo: Chuo Koron Shinsha).

Shiba, Ryotaro (1994b) *Meiji to iu kokka* (Meiji as a State), 2 vols. (Tokyo: NHK Books).

Shiba, Ryotaro (1996) *Kono kuni no katachi* (The Form of this Country), 10 vols. (Tokyo: Chuo Koronsha).

Shiba, Ryotaro (1998b) *Showa to iu kokka* (Showa as a State) (Tokyo: NHK Shuppan).

Shiba, Ryotaro (2000) *Shiba Ryotaro rekishi kandan* (Conversations with Shiba Ryotaro) (Tokyo: Chuo Koron Shinsha).

Shiba, Ryotaro (2002) *Shiba Ryotaro ga Kangaeta Koto* (Shiba Ryotaro's Thinking) (Tokyo: Shinchosha).

Shiba, Ryotaro, Naoki Tanaka, Hayao Miyazaki, Kenichi Ohmae, Morie Enomoto, Masayoshi Takemura and Ronald Toby (1997) *Taidanshu: Nihonjin e no yuigon* ([Shiba Ryotaro's] Last Words for the Japanese) (Tokyo: Asahi Shimbunsha).

Tanizawa, Eiichi (1994) *Shiba Ryotaro no okurimono* (A Gift from Shiba Ryotaro) (Tokyo: PHP Kenkyusho).

Tanizawa, Eiichi (1996) *Shiba Ryotaro no essensu* (The Essence of Shiba Ryotaro) (Tokyo: Bungei Shunju).

Wakamatsu, Kenji (2002) 'Globalization and Regionalization', *Journal of Japanese Trade & Industry*, vol. 4.

Yoshida, Naoya (1996) 'Kakegae no nai rashinban' (An Irreplaceable Compass), *Bungei Shunju*, March, pp. 120–6.

3
Surviving a Globalized World: Lessons to be Learned from Japan's Problem-Solving Incapability*

Yoshihiko Wada

Japan is notorious for its inability to change its actions in response to emerging environmental and social problems. Some problems have remained unsolved for what seems to be an unjustifiably long period of time. This problem-solving deficiency has spread like an epidemic across many levels of society, and can be traced across a wide range of social issues, from diplomatic and educational, to environmental and health and safety.

Japan's relationship with Asia, damaged by the militarism of the Imperial Japanese government during previous centuries, is just one example of that deficiency. Even today, those wounds are still raw for many Asian nations, as Japan is reluctant to admit fully its serious errors. The recent visit to Yasukuni Shrine by Prime Minister Koizumi, and the school textbook scandal exemplify these phenomena.[1] As a result, even though Japan is trying to improve its image among the global community, it has not yet gained the heart-felt trust and respect of other Asian nations.

It has recently been discovered that Japan's Foreign Ministry has repeatedly instructed first-class hotels to create and maintain, illegally, secret accounts by inflating figures on invoices for room charges over at least the past ten years. The Ministry's officials have then used these funds to pay for private parties, or even to find extra-marital affairs at those hotels. An internal inquiry team investigated the use of this secret money and discovered that more than US$1 m had been withdrawn from the unlawfully accumulated funds since 1996 (*Asahi Shinbun*, 2001a). No wonder the Kyushu–Okinawa G8 Summit in July 2000 cost nearly a hundred times as much as the one held in Birmingham, UK

(*Asahi Shinbun*, 2000a, 2000b)! It is regrettable that this practice of abusing taxpayers' money has been tacitly allowed for more than ten years.

Environmental and safety issues in modern Japan have also been weak areas. For example, Japan failed to prevent bovine spongiform encephalopathy (BSE), popularly known as 'mad cow disease', from affecting the Japanese livestock industry (*Nature*, 2001). Also, repeated serious accidents at nuclear energy facilities have caused human casualties and environment contamination through the emission of radioactive substances. The most serious incident was the nuclear criticality accident at the JCO Company in Tokai-mura, Ibaraki Prefecture, on 30 September 1999. There were two casualties as a result of exposure to lethal doses of radiation. In July 2000, it was discovered that the Mitsubishi Motor Company had secretly been recalling their defective vehicles for the previous thirty years (Kano, 2000). Safety has been seriously compromised as a result of this improper handling of manufacturing defects. Several accidents, some involving injuries, occurred because of defective parts.

In this chapter, I shall attempt to identify some barriers to real solutions to problems in Japanese society. My purpose is to suggest policy strategies for increasing Japan's problem-solving capabilities. Effective problem-solving strategies are a prerequisite for survival in this age of rapid globalization.

Below are several typical examples of environmental and health problems in contemporary Japan, from which I shall attempt to extract some common factors.

The Minamata Disease case

In Minamata City on Kyushu Island in Southern Japan, a hitherto unknown disease was discovered in 1956 (Ui, 1992, p. 110). Three years later, doctors at Kumamoto University, Kyushu, confirmed that the strange disease had been caused by an organic mercury compound present in the effluent discharge from a chemical fertilizer manufacturer, Nippon Chisso (Harada, 1972, pp. 52–3). Other scientists, most of them sponsored by the Japanese Chemical Industry Association, published a range of counter-arguments claiming that the cause of the disease was not organic mercury, but other substances (Harada, 1972, pp. 56–7; Miyazawa, 1997, pp. 227–9; Shimin Enerugi Kenkyujo, 1994, pp. 72–5). The article by Professor Raisaku Kiyoura of Tokyo Institute of Technology is typical of these studies in its strong support for the industry. However, the Kumamoto University team successfully refuted the claims made in those studies. In 1959, Dr Hosokawa, the president of the hospital affiliated to Chisso's Minamata factory, submitted his final report to the company. The report included a series of experiments involving the feeding of cats with fish caught in Minamata Bay. The report confirmed the earlier findings of the Kumamoto University study. The Chisso Company immediately banned the continuation of the experiment, and Dr Hosokawa resigned from the hospital and left the company (Harada, 1972, p. 68).

The Japanese government left patients anxious and hopeless for over ten years, as it delayed the official determination of the cause of their illness. Although, as early as 1957, the Ministry of Health and Welfare suspected that the discharge from Chisso was the real cause (Miyazawa, 1997, p. 121), the Ministry of International Trade and Industry and the government of Kumamoto Prefecture were reluctant to admit it.

Meanwhile, in 1965, a similar disease was discovered in a different part of Japan, in Niigata Prefecture. Doctors found twenty-six patients who had symptoms extremely similar to those of Minamata Disease (Miyazawa, 1997, pp. 373–82). The following year, the Ministry of Health and Welfare determined that the effluent discharged from the Showa Denko factory was the cause of the disease (Harada, 1972, pp. 98–104). It is highly possible that this repeated occurrence of the disease was connected to the delay in determining the cause of Minamata Disease.

Chisso continued to discharge untreated effluent until 1966, causing even greater pollution (Miyazawa, 1997, pp. 380–1), and it was not until 1968 (thirteen years after the first patient was reported in Minamata) that the government officially determined that the effluent discharged by Chisso was the cause of the disease. Chisso, however, was reluctant to provide victims with adequate compensation and denied the causal relationship between their effluents and the disease. Chisso even used 'Yakuza' (the Japanese Mafia) to threaten the families of victims, and doctors and journalists sympathetic to the dying individuals (van Wolferen, 1990, p. 121).

This industrial pollution incident had claimed the lives of 987 victims by December 1990 (Ui, 1992, p. 131), and many more have continued to suffer from 'symptoms such as severe convulsions, intermittent loss of consciousness, repeated lapses into crazed mental states and finally, permanent coma' (ibid., p. 110).

In 1995, the Japanese prime minister, Tomiichi Murayama, officially expressed 'regret' over the occurrence of the disease, and a political settlement was finalized. This was almost forty years after the official discovery of the disease. A slow process indeed!

The tainted blood incident

The Japanese government's tendency to neglect its responsibility to secure the safety of citizens against health risks can be observed in numerous contexts. Specifically, negative feedback[2] processes remain blocked, and the implementation of necessary measures is delayed unreasonably because of the pressure from a narrowly defined concept of economic efficiency.

One example of this neglect was the government's handling of processed blood products tainted with HIV in the early 1980s (Matsushita, 1996). In January 1982, a hemophiliac died of AIDS in Miami, Florida. The July 1982 issue of the *US Center for Disease Control (CDC) Journal* warned of HIV-tainted blood products causing AIDS among hemophiliacs. In January 1983, the *New England Journal of Medicine* published an article that recommended the use of alternative processed products for hemophilia treatment. In March 1983, the US Red Cross began to recall potentially risky blood products (Matsushita, 1996, p. 81).

In Japan during the same time period, such information was widely shared among specialists in the field, including officials in the Ministry of Health and Welfare. Even though they had access to the information from the USA, the Japanese government did not establish the AIDS Study Committee until June 1983 (Matsushita, 1996, p. 88). Most of the committee members were in support of banning the import of unsterilized blood products and of disposing of imported products already in stock. However, the chair of the committee, Dr Takeshi Abe, opposed the majority, and it was his recommendation that ultimately was followed (Matsushita, 1996, p. 89). Dr Abe was a staunch supporter of the Midori Cross Pharmaceutical Company, which had a large stock of imported unsterilized blood products. If the ban had been implemented immediately, the company would have lost enormous sums of money. The Japanese government finally banned the import and sale of unsterilized products and granted manufacture licenses for alternative blood products in August 1987, two years and four months after the US government had done the same (Hosaka, 1997, p. 293). During that period, approximately 2000 hemophiliacs became infected with the HIV virus through tainted products (Matsushita, 1996, p. 82). The result was a tragedy that claimed the lives of more than 400 hemophiliacs in Japan (Hosaka, 1997, p. 2).

On 28 September 2001, the Tokyo District Court announced its verdict on Dr Abe. He was found not guilty because the Court recognized that, as early as 1985, it was still difficult to know the health risks of the unsterilized blood products (*Asahi Shinbun*, 2001b). In light of the facts presented here, the verdict certainly appears unreasonable.

In fact, some of the senior managers of the Midori Cross Pharmaceutical Company had worked as medical researchers at the notorious biological weapons research institutes in China operated by members of the Japanese Imperial Army, known as Troop 731 (Matsushita, 1996; Yamaguchi, 1998). During the Second World War, the researchers at these institutes used innocent Chinese citizens in their experiments attempting to develop bacteriological weapons. It is estimated that at least 3000 Chinese people were victimized during these atrocious human experiments (Matsumura, 1997). However, the medical researchers of Troop 731 were never convicted as war criminals, since the US government made a secret deal with them. The researchers were set free in exchange for the release of their experimental results to the US government. A number of these researchers are now top people in Japanese medical circles. The mentality behind the activities of Troop 731, characterized by a lack of respect for human life, was a sad legacy that shaped the gloomy and inhumane history of postwar medical practices in Japan. This legacy can also be seen as a significant contributor to the tainted blood incident and to other numerous medical scandals in Japan (Matsushita, 1996; Yamaguchi, 1998). If these researchers had been convicted, the negative feedback mechanism would have worked effectively and subsequent medical practice in Japan would have taken a more humane approach.

The nuclear criticality incident at JCO in Tokai-mura

The nuclear criticality incident at the JCO Company in Tokai-mura in 1999 claimed the lives of two workers. It is generally believed that the cause of the incident was the improper handling of radioactive (uranium) materials by workers. It was later found that the JCO had been using a confidential and unauthorized in-house version of a work manual. This manual instructed workers to employ illegal procedures, different from those designated by the Japanese government, for the prevention of nuclear criticality incidents. Moreover, in order to save time, workers would skip important safety steps that were provided in the in-house manual. It became clear that the workers had not been properly trained with regard to the safety risks associated with nuclear processing operations (Genshiryoku Shiryou Joho-shitsu, 1999, pp. 33–6; Nishio, 1999, pp. 240–3; *Yomiuri Shinbun* Editorial Bureau, 2000, pp. 30–7, 186–97).

This account, however, only addresses some superficial causes of the accident. A deeper cause was the fact that the facility lacked a fail-safe design. Specifically, the settling tank was not designed to prevent nuclear criticality incidents. The JCO factory had been using unauthorized and unsafe specifications, and the JCO Company as a whole did not anticipate the possibility of nuclear criticality incidents (Genshiryoku Shiryou Joho-shitsu, 1999, pp. 36–7; Hirose and Fujita, 2000, pp. 220–3).

In addition, the safety inspections of nuclear facilities conducted by the Japanese government – specifically, the Nuclear Safety Committee of the Science and Technology Agency – were almost completely ineffective (Genshiryoku Shiryou Joho-shitsu, 1999, p. 37; Nishio, 1999, p. 243; Takagi, 1999, pp. 11–18; Hirose and Fujita, 2000, pp. 220–3; Tateno *et al.*, 2000, pp. 36–48, 172–5). The inspections did not detect the obvious failure of JCO's 'safety design'. The Nuclear Safety Committee's own Basic Safety Guidelines clearly state that each unit in a nuclear fuel facility must, from a technical point of view, take into consideration every imaginable situation in which nuclear criticality might occur and take appropriate preventative measures (Article 10, 'Nuclear Criticality Safety'). (See Nuclear Safety Commission of Japan (2004) for details of the Basic Safety Guidelines) Article 12 ('Consideration of Possible Nuclear Criticality Incidents') states that nuclear fuel facilities must take appropriate measures if there is the possibility of a nuclear criticality incident as a result of operational errors (Takagi, 1999, pp. 12–14). However, the guidelines left room for a wide range of interpretations. At the JCO and other facilities, the guidelines were implemented in an arbitrary manner, or they were not observed strictly (Genshiryoku Shiryou Joho-shitsu, 1999, pp. 37–9; Takagi, 1999, pp. 13–14). After the incident, nobody on the Nuclear Safety Committee, including the committee chair, Mr Kazuo Sato, was willing to take responsibility for the negligence that led indirectly to the deaths of two workers and the exposure of thousands others to radiation. Quite the reverse, in fact – the members of the committee inspected the site after the incident, as part of the Nuclear Criticality Incident Inquiry, and criticized the workers and the factory, as if they had been responsible for the serious flaw in the facility's safety design (Takagi, 2000a, p. 11).

The Mitsubishi Motor Company scandal

In July 2000, it became public knowledge that the Mitsubishi Motor Company, a major Japanese automobile manufacturer, had been concealing drivers' claims concerning defective parts, and had been repairing the defective vehicles in secret for the previous thirty years (Kano, 2000).

As early as 1969, the Japanese Ministry of Transportation had established regulations governing the recall of defective cars. Automobile manufactures were obliged to report and announce publicly the existence of defective parts in order to ensure vehicle safety, but because of unlawful vehicle recall practices by the Mitsubishi Motor Company, road safety had been compromised seriously. Several traffic accidents occurred because of defective vehicle parts, some involving injuries.

The culture of Japanese university education

After completing my graduate studies at a university in Canada, I returned to Japan in March 2000. I was fortunate enough to be offered a teaching position at a private university in Sapporo, Hokkaido. I was surprised to discover that the university had no system in place for students to evaluate the quality of the teaching process. (Of course, some progressive professors had been requesting such evaluations of their own volition.) The Faculty Development Committee was created and decided to introduce a student evaluation system starting in the year 2000. The results of these student evaluations were to be published in a semi-annual booklet, and I was given the task of compiling the data into a report format. To my disappointment, five out of thirty full-time faculty members did not ask their students for their evaluations at the end of the first term. This ratio increased to eight out of thirty in the second term. Arguably, some professors were afraid to ask for feedback from their students, but by so doing, they missed a precious opportunity to learn from their students' comments.[3]

A more surprising incident occurred on campus last summer. Most Japanese universities host annual open campus festivals, during which student associations and clubs present their activity reports and study results, or conduct fundraising activities. My former university employer[4] is no exception. Last summer, a student environmental group suggested the idea of measuring the environmental load on our campus, hoping that the findings of their research would help the university to reduce its ecological burden. They planned to investigate the university's energy consumption, waste generation rates and so on. To my surprise, the university rejected the students' proposal, arguing that potential unwanted findings might create a negative image of the university in the eyes of visitors. I was shocked to hear the news. However, this culture of minimizing or denying the existence of unpleasant facts exists at many levels of Japanese society.

Conclusions

Modern Japan is affected by a number of environmental, health, safety and educational problems. Behind most of these problems there appear to be some common underlying factors. One such common determiner is the Japanese tendency to deny the very existence or possible emergence of a problem in the first place. The tainted blood incident and recent BSE scandals are typical cases. As for the BSE case, the Ministry of Agriculture, Forestry and Fisheries (MAFF) only issued an administrative guidance to the industry not to use imported meat and bone meal. An administrative guidance is not a stringent policy regulation and does not usually entail penalties for those who ignore it. The fact that only the administrative guidance was issued in this matter shows that the government did not take the threat of BSE seriously. Farmers who used meat and bone meal from suspicious sources are also responsible for the occurrence of BSE in Japan.

The Mitsubishi Motor Company case is another example of the widespread practice of under-reporting inconvenient facts. The company believed that their practice of not publicizing the existence of vehicle component defects was not a problem as long as they repaired those defects (secretly) at the request of individual consumers. The Japanese have a culture of seeing a problem as not being a problem, or of denying the emergence or existence of a difficulty.

In fact, the Japanese have long been taught and trained not to look at or point out a problem, since it would disturb the harmony of society. The statue of the three monkeys in the Nikko Toshogu Shrine symbolizes this culture of 'don't see, don't hear, don't speak'. The examples from my own university are also illustrative of this culture. It appears that the purpose of education in Japan has long been to produce obedient subjects, not self-conscious citizens with critical minds of their own, and this tendency is still prevalent in the current educational system. The time to change this culture is now, as we realize that concrete problems are not resolved when they are left in the hands of incompetent high-ranking authorities. The traditional top-down, centralized approach alone does not work in a modern society, where problems have become more complex and diversified (Mori, 1999). Every individual in a society should be involved in the process of problem identification and problem-solving. This is particularly true at the start of the twenty-first century, as the world is moving towards globalization, which tends to bring about more complex and profound problems (Korten, 1995; Daly, 1996,

1999; Mander and Goldsmith, 1996; Chomsky, 1999; Cobb, 1999; French, 2000; Rees, 2000). For example, economic globalization is likely to widen the gap between the rich and the poor, and to increase social instability and environmental and health risks. The tainted blood incident and the BSE case discussed in this chapter are typical of the problems that were brought about by increased communications and exchange of materials across borders.

The purpose of education should be to cultivate the ability to perceive and identify emerging problems, as well as to assess the significance of those problems. Japanese society needs to promote value sensitivity and critical thinking. Perhaps, more importantly, Japanese citizens should cultivate a sense of 'ownership' of their own society, meaning that the citizens themselves should take responsibility for maintaining the health of the society by recognizing and eradicating threats to the system, as they emerge. In this respect, I am encouraged by the increasing participation of Japanese citizens in the activities of non-governmental and non-profit organizations (*Asahi Shinbun* Chikyu Project 21, 1998; Horiuchi, 1998; Mekata, 1998).

A second common determiner of the problems discussed above is the inability of Japanese authorities to identify the real causes of the problems. Even when a real cause is known, it is often denied, suppressed or marginalized by the powerful elites. Powerful elites consist of major industries, bureaucrats and politicians who work for the benefit of their constituencies (for example, pharmaceutical companies are the constituencies of the Ministry of Health and Welfare). These elites, as well as the 'scholars' who help to justify their decisions, often evade proper punishment. These groups of powerful elites sometimes cover up the facts and the real causes of problems (Takagi, 2000b, pp. 143–56). They mask the real problems (if they ever identify them) by shifting attention on to minor issues, claimed to be more important (Harada, 1972, pp. 56–7; Shimin Enerugi Kenkyujo, 1994, pp. 72–5; Miyazawa, 1997, pp. 227–9). They lack a sense of accountability and often monopolize information (Takagi, 2000b, pp. 136–40). Citizens are often given superficial or distorted information and excluded from serious and substantive problem-solving debates, either domestically or internationally. In other words, the elites have effectively blocked the negative feedback mechanisms, thus rendering large segments of society relatively powerless. Consequently, society, as a whole, lacks the ability to learn from previous mistakes and to adjust its policies according to what otherwise would have been important new information. Also, the measures that are sometimes implemented in the aftermath of such incidents as the ones described here are almost invariably superficial and ineffective.

Mass media are also responsible for providing superficial and distorted information to citizens. In the summer of 1997, while the Asia-Pacific Economic Cooperation (APEC) meetings were being held in Vancouver, Canada, I was working for a major Japanese newspaper company. At the same time, there were several parallel meetings and demonstrations organized by citizens' groups. Citizens were expressing their concerns regarding economic globalization, which APEC was trying to promote. Unfortunately, most of the Japanese media were not sensitive enough to the voices of citizens outside the walls of the luxurious conference center. They simply reported the 'official' statements made by the government representatives and the APEC Secretariat, without adding any critical perspectives (Wada, 1998). Such attitudes in the Japanese media reminded me of the notorious announcements from the Japanese military headquarter ('Daihon-ei Happyo') during the Second World War. These announcements often contained distorted reports of the damage inflicted on the enemy, which gave ordinary citizens in Japan a completely false image of the war. They thought that Japan was winning the war, while the reality was quite different: Japanese troops were being pushed back continuously, and casualty figures mounting. During the 1997 APEC conference in Vancouver, the Japanese media acted in a similar way. They portrayed a totally biased picture of the APEC meetings to their Japanese audience by reporting only the official statements. The Japanese media acted in a similar manner during other international meetings, such as the World Trade Organization (WTO) meetings and the G8 summits. I witnessed this phenomenon during the WTO Ministerial meeting in Seattle, USA. I was one of the thousands of peaceful demonstrators there. The Japanese media covered the demonstrations in a superficial manner and did not report significant facts about the nature of the WTO or the citizens' concerns. It is noticeable that, in Europe and North America, alternative media are more active than in Japan. Alternative information is easily available in those regions. Japan should foster such alternative media, as suggested by Katsuichi Honda (a radical journalist in Japan, who wrote extensively about the Nanking Massacre).

A third common factor underlying the problems addressed in this chapter is the inability of governmental policies to incorporate swiftly new scientific findings. The Minamata Disease case, the tainted blood incident, or the BSE contamination case, all illustrate this tendency. Japan should guarantee scientists a higher status, free from the pressures of the powerful elites (industry, bureaucrats and politicians). In their capacity as consultants or advisers to policy-makers, scientists and scholars must assume their proper share of the decisional responsibility.

Finally, it has been shown that all the incidents described above have also been caused by the rush for economic efficiency and private material gains at the expense of public values, such as the safety of consumers and workers, a healthy environment, natural beauty, the protection of human rights, stable communities and countless other life-quality factors that contribute to human well-being (Rees, 2000). Based on a narrowly defined concept of economic efficiency and in the search for short-term material gains, a range of deep-seated problems have been ignored or perceived as trivial. Japan needs to reclaim the importance of non-economic values.

At the time of writing, in the name of 'globalization', increasing emphasis is being placed worldwide on economic values by sacrificing public values (Korten, 1995; Mander and Goldsmith, 1996; Chomsky, 1999). Trade barriers are being loosened or abolished in order to secure freer and/or unregulated access to natural and financial resources as well as to the market. Free economic activity seems to be the most important value in this age of globalization. The regrettable incidents described in this chapter illustrate Japan's hasty engagement in the process of globalization and should offer timely warnings to the rest of the world.

In conclusion, I argue that the key to creating a vibrant and viable twenty-first century in Japan is the installation of effective negative feedback mechanisms at all levels of society. An equally important strategy is for Japan to emphasize non-economic values, such as public safety and environmental integrity. If Japan fails to implement these strategies, the nation will not be able to respond wisely to the range of problems that inevitably emerge in the process of rapid globalization. That failure would also threaten the environmental foundation and social integrity necessary for Japan's survival in the globalizing world. For Japan, the tide of globalization might well turn into a tidal wave. If, however, Japan succeeds in implementing these constructive strategies, it will be able to build a more viable and sustainable nation, and in so doing, Japan may become a model for other countries to follow rather than to avoid.

Notes

* I am is grateful to Mark Gibeau, Janette McIntosh, Alex Munteanu, and Donna Yeung for their editorial help.

1 Yasukuni Shrine was originally founded as Tokyo Shokon Shrine in 1869 (one year after the Meiji Restoration) and enshrines more than 2.5 million persons who are the war dead and victims of the Japanese civil war (which took place over the ten-year period 1860–1870), the Sino-Japanese War, the Russo–Japanese War and the Second World War. These persons include 57,000 female deaths, 21,000 Korean deaths and 28,000 Taiwanese deaths. The families of newly-found war dead continue to request enshrinement at Yasukuni Shrine.

The enshrining of the souls of people found guilty by the Tokyo War Tribunal began in 1959 and ended in 1978, when the souls of 14 Class-A war criminals were enshrined. There were no protests at all from China or any other country over the enshrining of the Class-A war criminals at this time and a number of Japanese Prime Ministers continued to pay visits to Yasukuni Shrine without any foreign protests until 1985. China protested the visit to Yasukuni Shrine by a Japanese Prime Minister (Yasuhiro Nakasone) in 1985 for the first time. The reason for their protest was that Yasukuni Shrine enshrines the souls of 14 Class-A war criminals. Since 1985 Japanese Prime Ministers' visits to Yasukuni Shrine received protests from China and South Korea.

Prime Minister Koizumi's visits to Yasukuni Shrine seem to continue receiving majority support from Japanese people for the following reasons, among other: Japanese Buddhism and Shinto religions allow for tolerance in that anyone becomes a deity after death so that Japanese enshrines not only friendly victims but also enemy victims; and the overwhelming majority of the Japanese people did not support the process of the Tokyo War Tribunal right after the second World War.

How to treat certain aspects of Japanese history in textbooks for Japanese elementary, and junior and senior high schools has always been a controversial domestic issue in Japan since the Second World War. Private companies present their new textbooks every year to the Ministry of Education (now the Ministry of Education, Culture, Sports, Science and Technology) for approval before they can be purchased by private and public schools. Usually local school boards select textbooks for public schools in their jurisdictions.

In 1982 the Ministry of Education asked the publishers of textbooks for senior high school social studies classes to replace the word 'invade' with 'advance' in sentences describing the Japanese Imperial Army's invasion of Asian countries in the Second World War. Both China and South Korea protested at this proposed change. Since then the treatment in Japanese history textbooks of various issues related to Japan's war-time behavior in Asia has received protests from China and South Korea. The most recent protest was about the new history textbook that incorporated the many positive contributions of Japan in modern history. The textbook was presented to the Ministry of Education for approval in April 2000. The textbook, after the revision requested by the Ministry of Education was made, was approved for public use in April 2001. Both China and South Korea protested at this time and asked for further revisions. But virtually all high schools decided not to adopt the textbook.

2 'Negative feedback' and 'positive feedback' are both control mechanisms within systems. These terms are usually employed in the contexts of ecology, biology or cybernetics. Positive feedback is 'deviation-accelerating' and necessary for growth and survival of organisms. In order to achieve control, negative feedback is also necessary. Negative feedback is a 'deviation-counteracting' input. Biologists

call the feedback mechanisms of living systems 'homeostatic mechanisms'. Critics of human society are using these terms increasingly in their fields. For example, social scientists point out that 'the positive feedback involved in the expansion of knowledge, power, and productivity threatens the quality of human life and environment unless adequate negative feedback controls can be found' (Odum, 1971, pp. 34–5). In this chapter, I use the term 'negative feedback' to refer to 'an input that counteracts the deterioration of systems'.

3 My former university employer, for whom I worked until last year, consists of six faculties, and is a well-respected university in Sapporo. We have exchange relationships with foreign universities, including Zhejiang University in Hangzhou, Zhejiang, China. Fortunately, the student evaluation report of my faculty received some attention, and became the model for the whole university. The Board of Directors of the university subsequently decided that all the departments must carry out student evaluation. Student evaluations are not yet widely conducted at many Japanese universities.

4 Sapporo University.

References

Asahi Shinbun (newspaper) (2000a) 'Extra-luxurious Summit', 24 July (evening edition) (in Japanese).

Asahi Shinbun (newspaper) (2000b) 'Foreign Ministry's Vice-Secretary Refutes the Criticisms of "Extra-luxurious Summit"', 25 July (in Japanese).

Asahi Shinbun (newspaper) (2001a) 'Secret Funds Amount to More than One Hundred Million Yen', 30 October. See http://www.asahi.com/politics/update/1030/004.html (in Japanese).

Asahi Shinbun (newspaper) (2001b) (evening edition) 'Summary of the Reasons of the Verdict of the Pharmaceutical AIDS Incident: Ministry of Health and Welfare Route', 28 September, pp. 1, 11 (in Japanese).

Asahi Shinbun Chikyu Project 21 (1998) *Shimin Sanka de Sekai wo Kaeru* (Transforming the World Through Citizens' Participation) (Tokyo: Asahi Shinbun) (in Japanese).

Chomsky, Noam (1999) *Profit Over People: Neoliberalism and Global Order* (New York: Seven Stories Press).

Cobb, John B., Jr (1999) *The Earthist Challenge to Economism: A Theological Critique of the World Bank* (London: Macmillan).

Daly, Herman E. (1996) *Beyond Growth: The Economics of Sustainable Development* (Boston, Mass.: Beacon Press).

Daly, Herman E. (1999) *Ecological Economics and the Ecology of Economics: Essays in Criticism* (Cheltenham, UK: Edward Elgar).

French, Hilary (2000) *Vanishing Borders: Protecting the Planet in the Age of Globalization* (New York and London: W.W. Norton).

Genshiryoku Shiryou Joho-shitsu (1999) *Kyoufuno Rinkai Jiko* (Horrific Nuclear Criticality Accident), Iwanami Booklet No. 496 (Tokyo: Iwanami Shoten) (in Japanese).

Harada, Masazumi (1972) *Minamata-byo* (Minamata Disease) (Tokyo: Iwanami Shoten) (in Japanese).

Hirose, Takashi and Fujita, Yuko (2000). *Genshiryoku Hatsuden de Hontoni Watashitachiga Shiritai 120 no Kiso-Chishiki* (Fundamental Knowledge on Nuclear Power Generation That We Would Really Like to Know) (Tokyo: Tokyo Shoseki) (in Japanese).

Horiuchi, Kozo (1998) *Chikyu Kankyou Taisaku: Kangae kata to Senshin-jirei* (Measures to Protect the Global Environment: Concepts and Advanced Examples) (Tokyo: Yuhikaku) (in Japanese).

Hosaka, Wataru (1997) *Koseisho AIDS Fairu* (The AIDS File of the Ministry of Health and Welfare) (Tokyo: Iwanami Shoten) (in Japanese).

Kano, Osamu (2000) 'Mitsubishi Jidousha no Rikoru Kakushi: Shohisha ha Mekaa nimo Gyosei nimo Tayorenai (Concealment of Recalls by Mitsubishi Motor Company: Consumers Cannot Rely on Manufacturers or the Government)', *Ekonomisuto* (Economist), 12 September, pp. 20–1 (in Japanese).

Korten, David C. (1995) *When Corporations Rule the World* (West Hartford, Conn.: Kumarian Press).

Mander, Jerry and Edward Goldsmith (eds) (1996) *The Case Against the Global Economy: and for a Turn Toward the Local* (San Francisco: Sierra Club).

Matsumura, Takao (ed.) (1997) *Ronsou: 731 Butai [Zouho-ban]* (Polemic: Troop 731 [expanded edition]) (Tokyo: Banseisha) (in Japanese).

Matsushita, Kazunari (1996) *Midori Juji to 731 Butai* (Midori Cross and Troop 731) (Tokyo: San-Ichi Shobo) (in Japanese).

Mekata, Motoko (1998) *Jirai naki Chikyu he: Yume wo Genjitu ni Shita Hitobito* (The World without Land-mines: Citizens Who Made Their Dreams Come True) (Tokyo: Iwanami Shoten) (in Japanese).

Miyazawa, Nobuo (1997) *Minamata-byo jiken: 40-nen* (The Minamata Disease Incident: A 40-year History). (Fukuoka: Ashi-shobo), p. 506 (in Japanese).

Mori, Satoko (1999) *NGO to Chikyu Kankyo Gabanansu* (NGOs and Global Environmental Governance) (Tokyo: Tsukiji Shokan) (in Japanese).

Nature (2001) 'Japan's Beef Scandal'. 27 September, (vol. 413, no. 6854), p. 333.

Nishio, Baku (1999) 'Uso datta Shisetsu no Anzensei de Saiaku no Jikoni (The Worst Accident Caused by the Fake Safety of the Facility)', in Baku Nishio (ed.), *Genpatsu wo Susumeru Kiken na Uso: Jiko Kakushi, Kyogi Houkoku, Deeta Kaizan* (Lies Behind the Promotion of Nuclear Power Generation: Accident Cover-up, False Reporting, and Falsifying Data) (Tokyo: Hachigatu Shokan), pp. 240–3 (in Japanese).

Nuclear Safety Commission of Japan (2004) *Basic Safety Guidelines* available from http://www.nsc.go.jp.

Odum, Eugene P. (1971) *Fundamentals of Ecology* (3rd edn) (Philadelphia, Pa.: W. B. Saunders).

Rees, William E. (2000) 'The Dark Side of the Force (of Globalization)', based on notes prepared for the LEAD Training Session on Globalization and Sustainability: Impact on Local Communities (Vancouver, BC, August 2000).

Shimin Enerugi Kenkyujo (People's Research Institute on Energy and Environment) (1994) *2010 nen Nihon Enerugi Keikaku: Chikyu Ondanka mo Genpatsu monai Mirai eno Sentaku* (Japan's Energy Planning for the Year 2010: A Possible Energy Option for the Future) (Tokyo: Daiyamondo-sha) (*in Japanese*.)

Takagi, Jinzaburo (1999) 'Tokai Uran Saitenkan Shisetsu deno Rinkai Jiko ni Tsuite (On the Nuclear Criticality Incident at Tokai Uranium Processing Facility)', *Agora*, no. 255, 10 November (in Japanese).

Takagi, Jinzaburo (2000a) *Genshiryoku Shinwa Karano Kaihou* (Liberation from the Nuclear Power Myth) (Tokyo: Kobunsha) (in Japanese).

Takagi, Jinzaburo (2000b) *Genpatsu Jiko ha Naze Kurikaesunoka* (Why Are Nuclear Accidents Being Repeated?) (Tokyo: Iwanami Shoten) (in Japanese).

Tateno, Jun, Noguchi Kunikazu and Aoyagi Naganori (2000) *Tettei Kaimei Tokai-mura Rinkai Jiko* (Scrutiny of the Nuclear Criticality Accident in Tokai-mura) (Tokyo: Shin-Nihon Shuppansha) (in Japanese).

Ui, Jun (1992) 'Minamata Disease' in Ui, Jun (ed.) *Industrial Pollution in Japan* (Tokyo: United Nations University Press).

van Wolferen, Karel (1990) *Nihon/kenryoku kozo no nazo* (The Enigma of Japanese Power: People and Politics in a Stateless Nation) (Tokyo: Hayakawa-shobou) (in Japanese).

Wada, Yoshihiko (1998) 'Vancouver karano tegami: bento haitatsugakari ga mita APEC (A Letter from Vancouver: APEC Meetings through the Eyes of a Bento Boy'. *Shukan Kin-yobi*, no. 209, 6 March (in Japanese).

Yamaguchi, Ken-ichiro (ed.) (1998) *Ayatsurareru seito shi: Seimei no tanjo kara shuen made* (Manipulated Life and Death: From Birth to the End of Life) (Tokyo: Shogakkan) (in Japanese).

Yomiuri Shinbun (newspaper) Editorial Bureau (2000) *Aoi Senkou: Dokyumento Tokai Rinkai Jiko* (A Blue Flash: Document of the Tokai Nuclear Criticality Incident) (Tokyo: Chuo Koron Shinsha) (in Japanese).

4

The Mind Roaming above the Ocean: Mental Health of Young Japanese Sojourners in Vancouver

Etsuko Kato

If globalization means merely that parts of the world are interconnected, then there is nothing new about this so-called globalization: it began centuries ago.... The only novelty is in the degree of expansion in the trade and transfer of capital, labor, production, consumption, information and technology, which might be enormous enough to amount to a qualitative change (Miyoshi, 1998, p. 248).

In this chapter I shall focus on a new type of migrant from Japan to Vancouver produced as a result of globalization – namely, those who are in an ambiguous status between sojourners and settlers. This type of migrant first presupposes an increasing number of short-term overseas visitors, then those wishing for a longer stay, then for permanent residency. It seems as if they are blurring the differences between traveling, months-long stay and permanent residency. Thus they represent a qualitative change of migrants as a result of a quantitative change.

I shall discuss the psychological and practical challenges that face this type of migrant. First, I shall describe a group of sojourners which consists primarily of young people – that is, those aged between 19 and 35, living in North America (and later in Vancouver) for more than a year with a student visa, a visitor's visa or a working holiday visa. Then, based on my thirteen months of field research and on theories of cultural psychology, I shall elucidate the unique problems confronting these young migrants.

Here three specific questions are raised: (i) What brings them to Vancouver? (ii) What problems confront them, and what are the causes? and (iii) What leads some of them to more self-destructive lives than others in Vancouver?

To answer the first question, I shall refer to Roy Baumeister's concept of 'identity deficit' – that is, lack of commitment to any values, which is observed among youth (including those who are well past adolescence) in industrialized countries in general. Then I shall point out some aspects of globalization that enable the young who have 'identity deficit' to cross national borders easily.

To the second question, my findings are that the 'identity deficit' itself is already a potential psychological problem, and that the problem can be magnified rather than solved, or even develop into (self-)destructive lives after going abroad, when the youth realizes with disappointment that just moving abroad does not change their lives dramatically. Here I shall refer to a Japanese psychological trait – namely, the situation-dependent perception of 'self', as a factor that puts young sojourners into vulnerable situations in North America.

To the third question, I argue that the young can be led into self-destructive lives in a higher possibility when they perceive themselves to be 'underachievers' or 'unfits' on leaving Japan. Failure to entering a suitable school or a problematic relationship with parents are examples of factor that make young people perceive themselves in a negative way. I will further point out that more serious cases, such as psychiatric problems and suicides, can be attributed either to the problems the youth already had in Japan, or their experiences in Canada.

General background of participants

Japanese migrants in Vancouver can be divided roughly into three subgroups: pre-Second World War immigrants and their descendants, postwar immigrants, and sojourners (with the potential to immigrate).

Vancouver, because of its location on the West Coast of North America and relative vicinity to East Asia, has been the most popular destination for Japanese migrants to Canada since 1877, when the first recorded Japanese settler arrived in the city. At its peak before the Second World War, Vancouver is considered to have held 95 per cent of about 22,000 Japanese Canadians (anecdotal and statistical data used here are from Tsubaki, 1998, pp. 142–3). Yet the wartime internment of Japanese Canadians in camps and the four-year prohibition of their return to the city after the war destroyed the once-established community.

A new phenomenon after the war was an increasing number of Asian immigrants, especially from the early 1970s to the mid-1980s, because of a migration policy change in 1966 which opened the doors wider for non-European immigrants. The development of air travel facilitated this influx. One statistical item shows that at least 101 Japanese households in total immigrated to the Greater Vancouver area alone between 1970 and 1974 (Tsubaki, 1998, p. 143). A Japanese postwar immigrant's impression is that, at its peak, Japanese immigrants to Vancouver numbered about 1,000 per year (Takeo Yamashiro, director of Japanese Community Volunteers' Association in Vancouver, personal communication, 2001). The immigrants from this period now constitute a distinctive group called 'postwar immigrants (*sengo-ijusha*)', differentiated from prewar immigrants and their descendants.

Following the waves of postwar migration detailed above is a new type of migrant: people who are sojourners at first, but are potential immigrants. This group consists of tourists and other kinds of visitors, students and 'working holiday-makers', whose number increased constantly from the mid-1980s and throughout the 1990s.

'Working holiday-makers' refers to Japanese nationals between the ages of 18 and 30 who are entitled to stay in Canada with up to a 12-month employment authorization under the bilateral agreement between Japanese and Canadian governments. Beginning in 1986, to promote intercultural exchange between the two countries, the agreement has been sending an increasing number of young people from one country to the other. At the time of writing, nearly 5,000 Japanese young people go to Canada each year, but fewer than 1,000 similiar Canadian people go to Japan. A questionnaire survey of eighty-one returned working holiday-makers conducted in 2000 indicates that the majority (32 per cent) of Japanese working holiday-makers stayed in Vancouver longer than in any other Canadian cities in 2000; the figure for Japanese working holiday-makers who stayed in Vancouver longest among Canadian cities was 42.2 per cent in 1999 (Nihon Working Holiday Kyokai, 2000, pp. 20, 54).

Besides working holiday-makers, more than 6,000 Japanese students per year fly to Canada to attend English as Second Language (ESL) schools, high schools, colleges or universities. According to 2001 statistical data at the Canadian Embassy in Japan, the majority (79.1 per cent) of these students are studying ESL, and more than half (56.89 per cent) are staying in British Columbia (see Figures 4.1 and 4.2). Considering all these situations, one may say that, on the whole, the Japanese sojourners in Vancouver are generally 'young' people.

While the 1996 census reports the number of Japanese Canadians in Vancouver as 21,880, the number of sojourners is difficult to measure because of their mobility, and often their neglect to register their arrival with the Consulate General. One estimation (or rumor) I heard in 2001

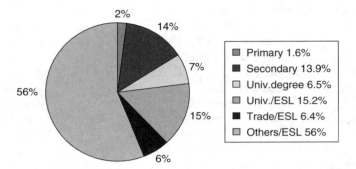

Figure 4.1   Approved applicants for student visa by level of study: 2001 (N = 6,615)
Notes: Univ./ESL: study English as a second language at a university; Trade/ESL: study English as a second language at a trade school; others/ESL: study English as a second language at other types of schools.
Source: calculated from statistical data provided by the Canadian Embassy in Tokyo.

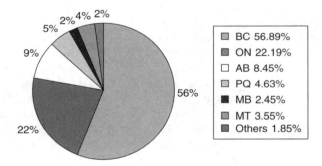

Figure 4.2   Japanese students in Canada by province: 2001 (*N* = 6,615)
Notes: BC: British Columbia; ON: Ontario; AB: Alberta; PQ: Quebec; MB: Manitoba; MT: combined Maritime provinces (New Brunswick, Nova Scotia; Newfoundland and Labrador, and Prince Edward Island); Others: Saskatchewan, Yukon, Northwest Territories and Nunavut.
Source: calculated from statistical data provided by the Canadian Embassy in Tokyo.

notes that the number of Japanese transients, including tourists, in the Westend area alone adds up to some 10,000 per year.

Despite the visibility of the young sojourners, the Japanese Canadian community in Vancouver has shown relatively little interest in them, because of their non-immigrant status and supposedly limited period of stay in Canada, which separates sojourners' interests from those of settlers. However, according to the 2001 statistical data from the Canadian

Embassy in Japan, the majority (78.1 per cent) of students are enrolled on courses lasting a year or more. Also, as I observe, students and other sojourners often prolong their stay for several years by extending their student visa, by switching from a working holiday visa to a visitor's visa, by marrying local Canadians, and so on.

Many of the sojourners express their wish to get a one- or two-year employment authorization (so-called 'work permit'), and from there permanent residency or citizenship of Canada. Moreover, those with visitors' visas are not necessarily short-term visitors, as they often switch to a student visa, or some switch from other kinds of visa to a visitor's visa, in order to prolong their stay. And not a few fly back and forth between the two countries at six-month to one-year intervals, returning to Canada often with a different kind of visa each time. Thus young sojourners are blurring the boundaries increasingly between visitors, sojourners and immigrants.

Another possible reason that the Japanese settlers in Vancouver have not actively contacted the young sojourners is that the sojourners seem to be a 'nuisance' to them. When the settlers hear about the sojourners, they are often in trouble; for example, hospitalized or detained at the police, or are in need of emergency shelter or an interpreter. These phenomena may suggest that the sojourners are especially vulnerable to troubles.

Methodology

The following discussions are based on my post-doctoral research at the University of British Columbia, conducted between April 2001 and March 2002, mainly through qualitative methods of interviews and participant observation. I undertook in-depth interviews with fifty-five individuals, whom I recruited through advertisements in two free Japanese magazines designed for sojourners and one newspaper published in Vancouver. I also recruited participants by putting posters on the bulletin boards of Konbini-ya, a Japanese-style 'convenience store' on Robson Street, and in several school information centers in the down-town area. In addition, I visited one international high school to recruit interviewees.

Recruitment took place in two stages. First, in April 2001, I released ads recruiting Japan-born Japanese 'youth'. I did not specify the ages group but presupposed 'youth' to be between 15 and the mid-thirties. The conditions were that (i) they should have either a working holiday visa, a student visa or a visitor's visa. I specified 'students' to be ESL students or college students and excluded degree students, because students of the latter category were in a minority group (6.5 per cent – see Figure 4.1) and (ii) who have lived or intended to live for more than one year in North America, including the United States. Eighty to a hundred people responded to this recruitment drive. Because of the limitation on time and budget (one interview usually took between 90 to 120 minutes, and often more; I paid a $12 honorarium for every interview), I met forty-one people, whom I chose as carefully as possible so that the distribution of their visa status, age and gender would reflect overall tendencies.

Then, in September 2001, I placed other ads, adding to the first conditions more specific ones requesting that interviewees should have experienced of, or be experiencing, (i) marijuana or drug-taking; (ii) alcohol dependence; (iii) unwanted relationships with partners; or (iv) school or work phobia, after coming to Vancouver. To this request, fourteen people responded, and I interviewed all of them. Figures 4.3, 4.4 and 4.5 show the demographic characteristics of the 55 interviewees by age, gender and visa status.

In addition to the interviews, I frequently observed young sojourners in the downtown area, mainly along Robson Street, which is the most popular residential and entertainment area for them, and sometimes at a school information center.

Another 'field' where I met my participants was the Japanese Social Services Network, later called Peer Net, which I co-founded with my colleagues at the Japanese Canadian Citizens' Association Human Rights Committee, serving as a representative from September 2001 to March 2002. Our original intention was to create and circulate a phone list of Japanese-speaking specialists, such as doctors, counselors and interpreters,

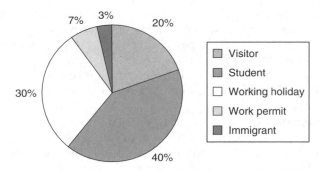

Figure 4.3   Interviewees by visa status (*N* = 55)

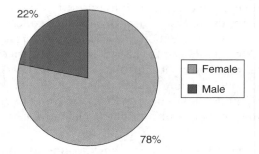

Figure 4.4   Interviewees by gender (*N* = 55)

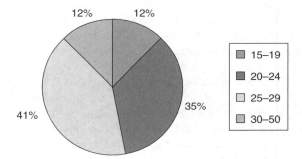

Figure 4.5   Interviewees by age (*N* = 55)

in Greater Vancouver who might help a person in trouble, but not to start a counseling service ourselves. However, as a representative, I occasionally received telephone calls and e-mails from troubled young sojourners or similar people.

In this situation, my research and community services often inter-sected and overlapped each other. Some of my research interviewees consulted me about their problems and I referred them to specialists; or a troubled client met through the Social Service Network later volunteered to be interviewed for my research. I am aware that my involvement with sojourners after releasing my name as a representative of the Network cannot be called participant observation in a strict sense, because my participants and I were in consultant–hierarchical client relationship rather than in an equal relationship. Yet, considering the mobility and lack of stable communities among sojourners, I believe that any opportunities for contact should be taken as chances for participant observation.

As well as such qualitative research in uncontrolled conditions, I also conducted quantitative research with Japanese college students in Vancouver in controlled conditions, to see the effects of an acculturation workshop I designed to measure changes in their self-esteem. However, because there were fewer participants than I had expected, I had to switch the methodology from quantitative to qualitative. Although the result was insightful, limitation of space in the current volume permits this chapter to focus on the uncontrolled, qualitative part only.

What brings them here? General background of young sojourners

I asked all the interviewees about their reasons for coming to Vancouver. The most popular answers, regardless of their visa status, were 'To learn English' and 'To experience overseas life'. Most of my interviewees had traveled or home-stayed abroad before, at which time they had developed a desire to live abroad for a longer period at sometime.

Noteworthy was a tendency among working holiday-makers to try living in all the English-speaking countries under the working holiday agreement with the Japanese government – that is, Australia, New Zealand and Canada – one after another. (Britain was added to this list in 2001. Korea and France have also taken part in the agreement since 1999, but their priorities as destinations among Japanese youth are low because these are not English-speaking countries.) Some mentioned relatively rare chances to be admitted to Canada – for example, the fewer working holiday visas issued, or stricter health checks compared to other countries – as a motive of their coming to Canada 'first' or 'applying early'. Asked why he chose Canada over New Zealand or Australia, a 29-year-old male working holiday-maker answered, 'You can be admitted to New Zealand or Australia anytime, so I could go there later. I thought I should come to Canada first because it's difficult.'

To my question 'What images of Canada did you have before coming here?', the most frequent answer from working holiday-makers and other sojourners was 'Nothing especially'. Other popular answers were general descriptions of Canada as 'big' or 'cold', or practical advantages of the country such as lower living costs and higher safety 'compared to the United States'.

Although some had visited or heard about Vancouver and were strongly interested in the city before coming, the two most popular reasons for them to choose the city were its mild climate and vicinity to Japan compared to other Canadian cities. Interestingly, sojourners choosing

Canada, or Vancouver, are often motivated by comparison and relativity, rather than necessity, personal attachment or the idiosyncrasies of the place itself: the relative competitiveness of getting a Canadian working holiday visa, the relative safety and low living costs compared to the United States, a relatively mild climate, and vicinity to Japan. In this situation, there seemed to be no strong reason for them to choose Canada, or Vancouver, except that they are English-speaking places.

In terms of why the sojourners want to learn English or to live in English-speaking countries, some had clear and concrete visions of developing their careers or lives by doing so. However, there were a substantial number of sojourners who expressed some confusion or uncertainty about their goal (for example, to develop a specific career) and the means to reach it (for example, to develop English skills). Some mentioned learning English as a temporary (*toriaezu*) goal and others mentioned it as if it was an ultimate goal of life, and both talked about their struggles in improving their knowledge of the language. As conversations proceeded, however, many made similar comments, which seemed to reveal their real struggles: namely, 'I don't know what I really want to do' (*yaritai koto ga mitsukaranai*). A 23-year-old female college student who has majored in ESL, hospitality management and business management, says, 'When leaving Japan, I said to my parents, "I guess I'll find what I want to do after going to Canada." But I cannot. Well, I have something I want to do, but not for a job.' A 22-year-old female ESL student says, 'I want to do what leads to professional skills, something useful after going back to Japan.' [Kato: For example?] 'Chinese language, though I don't intend to do it.' Some said explicitly that they did not find any meaning in learning English because they did not know what they really wanted to do. It seems that such young people come to Canada or other foreign countries with the expectation that the new, foreign environment will tell them what to do – something they were unable to find at home.

Identity deficit and globalization

The kind of struggle these young people are experiencing fits the description of 'identity deficit' described in Baumeister (1986). According to Baumeister, there are two kinds of identity crisis: 'identity deficit' and 'identity conflict'. Identity deficit 'refers to the inadequately defined self, characterized by a lack of commitment to goals and values. Without such commitments, the person lacks internal, consistent motivations' (Baumeister, 1986; p. 199). Baumeister, among other scholars, locates this type of identity crisis particularly among adolescents and among adults suffering a mid-life crisis. Or one can even argue that identity deficit is a normal process of human development for adolescents, because this age group is characterized by a ' "psychological moratorium" – an opportunity to experiment with different possible identities, free from the necessity for making a definite, firm commitment to one of them' (Baumeister, 1986; p. 200, discussing Erik Erikson's writings). Meanwhile, identity conflict 'refers to the multiply defined self whose multiple definitions are incompatible' (Baumeister, 1986; p. 199). The dilemma of immigrants, between their native culture and adopted culture is an obvious example of this kind of identity crisis.

Two points are noteworthy here. First, immigrants are usually associated with identity 'conflict', not identity 'deficit'. However, concerning my participants-sojourners' identity, the problem is more in its 'deficit' than its 'conflict'. Second, although Baumeister suggests that 'identity crises could occur at any stage in life' (Baumeister, 1986; p. 201, discussing Erikson's writings), he associates identity deficits particularly with adolescents and the middle-aged, suggesting that twenties and thirties age groups are generally the most stable period of life from the point of view of identity. However, my participants-sojourners are mainly in their twenties, with some in their early thirties.

Here, two things seem to be going on in parallel. First, a so-called moratorium, which was once believed to be the privilege of adolescents, no longer applies in many industrialized countries, including Japan and Canada. In today's world, 'we have no choice but to choose . . . choice is not a matter of permission but necessity, not a matter of liberation but, for many, of *shikata ga nai* [something one cannot escape from]' (Mathews, 2000; p. 178, discussing Giddens, 1991). In other words, 'doing what one really wants to do' is not a right but rather an obligation, which puts pressure on many. Meanwhile, in Japan, there is continuous pressure from parents and from society; as many of my interviewees described it: 'You must do this and that thing by this and that age in Japan.' Several female interviewees mentioned parental and social pressures for (happy) marriage, while they did not intend to marry, or had been divorced. The generation gap around marriage may be one of the reasons that make more women than men feel unfit in Japanese society and leave home (for ethnofigureic research on international 'romance' of Japanese women, see Kelsky, 1996a, 1996b). In these respects, many of my interviewees find a refuge in Canada, where 'Individualism rules and people don't care about what others are doing', or where 'You can enter or re-enter schools and change your life course at any age'.

Second, there is a global tendency that facilitates the international migration of people with an identity deficit in one country to another without much psychological tension. I would like especially to mention the mass media, the Internet and mass transportation as facilitators of this tendency.

The mass media blur the substantiality of foreign things by presenting them via newspapers, magazines or TV screens, bringing them to readers and viewers in their homes. They blur differences between foreign places and home; and the differences between one foreign place and another. If 'Medium is a message' as Marshall McLuhan says, foreign places brought into the home via the mass media tell receivers that they are the places odorless, temperate, harmless, easy, cozy and like home. The mass media makes it look easy for any Japanese in Japan to move to live on the corner of Haro and Bute from the following day, because s/he 'has seen' Bread Garden and Grand Robson Mall on TV or in guidebooks and 'knows' that there are shops there. But they do not know that in the same neighborhood homeless people are begging, drug addicts are trafficking, and sojourners are being cheated, threatened, robbed or raped.

Especially noteworthy about the Japanese media, and probably that of many other industrialized countries too, is that increasingly they are blurring the difference between 'visiting' and 'living in' foreign places. The phenomenon is typified by a series of best-selling guidebooks of overseas travel for young people published in Japan. Daiyamondo-sha, which has been publishing the most popular guidebook series *Chikyu no arukikata* (How to Walk on the Globe) since its first two volumes 'Europe' and 'America' in 1980, started a related series *Chikyu no kurashikata* (How to Live on the Globe) in 1995 with the volumes 'France', 'UK' and 'New York'. In almost exactly the same design and format as the 'How to Walk' series – thin paper, cheerful colors and many illustrations including photographs that show even shelves of a bakery with an explanation against each loaf, or how to use subway tokens, the 'How to Live' series makes readers feel that 'living in' a foreign place is as much fun and as easy as 'walking' by.

The Internet partly overlaps with the mass media in that it supplies detailed information about overseas lives. Anybody in Japan, for example, can read updated diaries from the private homepages of Japanese sojourners living abroad. At the same time, the Internet blurs the beginning of a journey or sojourning by enabling Internet users to virtually 'start' their overseas lives while still at home. An interviewee of mine said she opened her Royal Bank account via the Internet while she was still in Japan. Also, such Japanese newspaper and magazines as *Vancouver*

Shinpo, Vancouver Tonight and *Oops!* have their own homepages, where people in Japan can search for jobs or accommodation before travelling to Vancouver.

Along with the development of the media as mentioned above, the development of mass transportation has dramatically diminished people's sense of distance between places. Airplanes, which gradually replaced ships after the Second World War, now provide about six flights from major Japanese cities such as Tokyo, Osaka and Nagoya to Vancouver every day. Seven and a half hours' sitting or sleeping now take people from all over Japan to the other side of the Pacific Ocean.

In this environment, there is no wonder that one's search for a life-long pursuit, which would have taken place largely in one's own country in past decades, can now take place in almost any part of the world for almost anybody in Japan – or in industrialized countries in general. In fact, when I talk about my current research, Canadian listeners almost always respond by saying, 'Ah, how true it is, with many North Americans teaching English in Japan!' One said that India is also a popular destination for North Americans searching for a life aim. It seems that today, peoples on both sides of the Pacific Ocean believe that the other side of the ocean will give the answer to their life's quest.

When one's struggle with identity deficit is expanded to a cross-national level, the confusion also expands. I frequently encountered sojourners who said 'It depends' when asked about which country they want to settle in, what kinds of jobs they want to have, and what kinds of resident status they finally want to obtain in Canada. They seemed unable to decide to which factor they should give priority in order to plan their future. Here are two examples. Yusuke is a 30-year-old male who was running his own bar in a big city in Japan. He has traveled around Canada with a visitor's visa, and now lives in Vancouver with a student visa. He studied English in England for two years, has traveled to many countries, and stayed in Australia 'not for 10 days as originally planned, but as long as for two months, unexpectedly'.

Kato: What made you choose Vancouver for your studies?
Yusuke: Its climate. On my last visit to Canada, I wanted to live in this country permanently, and actually I had a job offer in Toronto. But I found the climate there so harsh, and preferred here. [But] when I came to Vancouver, I was wondering in what I should major. I had three choices for study: hairdressing, tourism and TESL [Teaching English as a Second Language]. I chose TESL, because the certificate might be useful when I go back to Japan to

open my own English school. But I wonder if I should really go back to Japan; I guess I fit this place [Canada] better.

Kato: When did you start thinking about living abroad permanently?

Yusuke: Since I was in Japan, I have been thinking about whatever country may give me permanent resident status.

Kato: Did you make a trip to Australia with the idea that you might live there permanently someday?

Yusuke: Yes . . .

. . . . . .

Kato: Were you thinking about settling down in Vancouver when you came here [with a student visa] last year?

Yusuke: I was. But once I came to the stage where I had to decide, I was thinking about over and over. I am undecided because I don't have something I definitely want to do. It's nice that I don't have to care that other people's eyes are watching me [in Canada], but if that's the only reason for immigrating, perhaps I had better go back to Japan? And, if I wanted immigrate, I should have majored in tourism [for better job opportunities], but I didn't.

The second example is Yoko, a 27-year-old female with visitor's visa. She was a nursery school teacher before her first visit to Canada as an ESL student. She has flown back and forth between Canada and Japan three times, once with student visa and twice with her visitor's visa, and has now lived in Vancouver for a total of 1 year and 10 months.

Kato: Did you say on the phone that you wanted to get a 'work permit'?

Yoko: I am just thinking about many things. Maybe I will come [to Canada] again with a working holiday visa. But a working holiday visa won't lead to a life-long job. I am just in the middle of conflicts. I could get a work permit as a skiing instructor, if one of the [Japanese] teachers [at my skiing school] quits her job . . . Or I am thinking about working in other countries than Canada. I found on the Internet a nursery school teacher's job in England, so I may apply for this. I don't want to go to England, though.

Kato: Why not?

Yoko: They speak another kind of English. Also, people look cold and the cost of living is high there.

Kato: Don't you think about working in Japan [again]?

Yoko: Not at all . . . I don't know what I should do back in Japan. In this respect I like to be here [in Canada], because I can think clearly about what I want to do – like, I want to go to school or I want to save money.

She did not say, however, why she wanted to go to school or to save money. In between their overseas stays, Yusuke, Yoko and many other sojourners who fly back and forth work in Japan as part-timers, to save money for their next sojourn. They humorously call themselves 'migrant workers (*dekasegi*)' in Japan.

Relationship troubles: destructive life

Sojourners who left Japan in the hope of finding a life's pursuit first enjoy the abundant free time they are enabled to spend in search for 'What I really want to do.' Soon, however, many of them realize that just coming to Vancouver does not make a dramatic change to lives. According to one interviewee, 'All working holiday-makers are frustrated, and unable to find their ways (*asetteiru*).' Some sojourners get, or feel as if they have got, an endless choice of work and studies, and thus further fragment their future visions, having a further identity deficit, as seen in the cases of Yusuke and Yoko described above.

When a person has a lot of free time, some money, nothing to do and is very anxious in a foreign environment, s/he may be tempted to change her/his life dramatically through a relationship with local people. One most common form of destructive life that Japanese sojourners, especially women, experience in Vancouver is an unequal relationship with Canadian partners.

Hiromi, a 26-year-old former civil servant, had visited Vancouver three times with a working holiday visa, a visitor's visa and a student visa, first 'to learn English' and then over time in a more conscious search for a life's pursuit. Hiromi started living with her Canadian boyfriend on her third visit, but she soon found his attitude changed, and she finds herself totally responsible for household chores. She had also been physically threatened by him. She said she was not this passive person when she was in Japan, and was now wondering, 'Am I now really me?' The following is an excerpt from my interview with her.

Kato: Do you think he is a good match for you?
Hiromi: He is a good match for 'me in Canada'.
Kato: What do you exactly mean by 'you in Canada'?
Hiromi: I can't speak English well. I am a foreigner. And I don't have basic rights.
Kato: What kinds of rights?

Hiromi: If I was in Japan, I could, of course, work anywhere I like, study as long as I like, and have the right to vote. Here I am not even covered by any kind of health or other insurance.

This derogatory perception of herself by a Japanese sojourner can be explained in two stages. First, some psychological surveys have pointed out that Japanese perception of 'self' in general tends to be situation-dependent, in contrast to North American perception of 'self' as a distinct and consistent entity. For example, asked to describe themselves, American students tend to answer using abstract psychological traits such as 'I am optimistic', while Japanese students tend to give a concrete and specific self-description such as 'I play chess at weekends'; only when a particular context is specified such as 'Describe yourself at home with your family' do they use psychological attributes (Marcus and Kitayama, 1998; p. 76, referring to Cousins, 1989). Also, when given specific contexts such as 'alone', 'with a friend' or 'in a professor's office', the Japanese respondents gave different types of self-descriptions for the different contexts to a significantly greater extent than did American respondents (Marcus and Kitayama, 1998).

If 'self' tends to be situation-dependent in the Japanese mind, then such ideas as 'human rights' or 'self-esteem', which presuppose a distinct 'self' separated from situations, may be somewhat foreign to the Japanese. (In fact, there is no exact translation of the English term 'self-esteem' into Japanese; see Heine *et al.*, 1999, p. 779.) Once Japanese people travel to North America, they can easily be controlled by North Americans because, by North American standards, they seem to lack self-esteem and make no demands for human rights.

For example, according to a North American psychology book, 'people with low self-esteem are more at the mercy of situations and events, because they lack a firm sense of who they are' (Baumeister, 1993, p. 207); the book also views 'low self-esteem' as 'a weakly or inadequately satisfied desire for self-worth' (ibid., p. 203). From this point of view, a normal Japanese individual may seem in North America to have 'an inadequately satisfied desire for self-worth', just because s/he is more sensitive to situations, or pushes her/himself forward less than regular Americans do. Interestingly, two women interviewees who told me about their unequal partnerships with Canadian men said that their boyfriends were groundlessly confident, and they did not know why.

Another relevant anecdote is that prewar Japanese immigrants to Canada, who brought such Japanese values as modesty (*enryo*) or patience (*gaman*) with them from home, were unfamiliar with the idea of 'human rights' and reluctant to accuse the Canadian government of its wartime mistreatment of them. It was younger-generation Japanese-Canadians who were at the center of the movement to gain redress for their parents in the 1980s (*Bilingual Human Rights Guide for Japanese Canadians*, 1995, pp. 10–13).

Contemporary Japanese sojourners are different from prewar immigrants in that they have learned the concept of 'human rights' in school education. Still, Hiromi's confusion between human rights and the vote/ citizenship above suggests that a Japanese education does not teach children about human rights. Two possible reasons are: (i) school education in Japan, or in Confucianism-influenced societies in general, still has more emphasis on nurturing sensitivity to situations than skills to express personal demands that could conflict with the demand of others; (ii) children's encounters with the concept of '(basic) human rights (*kihonteki jinken*)' are often paired with learning about the Japanese Constitution (at least it was the case when I was at school). This combination can mislead children into believing that their human rights are effective only in Japan, and not in countries whose citizenship they do not have.

As well as these cultural confusions, many Japanese sojourners struggle with identity deficit, and their self-perception is particularly vulnerable to situational changes. In fact, when I asked 'Do you like yourself?' (by which I was asking whether s/he has self-esteem), Yoko answered, 'I haven't liked myself for the past three months, but I will like myself in ten days time, when I shall hear about a job opportunity and may get a work permit!'

Young Japanese sojourners, who are even move vulnerable to situational changes, may look, through the eyes of Japanese settlers as well as of non-Japanese Canadians, easy to control. In fact, I heard from my interviewees about Japanese settlers' mistreatment of them such as using them as unpaid labor, sudden lay-offs or sexual harassment only a little less often than I heard about troubles they had with non-Japanese Canadians.

Marijuana and drugs: self-destructive lives

Another possible temptation for young sojourners who have free time and money but are uncertain of their future in a foreign environment is to satisfy their curiosity about new things as opportunities arise. The 'experiences' (*keiken*) of my interviewees varied from doing a job 'I would have looked down in Japan', such as being a waitress at a Japanese-run noodle shop, going to an ESL school near a drug-trafficking area, or accepting an invitation to a party or a show from a stranger met on bus. Here 'safe' or 'dangerous' does not seem to count as much as novelty, because, as far as one is doing something new, one is adding new experiences to life and thus life seems to be evolving. Also, these new things have extra value because they happen in a foreign environment; working at a Japanese-run noodle shop or sushi bar would be nothing special in Japan, but it has a unique meaning for some people as an 'experience' in Vancouver because it takes place in Canada.

Such an unconditional inclination toward novelty, however, sometimes leads to self-destructive behaviour. A popular form of Japanese sojourners' self-destructive behaviour in Vancouver seems to be the use of marijuana, and drug dependence. This is not surprising, considering the availability of, and relative social tolerance for, marijuana and drugs in Canada, particularly on the West Coast, compared to Japan. The three most popular substances my interviewees said they had experienced were 'weed' (marijuana), 'ecstasy' or 'E' (MDMA), and 'speed' (a stimulant drug). Other drugs my interviewees mentioned as something they knew of, directly or indirectly, are LSD, cocaine, magic mushrooms and 'something that has three letters but not LSD (which my interviewee could not recall)'. Opportunities for the sojourners to obtain these substances are frequent: from Canadian friends or partners, from Japanese friends or ESL classmates or from ESL teachers. One said her friend obtained marijuana from the host family of her farm-stay. Drugs are available at raves or clubs.

The young Japanese sojourners' use of marijuana, as told by my interviewees, is almost as common as smoking tobacco. An interviewee said that, according to her Japanese friends, she was 'the only working holiday-maker in Vancouver who doesn't do marijuana'. Some had experienced marijuana when they were in Japan, or during their overseas trips to other countries such as the Netherlands, but the majority tried it for the first time in Vancouver. According to my interviewees, Canadians offer marijuana to them, saying, 'Marijuana is not dangerous', 'Tobacco is addictive and bad for your health, but marijuana is not', 'Even the police are doing marijuana'. Along with these words, the facts that marijuana is passed around just like cigarettes at gatherings of Canadians, or that Canadians of various ages and genders (such as a boyfriend's mother, or a farm-stay host family) take marijuana lowers Japanese young people's psychological barriers against it.

Interestingly, a few interviewees pointed out different marijuana-smoking habits between the Japanese and Canadians, which could be explained by a North American orientation toward independence and a Japanese one to interdependence. Canadians, according to them, tend not to force the matter when an offer of drugs is rejected, while the Japanese tend to use high peer-pressure. Two interviewees said that, when they refused marijuana offered by Japanese ESL classmates, the friends responded with exaggerated surprise, saying, 'Aren't you doing it? No kidding!

(*yattenaino, uso*)' or 'Oh, how come, it's fun (*e, nannde, tanoshiinoni*)?' At the same time, Japanese sensitivity to surrounding situations, including people's feelings, discussed above, can lead to weakness in the face of peer-pressure. A 27-year-old college student said, 'I smoked my friend's marijuana in return for her helping me moving out. She wanted to share it with me. I don't like marijuana, but she would be offended (if I rejected her offer).'

Experiencing marijuana does not always lead to addiction, however. According to a 17-year-old female high school student, 'Everybody does it to some degree, and quits it when they think they don't need it. Or they do it just for a change (*kibuntenkan*).' However, it seems that sojourners are more likely to use addictive substance in a self-destructive way when they consider themselves to be 'underachievers' or 'unfits' at the time they left Japan.

A 21-year-old woman became addicted to drugs and alcohol during her stay on Vancouver Island as an ESL student. As a high school student she had had a dream of becoming a pianist, but injuries to her arms prevented her from entering a good music college. She left Japan on graduating from high school. Not motivated to study English, she soon stopped going to the ESL school. She first became dependent on alcohol and continued drinking for four months, until she was hospitalized. After giving up drinking, she went to raves for nearly a year and became dependent on various drugs. She found this habit destructive to her body, and gave it up. Now she reflects on herself and says, 'I was a loser'; 'I had my dream broken, and came here to escape.'

The younger the sojourners are, the more the feeling of 'underachievement' seems influenced directly by their parents' attitudes toward them. Such people seem especially vulnerable to a self-destructive life. An 18-year-old male high school student said, 'I am disappointed with the quality of people I have met here.' 'I have been making efforts to some extent. But there are lots of people who came here not of their own free will but because they couldn't make it in Japan; and maybe their parents abandoned them. Such people make up 80 per cent of the Japanese I know in Vancouver. Some left, or failed even to enter high schools in Japan. Some are old enough to work but live on their parents' money. They go to clubs and raves, do 'ecstasy' or 'weed', or binge drink alcohol.'

Unfortunately, none of these 'kicked-out' sojourners responded to my recruitment request for interviewees. This is probably because such young people are too indifferent to their surroundings, including newspaper advertisements, or are too self-protective to talk about themselves.

Psychiatric problems and suicides: serious cases

Finally, the more serious, and fatal, cases – such as psychiatric problems and suicide – are also present, even if they are fewer in number. An emergency interpreter in Vancouver reported in 2001 that she saw a couple of sojourners (usually 'young women') per month who had just arrived from Japan and needed immediate hospitalization for psychiatric care.

The number of suicides of sojourners, including attempted suicide, reported to the Consulate General of Japan in Vancouver between April 1997 and December 2000 range from zero to six per year. Cases related to psychiatric problems ranged between two and nine per year over the same period. These numbers should include not only the cases of young, single sojourners but also of workers in corporations, their family members, or tourists. Yet the rumors I heard just after I arrived in Vancouver in March 2001, to the effect that 'One/two young people recently threw themselves from Burrard/Grandville Bridge' indicate that young, single sojourners need special attention. They, after all, do not have any such affiliations as companies or schools that could care for them in crisis.

Many serious cases may have their causes in the sojourners' lives back home, while some seem to be caused by their experiences after coming to Canada. Two of my interviewees told me about their past suicide attempts.

A 20-year-old female college student said she was diagnosed as being mentally ill as a child. She gave up junior high school at the age of 14. Her parents sent her to schools in New Zealand and Hawaii. Neither helped to improve her health, and she made her first suicide attempt in New Zealand. She also made a few more attempts after going to Vancouver as an ESL student at the age of 18. She said, 'I didn't like myself [when I first came to Canada]. I was feeling empty, thinking, "Why am I alive?" ' She was also feeling guilty about being ill and bothering her parents.

In contrast, the other interviewee, a 29-year-old female permanent resident, said she was full of confidence in her career and liked herself when she came to Canada seeking life's challenges. However, her boss at a Japanese-Canadian company, who apparently had a psychiatric problem himself, undermined her mental health by verbal abuse. She put up with it for two years in order to get a work permit, but finally gave up the job because of depression. Since then, she has attempted suicide. She says, 'Listening to the manager, I became unable to tell what was right and what was wrong. I have completely forgotten what I was confident about in me. Since then I cannot stop hurting myself.'

Helping young sojourners to live positively

So far I have described the challenges that young Japanese sojourners in Vancouver are facing, from the general, potentially problematic situations to more serious cases. I have also discussed the possible causes of such problems, first 'identity deficit' and then culturally different perceptions of 'self' between the Japanese and North Americans, mainly from the viewpoint of cultural psychology. But there are several points I did not discuss, or did not emphasize, while they still seem to be relevant.

First, the majority of young Japanese sojourners in Vancouver are psychologically healthy, even if many are experiencing some degree of identity deficit. For example, among the forty-one individuals I met through my first recruitment, only eight (one male and seven females) seemed to me to be psychologically unstable (though not necessarily 'sick'). Thus, generally speaking, the sojourners' presence in Vancouver, or in Canada, itself is by no means a problem. The question is whether local people in Canada, especially Japanese settlers, are aware of the sojourners' vulnerability, and are ready to support them when in trouble. At the same time, they should provide sojourners with preventative education, discussing with them, for example, various survival skills and mental health care. And, as some of my sojourners said, it is hoped to have a place where both settlers and sojourners can just drop by and chat 'whether there is any special event or not (*naniwa nakutomo*)'.

Second, living in Canada seems to have a positive overall effect on the majority of sojourners, unless they had serious psychiatric problems when they left Japan. The woman who came to Vancouver Island after failing to be a pianist (discussed above) says, 'I was cured mentally by the slow pace [of Canada]. Though I was physically destroyed [by drugs], I will give them up.' She also says she has finally found what she wants to do, namely fashion designing.

The woman whose attempted suicide was discussed in the second example above is now attending support meetings for suicide survivors held at a local hospital. She also says that living in sparsely populated Vancouver is better for her mental health than living in overcrowded Japan.

The woman whose attempted suicide was detailed in the first example given above was suffering from a psychiatric illness when she left Japan.

But she went to various support meetings after arriving in Vancouver, was treated by Canadian psychiatric specialists, and is now going to college regularly. Because she had had bad experiences with Japanese psychiatric specialists since childhood, she says, she is more comfortable with Canadian doctors and counselors. Thus she made the best use of the abundant mental health services in Canada. Her case, however, may be exceptional, as she had relatively high language skills and an outgoing personality that eventually beat her illness.

As mentioned earlier, many of the young sojourners are wishing to stay in Canada for longer periods and, if the situation allows, to gain permanent residency. This new type of migrant, originally a traveler, ESL student, working holiday-maker or other kind of sojourner, may constitute the majority of future Japanese settlers in Canada. It is hoped that the Japanese settlers' community, as well as related industries and organizations such as colleges, ESL schools and school information centers in Vancouver, will approach the Japanese sojourners in practical, supportive ways without trivializing them as 'just fun-seeking, short-term visitors', or pathologizing them. At the same time, it is hoped that researchers of various disciplines, including anthropology, psychology, psychiatry, sociology and human geography will further study this new type of diaspora, which does not fall into such established categories as immigrants, refugees, international students, overseas corporation workers or satellite kids.

Note

This chapter was originally presented as a paper at the Center for Japanese Research (CJR) Seminar at the University of British Columbia on 8 February 2001. A Japanese version was presented at my open lecture co-hosted by the Immigrants' Association and Kiyukai, held at Tonari Gumi (Japanese Community Volunteers' Association) on 28 February 2001. I am grateful to Professor Masao Nakamura, chair of CJR, and Mr Tatsuo Kage and Mr Katsumi Kubo, representatives of the Greater Vancouver Japanese Immigrants' Association, for making the two presentations possible. I also give my special thanks to Professor Darrin Lehman and Professor Steven Heine, of the Department of Psychology, who were hosts and advisers during my research period at UBC. Lastly, I am thankful to Government of Canada for financial support through a Postdoctoral Research Fellowship.

References

Baumeister, Roy (1986) *Identity: Cultural Change and the Struggle for Self* (New York: Oxford University Press).

Baumeister, Roy (ed.) (1993) *Self-esteem: The Puzzle of Low Self-Regard* (New York: Plenum Press).

Bilingual Human Rights Guide for Japanese Canadians Edited by Japanese Canadian (1995) Citizens Association Human Rights Committee.

Cousins, Steven D. (1989) 'Culture and Self-perception in Japan and the United States', *Journal of Personality and Social Psychology*, vol. 56, pp. 124–31.

Giddens, Anthony (1991) *Modernity and Self-identity: Self and Society in the late Modern Age* (Stanford, Calif. Stanford University Press).

Heine, Steven J., Darrin Lehman, Hazel Rose Marcus and Shinobu Kiayama (1999) 'Is There a Universal Need for Positive Self-Regard?', *Psychological Review*, vol. 106, no. 4, pp. 766–94.

Kelsky, Karen (1996a) 'The Gender Politics of Women's Internationalism in Japan', *International Journal of Politics, Culture and Society*, vol. 10, no, 1, pp. 29–50.

Kelsky, Karen (1996b) 'Flirting with the Foreign: Interracial Sex in Japan's "International" Age,' in Rob Wilson and Wimal Dissanayake (eds), *Global/Local: Cultural Production and the Transnational Imaginary* (Durham and London: Duke University Press).

Marcus, Hazel Rose and Shinobu Kitayama (1998) 'The Cultural Psychology of Personality', *Journal of Cross-Cultural Psychology*, vol. 29, no.1, January, pp. 63–87.

Mathews, Gordon (2000) *Global Culture/Individual Identity: Searching for Home in the Cultural Supermarket* (New York: Routledge).

McLuhan, Marshall, Quentin Fiore and Jerome Agel (2001), *The Medium is the Message* (New York: Gingko Press).

Miyoshi, Masao (1998) ' "Globalization" and the University,' in Fredric Jameson and Masao Miyoshi (eds), *The Cultures of Globalization* (Durham and London: Duke University Press), pp. 247–70.

Nihon Working Holiday Kyokai (2000) *Working holiday seido riyosha no foroappu chousa kekka hokokusho* (Report on the follow-up research on working holiday-makers).

Tsubaki, Machiko (1998) *Tabunka-shakai Kanada ni okeru nikkeijin-shakai no henyo to bunka-keisho: Ethnic-bunka wa sonzoku suruka* [Changes and cultural transmissions in Japanese Canadian communities in multicultural Canada], *Tokyo-Gakugeidaigaku Kiyo*, vol. 3, no. 49, pp. 141–56.

5
Okinawa after the Cold War and the Return of American Military Bases*

Keisuke Enokido

The social impact of ongoing economic globalization on cities and regions has become a matter of great interest for both local governments and civil society, specifically from the 1990s onward (Stöhr, 1990; Cox, 1997; Douglass and Friedmann, 1998; Edgington *et al.*, 2001; Stöhr *et al.*, 2001). The dynamics of globalization is often characterized by the magnitude of speed and geographical expansion of material and non-material flows transcending the boundaries of nation states (Castells, 1996). Thus, for cities and regions, how to take advantage of and/or cope with changes in external dynamics has recently been seen as a policy imperative. In particular, the opportunities and risks embedded in new global–local linkages are critical issues for 'backward' regions – that is, those in relative isolation from mainstream national politics and metropolitan markets.

Currently discussion of global–local linkages often focuses on the impacts of economic globalization on local society (see for example, Stöhr, 1990). These discussions often neglect the substantial impacts of other influential global changes, such as changes in global geopolitics in 1990 following the end of the Cold War, which have yet to be sufficiently addressed (Markusen *et al.*, 1991; Accordino, 2000).

A general argument in the literature (see, for example, Castells, 1997) regarding the intensification of global–local linkages under the advance of economic globalization is that the power of the nation-state to protect local society has declined, and that the latter has become more eager for greater local autonomy or political and/or administrative decentralization. In this chapter I shall address the local impacts of global geopolitical changes using the case of a Japanese peripheral region, Okinawa (see Figure 5.1). During the period 1945–90, Okinawa fell more directly under the influence of Cold War geopolitics than other region of Japan because

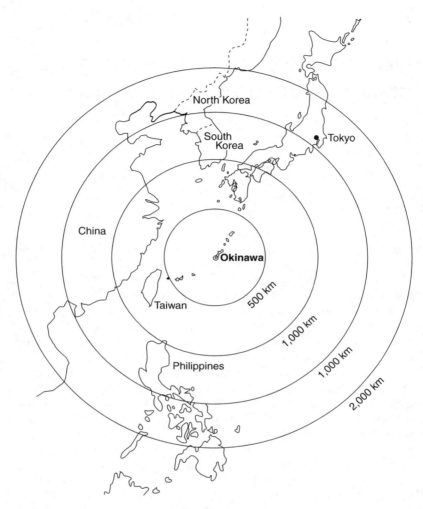

Figure 5.1   The location of Okinawa Prefecture
Source: *US Military Bases in Okinawa* (Japan: Okinawa Prefecture Public Brochure, 1998).

of the greater number of US military bases it hosted (see Johnson, 2001) (Figure 5.2). During the 1990s, conditions changed dramatically in Okinawa because of the perceived reduced need for the 30,000 troops stationed there, as well as the many others stationed elsewhere in East Asia. None the less, the interplay between Okinawa, Japan and the US administration through negotiations for the removal of US bases, and

Figure 5.2 The location of US military bases on Okinawa Honto (main island)
Source: Summary Report of International Workshop on Regional Development, 10 February 1997 (Japan: Okinawa Prefecture Cosmopolitan City Development Promotion Office).

the return of military land to local owners, represents an interesting case study of global–local relations, one in which governmental and civic actors each attempted to promote their respective interests.

This case study of Okinawa illustrates the linkage between changes in the global military balance and changes in local politics and society in

Japan. As such, its contribution to the growing literature on globalization is a focus on the restructuring of local–national political and administrative relations under the new global geopolitics. Findings are based on fieldwork conducted in Okinawa and Tokyo between 1998 and 2001, and deal with events surrounding the return of American military bases from the 1995 'rape incident' to the G8 summit held in 2000.

In this chapter, I shall first examine the position of Okinawa as a peripheral region within Japan, focusing on the impact large US military installations have on civil society. I shall then discuss events arising from the end of the Cold War in 1990 and political manoeuvring on the part of both national and local governments geared to giving back land used for military bases to local property owners. Finally, I conclude by making generalizations from the Okinawa case study about the impact of globalization on society.

Background

In this section, I offer an introductory background on Okinawa as a peripheral region of Japan, and identify the changing relations between Okinawa, the Japanese government and the US military after 1989. The section ends with an examination of the local stakeholders' political and economic interests in the return of US bases.

Okinawa's history

Since 1609, Okinawa has been part of Japan, but has remained a distinct political, economic and cultural region, consisting of one main island, called Okinawa Hontō, and additional smaller islands located on Japan's southern periphery (see Figure 5.1). Okinawa was once an independent kingdom, with a tributary relationship with the Chinese Ming dynasty around the fourteenth and fifteenth centuries. A Japanese feudal lord secured the territory of Okinawa by force under the shogunate system in the seventeenth century and the process of assimilating Okinawa into Japan was complete by the time of the Meiji Restoration in 1868. But given its distinctness from other regions of Japan, Okinawa was thought of as an exotic and backward region because of the area's geography as well as its culture (see Morris-Suzuki, 1998).

In the modern era, Okinawa was occupied by the Allied Forces at the end of the Pacific War, and put under the US administration in 1945 until it was returned to Japan in 1972. During this period, many US bases were built on Okinawa Hontō; even after the 1972 reversion of Okinawa to

Japan most of these continued to operate with a heavy US military presence. Specifically, 40,000 military troops were present in 1972 and 25,000 were remaining in 2000 (Okinawa Prefecture, General Affairs Department, 2001). Such an intensive concentration of both US army and air force troops was considered necessary to maintain US military commitments during the Cold War period (1945–90) (see Johnson, 2001). Indeed, the presence of US bases on Okinawa was disproportionately high compared with the rest of Japan: Okinawa hosted about 63 per cent of total US personnel in Japan as of 1990. At the time of writing, the majority of the population of Okinawa Hontō, numbering nearly one million, inhabit settlements – including Okinawa City, Ginowan City and Kadena Town – which lie adjacent to bases (see Figure 5.3). The continuing presence of US bases was legitimized by the Japan–US Security Treaty signed in 1951, although there are no legal grounds that justify the concentration of such an excessive number of bases on this island. The problems associated with US bases have not been shared by the rest of the nation, mainly because of the remoteness of Okinawa from the central areas of Japan. Thus the current situation, where US military bases occupy approximately 20 per cent of Okinawa Hontō's land area, is a product of both history and national and international politics.

It is well known that activities on large military bases are not compatible with local civic life; consequently, the people of Okinawa have been threatened continuously by serious incidents and accidents caused by US military service personnel (Okinawa Prefecture, General Affairs Department, 1998). Although there are US bases on the Japanese mainland, the frequency and seriousness of incidents (such as rapes, other acts of violence and property crimes) originating with the US military in Okinawa is incomparable. In fact, compared with countries such as Germany and Italy, which have also hosted US bases, the number of problems in Okinawa has been distinctly higher (Johnson, 2000). The Okinawan public have pushed for the consolidation and reduction of military sites to be based on a national policy (see Wakaizumi, 2002), but in fact there has been little change in the proportion of island land area that US bases cover (Okinawa Prefecture, General Affairs Department, 1998). Thus the people of Okinawa have remained marginalized on the issue of US military presence, mainly because access to the national political arena was greatly restricted under the conservative 'top-down' system in Japan (see Nagata, 1996). Okinawans remained essentially voiceless until the 1990s (Smith, 2000).

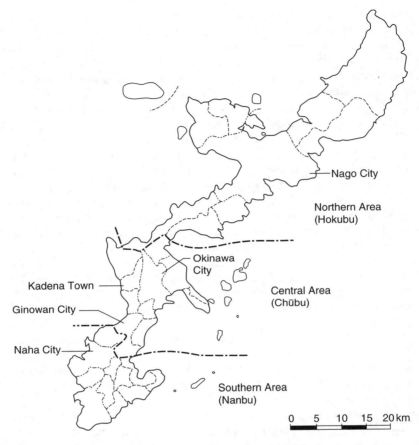

Figure 5.3   Municipalities in Okinawa Hontō shown in this chapter
Source: *A Minute Guide to Okinawa: Society and Economy*, July 1995 (Bank of the Ryukyus International Foundation).

Change in the mindset of Okinawans after the end of the Cold War

The Cold War paradigm that had justified the presence of US bases since 1945 suddenly changed in 1989. Immediately after the announcement of the end of the Cold War at the US–Soviet Summit in Malta on 3 December 1989, the possibility of a large-scale reduction in US military bases on Okinawa began to draw greater local attention. Soon afterwards, in April 1990, the then US Defense Secretary, Dick Cheney, announced the reduction of US bases in Okinawa, Korea and the Philippines. Moreover, the return of Clark Air Base in 1991 and Subic Bay Naval Base in 1992 (both in the Philippines) heightened expectations that US bases stationed on Okinawa would also be reduced (see Gabe, 1993).[1]

In the event, however, this apparent turnaround in US military policy was not as favourable as expected for Okinawa. The East Asia Strategy Report issued by the US Defense Department in 1994 (known as the Nye Report) announced the continuation of some 100,000 troops being posted in Japan and South Korea until at least the year 2015 (see Johnson, 1999). Moreover, the fact that the US bases on Okinawa were used to deploy troops during the Gulf War with Iraq in 1990 suggested the end of the Cold War would not automatically result in a reduced US military presence there (Gabe, 1993).

The 1995 rape incident and subsequent protests

In 1995 an event occurred that caused a dramatic change in attitude among the local populace toward the presence of US bases, namely the rape of an Okinawan schoolgirl by American servicemen. Despite the local outcry, the military authorities planned to send the soldiers involved back to the USA, effectively avoiding prosecution under Japanese law. In response, civic groups and labour unions organized a large-scale rally of some 85,000 protestors. The protestors were not only against the rape incident and perceived leniency toward the offenders, but for the first time expressed objection to the prolonged presence of US bases and the failure of the Japanese government to reduce military troops on Okinawa (Okinawa Prefecture, General Affairs Department, 2001). Although American soldiers had previously committed similar, and sometimes more violent, acts to the 1995 rape, no organized protest on this scale had ever taken place since Okinawa's reversion to Japan in 1972. The protest rally heightened political tensions between Okinawa and the Japanese government, as well as the USA.

At the same time, political tensions within Okinawa itself also began to intensify, mainly because local attitudes to the presence and return of bases varied widely. In fact, public opinion in Okinawa was divided, reflecting a divergence in viewpoints concerning the region's long-term economic development. On the one hand, many local citizens took an anti-US-base stance rooted in a long-standing desire for greater local autonomy, or the power of self-government in regional affairs. On the other hand, many landowners and business people feared the removal of US bases on economic grounds, and wanted greater developmental assistance and support from the Japanese national government in Tokyo. It is important to note that the areas were closely linked, in that the traditionally weak local economic power of the peripheral region engendered its political and economic dependence on the nation's centre. Conflict between these two viewpoints has meant the situation in Okinawa is both dynamic and complex.

American bases and local landowners

Yet another important background issue is the perspectives of local landowners. Historically, any decision to return land occupied by a base to local property owners has been at the discretion of the USA, and no plan for return had ever been made public. Accordingly, not only Okinawa Prefecture but also the Japanese national government has never been aware of the exact timing (or even the possibility) of the return of a base. This uncertainty has proved frustrating, mainly because of the ongoing threat the presence of US bases poses to civilian life – for example, violence, property damage, plane crashes and military vehicle accidents. It has also been a problem for local landowners whose properties host military installations. Because such property owners receive rent from the Japanese government as compensation, they stand to lose this income as soon as the land is returned. Moreover, the subsequent reuse of the land on which bases were built has opened questions as to whether the transition to civilian activities (for example, residential use) could be implemented smoothly (see Kurima, 1998). As the economic dependence of numerous landowners on government-sponsored rent is high, there is a correspondingly strong stake in the military's continuing presence as a source of income (see Ginowan City, 1993). About 7,990 ha, or 33 per cent, of the land occupied by the US military is the private property of 31,000 separate owners (Okinawa Prefecture, General Affairs Department, 2001). Although a minority of landowners have opposed the occupation of their land for military purposes, the majority of those affected have not wanted to lose the rental income available as compensation when the feasibility of the redevelopment of returned sites is low.

The earlier return of US bases has often been discouraged by the lack of any real political pressure exerted by landowners on their own behalf. Because those who own occupied land were afraid to prompt the initiation of a joint process for return of land holdings between the national and US governments, they did not suggest any redevelopment proposals. There were no set rules that defined the administrative details for the return of bases. While responsibility fell under the jurisdiction of local government, most municipalities did not want to begin a return process when there was no interest among landowners (Kurima, 1998). Because the governments of Japan and the USA tend to make decisions regarding base return without due consideration of the opinions of landowners and local governments, the conversion of returned lands to profitable, non-military uses will not be smooth. Hence, there is a dilemma between practical and political concerns, and frustrated local communities, so the necessity for an official schedule of return remains high.

Okinawa's local economy and the claims of different stakeholders

Interrelationships between the historical and structural weaknesses of Okinawa's economy, together with the post-1945 presence of US bases, have generated a unique set of economic stakeholders in the region. In addition to landowners, the employees of military installations were also economically dependent on the US presence. As of March 2001, there were 8,500 base employees, accounting for 1.3 per cent of Okinawa's total labour force of 630,000. Because of a lack of alternative job opportunities, these employees were at high risk from the possible closure of US military installations. As one example of the significance of US bases for job creation, they are among the most common workplaces for university graduates. Many people in Okinawa felt their economic life was embedded in a 'base-dependent economy' (*kichi keizai*). As a group, base employees do not necessarily support the US military presence, but they do oppose the closure of bases in the absence of government compensation.

In terms of local economic structure, Okinawa's public spending has been largely dependent on financial transfers from the national government since the 1972 reversion. Indeed, the share of independent revenue sources, such as local taxes (23 per cent), in the prefecture's budget is the lowest among the forty-seven prefectures of Japan (data as of 2001). The dependent structure of Okinawa's prefectural gross product is also related to the relatively small share that secondary industry (that is, manufacturing and construction) represents in the prefectural economy. In Okinawa, this sector comprised 18 per cent in 2001, while tertiary industry (that is, wholesale, retail, finance, insurance and real estate) ranked first, followed by Tokyo in second place, among the forty-seven prefectures. Among secondary industries, construction activity (characterized by a high share of public works funded by national subsidies) in 2001 amounted to 12 per cent (ranked eleventh). The fact that construction is proportionately greater than manufacturing is a unique characteristic of Okinawa within Japan. For example, in terms of the share of the construction industry in Gross Prefectural Product (GPP), Okinawa ranked within the top ten among the forty-seven prefectures. Remoteness from the mainland market, the relatively narrow base of the Okinawan market (the total population of the prefecture was about 1.3 million in 2001), and the forced transformation from an agricultural society to a military-dependent society during the US administration, hinders new areas of economic growth (see Tamamori and James, 1995). The overall effects of this weak economic structure are evident in a prefectural unemployment rate that was twice as high in 2001 as the national average – 10 per cent and 5 per cent, respectively.

This unique local economic structure has had several political implications. Thus, from the viewpoint of the construction industry and related industries, they had been highly dependent on public works spending, so an increase in political tension between the prefectural government and the national government was something to be avoided, or the high level of public works spending in the prefecture might suffer. Moreover, in the local pursuit of the return of US bases, competing stakes came to the fore, in particular the promotion of the relocation of Futenma Air Station in Ginowan City (see below).

A post-1990s restructuring of centre–periphery relations between Tokyo and Okinawa

This section shows the complex and dynamic interplay between the national and local governments following the 1995 rape incident, as well as non-governmental actors. The narrative here consists of seven policy events that took place between 1995 and the year 2000 (see Table 5.1). The first event was the establishment of an international policy forum by the Japanese and US governments (the Special Action Committee for Okinawa – SACO) in the face of increasing local antagonism against US bases and their involvement in defusing it. The second discusses the establishment of a prefectural–national policy forum, the Consultative Body on the Problems of US Military Bases (*Okinawa Beigun Kichi Mondai Kyogikai*),[2] set up to satisfy the prefectural government's desire to represent local interests in talks with both the Japanese and US governments about the presence of US bases. The third event to be discussed concerns the Round Table on the Municipalities of Okinawa Accommodating US Military Bases (*Okinawa Beigun Kichi Shozai Sichoson ni Kansuru Kondankai*),[3] which was a mechanism established by national

Table 5.1 List of policy events, 1995–2000

October 1995	Protest rally against the rape incident
November 1995	The establishment of SACO
November 1995	The Consultative Body on the Problems of US Military Bases
August 1996	The Round Table on the Municipalities of Okinawa Accommodating US Military Bases
December 1997	Nago City referendum
February 1997	Nago City mayoral election
November 1998	Prefectural gubernatorial election
July 2000	The 2000 Kyushu/Okinawa G8 Summit

Source: Okinawa Prefecture, General Affairs Department 1998, and *Okinawa Times* (various issues).

cabinet members in order to respond better to the economic and social needs of municipal governments that hosted US bases, and to build national–local cooperative relationships. The planned provision of extra subsidies to the municipal governments in question played a central role in restructuring the relationship. The fourth event presented the rise of social and political turmoil at the municipal level, caused by the recommendation of SACO (see above) that a new air base be imposed on a particular local community, Nago City, in exchange for the provision of financial compensation from the national government. The fifth event presented a change in political dynamics at the prefectural level as a result of the heightening of national–prefectural tension caused by the hard-line attitude of the prefectural governor toward the national government. This change was shown by the replacement of the existing governor in 1998 for a more 'practical' candidate, one who emphasized the building of a more cooperative relationship with the national government. This last event illustrated a gradual improvement in national–prefectural relationships after 1998 as a result of the inception of the new prefectural administration. Finally, the prime minister of Japan decided to hold a major international conference in Okinawa as part of the Japan G8 summit held in 2000, which raised the Okinawan peoples' expectation of an increased profile for the region at both national and international levels.

The effects of local political movements on the international political community (establishment of SACO)

The 1995 protest rally initially provoked changes at the international level with the establishment of SACO in November of that year, following the initiative of both Japanese and US politicians. This committee aimed to deal with the issues of the return of bases in order to relax the heightened antagonism of the Okinawan public against both US bases and the Japanese government.

The SACO committee met several times during 1995–6 in order to finalize a schedule for the eventual return of military bases in Okinawa to the landowners. However, the base return scheduling proposed by SACO only resulted in raising the tension between Okinawa and the national government as well as inside Okinawa itself. This was because the Okinawan public requested the full closure and return of bases, but most of the 'actual' return of bases authorized by SACO were just the relocation of bases to other existing sites within Okinawa, or even to a new site within the island. The local public had not anticipated this option, involving complete closure, consolidation and relocation. In particular, the construction of any new bases was wholly unacceptable to the people of Okinawa, and thus the final report of SACO in 1996 was not compatible with their original requests following the 1995 protest rally.[4] Bases scheduled for return are categorized as shown in Table 5.2 (see also Figure 5.4).

On completion of the SACO Report, the USA gave responsibility for implementation to the Japanese national, prefectural and municipal governments. In particular, Nago City (see Figure 5.3), designated by SACO as being the most suitable community for new air base construction, became a site of intense political conflict.

Table 5.2   List of US bases agreed for return in the Special Action Committee for Okinawa (SACO) final report

Full return	Aha Training Area (approx. 480ha)
Partial return	Northern Training Area (approx. 3,987ha of 7,513ha)
Consolidation to existing bases	Gimbaru Training Area (approx. 60ha)
	Sobe Communication Site (approx. 53ha)
	Yomitan Auxiliary Airfield (approx. 191ha)
	Camp Kuwae (approx. 99ha)
	Senaha Communication Station (approx. 6ha)
	Makiminato Service Area (approx. 3ha)
	Naha Port (approx. 57ha)
	Housing consolidation (Camp Kuwae and Zukeran, approx. 83ha)
Relocation to a new site	Futenma Air Station (approx. 481ha)

Notes: Some conditions are attached to the return of each land site (see the SACO final report for further information). As of 2002, only the Aha Training Area was returned in full (Tokyo: Japan Defense Agency, 2002).
Source: SACO Final Report, December 2, 1996 (Tokyo: the Ministry of Foreign Affairs of Japan).

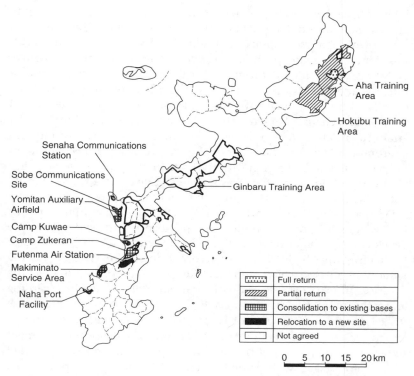

Figure 5.4 US bases agreed for return by the Special Action Committee for Okinawa (SACO) final report, by method of return
Source: The SACO Final Report, 2 December 1996 (Tokyo: The Ministry of Foreign Affairs of Japan).

The reformation of Okinawa–Tokyo–Washington DC relations

As mentioned above, because SACO was an international policy forum involving the governments of Japan and the USA, there was no way for the Okinawa prefectural government to be involved. When SACO began, the prefectural governor of Okinawa, Masahide Ota, asked the then prime minister, Tomiichi Murayama, to set up another policy committee, one that could discuss the base issue between the prefectural and national governments, in order to reflect local interests in decisions at SACO. Because the prime minister was a leader of the Japan Socialist Party (JSP), a party that supported Prefectural Governor Ota, a national–prefectural policy forum to discuss the issues of the return of bases was established in 1995.[5] This was called the Consultative Body on the Problems of US

Military Bases. Historically, this type of intergovernmental arrangement to discuss the return of bases had not been possible under the traditional 'top-down' Japanese political and administrative system, and so this was something of an epoch-making event. The aim of the consultative body was to provide opportunities for the prefecture to voice its own interests and discuss the issues of the presence and return of US bases directly with the national government. These voices were then expected to be included in SACO meetings. In sum, SACO was the first-tier arrangement at the international level, and the consultative body was a second-tier forum that was national in nature. It was a mechanism for linking a sub-national region with the domain of an international policy arrangement; however, there was no agreed rule as to how SACO could take local Okinawan interests into consideration.

During 1996, Prefectural Governor Ota quickly initiated policy innovations in order to promote the planned return of the bases. He developed two major plans and presented them at the first meeting of the consultative body. The first involved an Action Program for the Return of US Bases, which proposed three phases for the return of all the US bases in Okinawa.[6] Because of local political constraints regarding any active promotion in support of the return of bases by the prefecture (that is, because of the loss of landowners' income, discussed above), and the lack of any real political capacity to press the national government to facilitate the process of the return, the prefectural government had never before taken such proactive action. The plan developed by the prefecture was in fact 'a wish list' in its nature, because it was hardly conceivable that the USA would return the existing bases so easily. Yet this initiative drew the attention of liberal intellectuals on the Japanese mainland, including academics and human rights advocates, because it was such a novel action by the prefecture toward greater humanity made possible through a reduction of the number of bases (Broad National Combination for Independence, Peace and Democracy, 1997).

The second plan developed by Prefectural Governor Ota in 1996 was the Cosmopolitan City Formation Concept. This was a regional economic development plan targeting the promotion of cross-border linkages between Okinawa and nearby Asian markets (for example, Taiwan), based on the assumption that the phased return of the bases would be implemented and therefore space for local economic activities (for example, resort development and industrial districts) would increase. Since 1972, regional development (or reconstruction) planning in Okinawa had been conducted with the strong intervention and control of the national government, especially when compared with other prefectures, and thus such an attempt by the prefecture to plan its own future was also unprecedented.

Overall, for the prefecture, the two plans were considered to be strategic tools to promote long-standing issues over the return of the bases and local economic development. Their main thrust was to obtain greater local autonomy for decision-making in the return of the bases, and special assistance from Tokyo for more effective economic and social development.

The results of the national–prefectural discussion taken in the consultative body were rather mixed. Many bases included in the prefecture's Action Program for the Return of US Bases were also included in the list of bases to be returned, which was issued in the SACO Final Report. Yet the SACO plan did not mention the closure of all the bases existing in Okinawa. Prefectural Governor Ota, however, contended that the prefectural plan had been respected, if not fully (Ota, 1996). In particular, an agreement was reached to relocate Futenma Air Station, one of the largest bases in Okinawa and the most 'dangerous' because of its location in the heart of an urbanized central area called Chūbu (see Figures 5.2 and 5.3). This decision was made in 1996 by the then prime minister, Ryutaro Hashimoto, with the then US Ambassador to Japan, Walter Mondale, and its planned closure was a shock to the local community because its return was considered to be almost impossible, surprising even bureaucrats working at SACO (*Okinawa Times*, 2 December 1996).

However, the final SACO agreement provided that the air station should be relocated within Okinawa, and not simply closed. This condition caused confusion in Okinawa at first, because it was difficult to find a relocation site for such a large base that would not affect an existing residential community. And from an Okinawan perspective, the construction of any new base was unacceptable because it would further extend the presence of US military personnel, and so would be against the prefecture's policy on the reduction and consolidation of bases. It should be noted that no localities on the mainland made any offer to take on the relocation, and as a result the issue of the relocation was not shared with other prefectures, despite a national interest in peace and security.[7]

The formation of a new link between the national and local governments in Okinawa

Besides finalizing its own schedule for the consolidation or relocation of the bases, the national government also sought to provide more funding to Okinawa as a kind of compensation for the events of 1995 and 1996. However, this soon required special arrangements with the municipalities concerned. Fifty-three municipal governments administer the territory of the Okinawa region under the coordinating control of the prefectural government. Municipal governments (each having a municipal assembly) are the closest governmental body to local residents, and so are a fundamental unit of local politics. Their cooperation was therefore necessary to enable the national government to facilitate the process of base relocation. While opposition to the relocation remained strong, as represented by the prefectural referendum, national politicians began to strengthen their intergovernmental relationships with municipal governments in Okinawa by establishing a new policy forum, one designed to promote local economic development subsidized by the national government.

This forum was established on 20 August 1996 and called The Round Table on the Municipalities of Okinawa Accommodating US Military Bases. The Round Table was set up as a private advisory body (*shiteki shimon kikan*) reporting to the then chief cabinet secretary, Seiroku Kajiyama, under Prime Minister Hashimoto's administration (*Ryukyu Shimpo*, 20 August 1996). This arrangement was considered to be a new kind of national intervention in municipal governments. It was unique in that it acted as a catalyst between the centre and the local areas, and because national politicians mobilized non-governmental actors in Okinawa and the mainland, including academics, journalists and business people, as members of the forum. It should be noted that the director of the Round Table, Haruo Shimada, was a university professor and had been consulted by the Liberal Democratic Party on economic policies. Such a mechanism of intervention depending on non-governmental actors and regarding issues related to the presence of US bases was unprecedented. Its aim was to empower municipal officials to manage their own economic development and thus increase the effectiveness and efficiency of the supplementary financial assistance provided to Okinawa in the form of subsidies.

The Round Table was expected to ease the frustration of municipal governments that had to continue to undertake the burden of hosting US bases within their jurisdiction. At a series of meetings of the Round Table in 1996 and 1997, economic development plans and projects were discussed between the Round Table members and the municipal planners. The Round Table eventually confirmed a number of plans for economic projects based on various criteria, and reported back to national politicians with a proposal and request for special finance grant. The scale of assistance finally approved by the national government coalition in power at the time[8] was quite remarkable, and a special budget was passed on 24 March 1997 (*Okinawa Times*, 27 March 1997). The maximum amount in this budget dedicated to municipal projects in Okinawa was ¥100,000 million (US$833 million using the exchange rate of ¥120 per dollar) over the eleven years from fiscal year 1997 to fiscal year 2007 – or US$76 million per year. Considering that the average annual budget for the development of Okinawa (*Okinawa Shinko Kaihatsu Jigyo hi*) from fiscal year 1992 to fiscal year 2001 was ¥190,000 million (US$15,833 million, using the exchange rate of ¥120 per dollar), this special assistance accounted for only 5 per cent of the average regular assistance. However, for those municipalities that had been dependent on subsidies, the special financial arrangement made between the director of the Round Table, the chief cabinet secretary and the then minister of finance, Hiroshi Mitsuka, was particularly attractive.

For national politicians, this process was necessary to show greater responsiveness to local economic needs and interests. Put another way, it showed that the existing system of providing national assistance to Okinawa was not very satisfactory. The process was also important for national-level politicians to legitimate the provision of extra financial assistance by negotiating with the specific municipal governments. It was especially important in enabling follow-up on the effects of the extra spending to ensure that it would not be used inefficiently, based on project evaluation criteria developed by the Round Table.[9]

The establishment of the Round Table showed that the national government had the power to intervene in local politics while its relations with the regional (that is, prefectural) level were unstable, because of the extreme anti-base stance taken by Prefectural Governor Ota at that time. In particular, the issues of the implementation of the relocation of Futenma Air Station was negotiated between then Prefectural Governor Ota and Prime Minister Hashimoto, who were of different political persuasions. Consequently, a new national–municipal intergovernmental relationship was being formed through the Round Table. In this process, the role of the prefecture in managing local affairs was weakened by the national government's intervention, if only temporarily.

Proliferation of intra-local conflicts

The restructuring of national–municipal intergovernmental relations continued in 1996–7. In particular, Nago City, designated by SACO to host a new air base following the closure of Futenma Air Station, opposed such a recommendation and took the initiative to invalidate the base's relocation. Thus Nago City held a special municipal referendum over the relocation of Futenma Air Station to a district within the city in

December 1997. When SACO first proposed the idea of the relocation of the air base to Nago, the then city mayor, Tetsuya Higa, opposed the idea in principle (*Ryukyu Shimpo*, 18 November 1996). However, the mayor eventually disclosed his intention to allow the national government to conduct an on-site feasibility study for the construction of the new base in return for extra financial assistance. Accordingly, local anti-relocation civic groups and labour unions took action to set up the municipal referendum to oppose the mayor's apparent change in attitude. Toward the voting day, a sharp division of opinion in the local community was noticed. As well as those citizens and groups opposed to relocation, there were supporters of the relocation who were in favour of obtaining special national subsidies. This latter group included the municipal mayor, the majority of municipal assembly members, and workers in the construction industry. The national government also tried to influence the result, in favour of the acceptance of the relocation, by mobilizing the officials of a prefectural branch of a national agency (the Defense Facilities Administration Agency, Naha branch) to encourage local citizens to vote for the relocation. The referendum eventually resulted in victory for the anti-relocation voters. However, it should be noted that this referendum was not legally binding. None the less, it required the municipal mayor to undertake certain actions in response to the referendum results.[10] Finally, despite public opposition, Mayor Higa rejected the result of the referendum on 24 December 1997 in favour of the relocation, as he believed that moving Futenma Air Station to Nago City would secure specially allocated financial assistance from the national government. Simultaneously, he announced that he would step down as mayor, apologizing that he was responsible for splitting the community over the process of the referendum (*Ryukyu Shimpo*, 26 December 1997). But a political reason for his seemingly irresponsible action was also possible. According to Arasaki (1999), if Higa had not resigned, he would have been recalled, which would have been a personal disgrace, and furthermore, it was highly likely that he would not have been re-elected; thus resignation was the only realistic option. It is important to note here that the national government put pressure on the mayor to accept the relocation by proposing various economic development projects, such as the redevelopment of Nago's central district and the construction of local cultural and tourism facilities (see *Ryukyu Shimpo*, 8 December 1997).[11]

This policy conflict between anti- and pro-relocation groups carried over into the subsequent mayoral election in 1997. Despite the victory of the anti-relocation groups, a pro-relocation candidate, Tateo Kishimoto, who was the deputy mayor under Higa's administration, was elected on

8 February 1998. In sum, the new mayoral candidate focused more intensively on local economic issues than his anti-relocation opponent, Yoshikazu Tamaki, while leaving the decision to accept relocation to the prefectural governor, Masahide Ota. Because the governor announced his own rejection of the relocation of Futenma Air Station before the municipal election, Kishimoto did not need to argue this issue further, and could concentrate on local economic development issues. It should also be noted that in Nago, as in other Okinawan localities, micro-politics become rather complicated around the time of elections. Thus voters do not necessarily vote on the basis of their own rational preferences and values. For example, in some cases votes were cast based on the candidates' hometowns rather than their election campaign slogans. An individual voter may even support candidates from different parties at the various levels of administration – that is, at national-, prefectural- and municipal-level elections (interview with Toshio Tajima, urban planning consultant, *Chiiki Keikaku Kenkyujo*, Tokyo, 8 August 2001). Out of these kinds of local political dynamics, the new pro-relocation mayor was elected.

In Nago City, political conflicts also occurred at neighborhood level. Thus, prior to the acceptance of the feasibility study for the relocation, it was necessary for Mayor Higa to obtain the approval of each neighborhood within the city. This was done in order to assure a full democratic process and to carry out the study smoothly. The proposed relocation site was off the coast of a small fishing village within the city boundary, called the Henoko district. The consensus of the people of Henoko and neighboring villages was essential. But at this neighborhood level there also developed a tension between anti- and pro-relocation residents. This comprised a conflict between those who worried about the diverse and long-term social, economic and environmental impact of the new base, and those who favored the availability of short-term special subsidies expected from the national government to increase employment and so prevent village depopulation. Because of this political difficulty, the neighbourhood committees of residents in Henoko gave up the task of building a consensus and left the decision-making to the mayor. Thus neighborhood politics became rather heated when the new mayor, Kishimoto, accepted the relocation under a newly elected prefectural governor, Keiichi Inamine, which will be discussed below.

A new governor and the depoliticization of national–prefectural relations

After the mayoral election of 8 February 1997, a new gubernatorial (prefectural) election was held on 15 November 1998 on the completion of

Ota's second four-year term. The election was a competition between the anti-base governor, Ota, and the local leading businessman, Keiichi Inamine, who eventually won. The latter had a more flexible attitude toward the presence and relocation of the bases, and it should be noted that he was an appointed member of the Round Table mentioned earlier, and so was supported by the national LDP government.

Prior to the election, the national government had ended all communication with Governor Ota after he had announced his rejection of the relocation, and upset Prime Minister Hashimoto. This shutdown of communication raised severe criticism in Okinawa against Ota's hard-line attitude toward the bases and the national government. It is important here to remember that Okinawa was a somewhat backward peripheral region, and so its economic dependence on funds from the centre – that is, the Japanese national government – is significant. Therefore, the initiation of direct and frequent centre–local dialogue after the 1995 protest rally raised local expectations that issues surrounding the bases and Okinawa's economy would improve.

Despite the fact that Okinawa was protected under the Japanese Constitution, the change in the prime minister's attitude toward the governor and Okinawa put a certain psychological pressure on the people of Okinawa. Interestingly, the change in the national attitude did not provoke anger among local people against the prime minister, but rather against the governor, as shown in Inamine's election campaign, which accused Ota of having a dogmatic, unrealistic policy. Since the 1995 rape incident, the governor's constituents had supported his stance against the national government. But when they felt that the governor's attitude was so hard-line that it provoked the prime minister's anger to the extent that national–prefectural relationships began to collapse, their attitude toward the governor changed. Because the return and relocation of US bases was a political issue that could not be handled by routine administrative procedures, any weakening of national political support would be disadvantageous to Okinawa. As a result, in the gubernatorial election, Ota's contender Inamine won because he put a stronger emphasis on the regional economy in his political manifesto, and insisted that Okinawa should maintain communication with the Japanese government, and take advantage of the special financial assistance offered in exchange for base relocation. Inamine secured 52 per cent of the popular vote, while Ota only maintained 47 per cent.

After the Inamine administration began in 1998, a more cooperative relationship developed between the national, prefectural and municipal governments for the promotion of base relocation. It is important to note that the relocation accepted by the new governor Inamine was conditional, and the new governor requested that the relocated Futenma Air Station should be used both by military and civilian airplanes (as is the case at Honolulu International Airport), and also be returned to Okinawa in its entirety after fifteen years of joint use. This condition was based on his policy that the air base should function as an asset for the long-term development of Okinawa. While the US repeatedly rejected the possibility of accepting these conditions, the national government did not raise the issue with its American counterpart, and began to arrange special financial assistance to Nago City and surrounding municipalities.

Together these districts comprised the northern area of the Okinawan main island, Hokubu (see Figure 5.3), where economic development has been rather disadvantaged because of the mountainous landscape and remoteness from urbanized areas in the central and southern areas of the island (see Figure 5.3). Hokubu, however, is a resource-rich area; for example it provides the water supply for other areas as well as to the US military bases.

Thus, although it was clear that extra financial assistance – that is, subsidies – was linked to the presence and relocation of bases, political leaders of municipalities in Hokubu claimed the assistance should not be linked to the relocation of bases *per se*, but rather should be provided independently of the acceptance of relocation. Eventually, in 1999, special committees for the preparation of the relocation of Futenma Air Station to Nago City were established by the national government, in which the prefectural governor and related municipal mayors participated. However, because the conditions of Governor Inamine were not satisfied, the implementation of the relocation was suspended during 1999 and 2000. Still, various economic projects awarded to Nago City by the national government continued (for example, a Free Trade Zone development). In 1998 there was further opposition to progressing the relocation planning – for example, an environmental group was concerned about the impact of the planned offshore air base on the dugong, an endangered sirenian species, which inhabited the waters in the coastal area. However, various national-level bureaucrats, namely the prefectural governor and affected municipal mayors, acted in support of relocation from 1998 to 2000.

The 2000 Kyushu Okinawa G8 Summit

The new cooperative style of national–prefectural relations was further promoted by the new Prime Minister Obuchi's personal decision in 1999 to select Okinawa as the location for a main conference at the Japan G8 summit, to be held in July 2000. This was the first summit conference held in any non-metropolitan city in Japan. Although Prefectural Governor Inamine had approached the prime minister to host the G8 Summit in Okinawa, a positive outcome was not expected, because of Okinawa's lack of experience in holding such a major international conference. Therefore, Prime Minister Obuchi's decision was interpreted as a 'gift' to the people of Okinawa, and as a sign that he would promote the internationalization (*kokusaika*) of the Okinawan society and economy.

Nago City, the candidate site for the new air base, was also chosen as the location for the main conference, and a new and expensive convention hall was built in 2000. In addition, the national government financed the improvement of the relevant infrastructure, including the repair and improvement of arterial roads, and the building of various meeting facilities. Ultimately, approximately ¥80 billion (US$754.7 million using the exchange rate of ¥106 per dollar) was invested, local construction companies being the recipients of this funding.[12] As a result, the national government's financial assistance to Okinawa was named as the summit budget for 'special procurements' because of the volume of public works it generated (*Okinawa Times*, 11 May 2000). Meanwhile, anti-base citizens and groups used the summit as an opportunity to protest at the presence of US bases – for example, by surrounding the fence of Kadena Air Base, the largest air base in Okinawa, with a circle of people. Unfortunately, Prime Minister Obuchi died suddenly before the summit began, and Okinawa lost a national politician who seemed to be most sympathetic towards the prefecture.

Thereafter, no significant development occurred over the proposed relocation of Futenma Air Station, but the plans to relocate other small bases and installations agreed by SACO were gradually implemented. Both national and prefectural actors put more emphasis on local economic development in Okinawa and selected key projects, such as the establishment of an international university with a graduate school curriculum (*daigakuin daigaku*), and the authorization of an Okinawa Free Trade Zone.

In November 2002, a further gubernatorial election was held as Inamine completed his first four-year term. A deputy governor under Ota's administration, Masanori Yoshimoto, who was opposed to the relocation of Futenma Air Station within Okinawa, ran in the election as Inamine's main contender. While there was criticism of Inamine for his lack of success in moving the national government toward fulfilling the conditions stipulated for the acceptance of the relocation of Futenma

Air Station, US bases was not seen as a major campaign issue in 2002. Instead, Governor Inamine focused on the regional economy, compared to Yoshimoto's emphasis on base-related issues. Consequently, Inamine won 64 per cent of the popular vote, while Yoshimoto secured only 26 per cent, and the destabilization of national and prefectural inter-governmental relations was avoided. Tokyo–Okinawa dynamics continued to concentrate on the promotion of economic development projects (such as those mentioned above) and bureaucratic arrangements became more important, while the role of the prime minister became less visible.

Conclusions

A number of issues relevant to the impact of globalization on society are observable in this Japanese case study.

The impact of global change on local perception

The interplay between different levels of governmental and non-governmental actors (civil society and local landowners) demonstrates that the end of the Cold War and the resulting change in global geopolitics had a variety of impacts on a peripheral region hosting numerous foreign military bases. These were not necessarily material impacts, but rather psychological in their inception. Thus, as shown in the early initiative over the reuse of Futenma Air Station taken by Ginowan City, a change in the mindset of the Okinawan public toward the presence of US bases was apparent following the end of the Cold War in 1990. This renewed planning effort represented a process of linking changes in global dynamics with local society.

It is important to note that local and national contingency – that is, the rape incident in 1995 and a change in the national political climate (namely, the election of the Japan Socialist Party), also coincided with this changing local mindset, and possibly triggered the action of local citizens against the state and the US military. However, as detailed above, this was a complex political and social process, one in which agents of change and external political structure interacted dynamically. This case study demonstrates that local society had become more active in addressing the impacts of globalization (for example, the Nago referendum), and the historical relations between Okinawa and the central state had changed, especially when the legitimacy and capacity of the central state to manage local affairs in Okinawa came to be questioned.

Thus the case study basically supports the argument that global dynamics (in this case changes in the geopolitical situation) had an increasing effect on local societies, and that the role of the nation-state had also changed. However, the power of the state to control the prefecture through financial inducements is still vital, and local governments and society in Okinawa both continue to rely on external subsidies. As a result, the direction of change does not necessarily seem to be unidirectional toward the weakening of the nation-state. A characteristic development at the local level in Okinawa was that local communities became more concerned about political and social inequity in relation to the excessive presence of US bases. They also became more concerned over their regional or local autonomy for decision-making, as well as their capacity for self-reliant economic and social development. This suggests that local awareness of political, economic and social rights in Okinawa was heightened in the face of the global geopolitical changes of the 1990s.

Challenge to the state power and its resilience

The rise of local civil society in Okinawa, manifested in the 1995 protest rally, was a challenge to the role and capacity of the national Japanese government in controlling local events, and to a lesser extent to the capacity of the prefectural government, which was supposed to represent and promote local interests. As the literature discussing the impacts of economic globalization on the power of the nation-state to govern its territory suggests (see, for example, Castells, 1997; Hirst and Thompsion, 1999), this case indicates that the state's power to deal with regional and/or local problems was deeply questioned. The inception of SACO and the consultative body suggested that the conventional measures for administering the presence and return of US bases were considered to be ineffective by both the Japanese and US governments, and so alternative measures and arrangements became necessary. The national government wished to maintain the legitimacy of its policies and actions with respect to the US bases, yet this had to be carried out by balancing national interests (that is, peace and security) as well as local interests, such as social inequity with respect to the unequal burden of hosting US bases. The case study shows that, while the state wanted to control the region, it could not continue its traditional top-down bureaucratic approach. It should also be noted that the new measures taken by the national Japanese state were not really oppressive, but rather 'softer', with a focus on a new centre–local coalition-building represented by the Round Table. The subsequent reformation of Tokyo–Okinawa relations suggests that the state tried to be more responsive to local interests, but it also became more strategically selective in terms of its actions for maintaining power to control local governments and civil society.

Conflicts of local interests

In the process of restructuring centre–local relations, national politicians concentrated on rebuilding an intergovernmental coalition while a significant part of local civil society continued to challenge the traditional policy and practice of the state. However, new political conflicts within the local society took place concerning the relocation of Futenma Air Station. This local conflict was a result of the existence of opposing views toward the planned new air base: one group viewing it as a new and irreversible threat, and the other as a new economic opportunity. But as represented by the results of the municipal referendum and the mayoral election held in Nago City, the local political community was not divided simplistically into two opposing groups. Rather, as the two elections showed, local politics was dynamic and no driving force that could unite the region under the principle of anti-state or anti-military-base movement was formed. This suggests that a simple dichotomy of centre versus local over the bases issue was not realistic, and a more interactive and interdependent relationship (albeit one in which not all were equal), needs to be acknowledged. The issue of the relocation of Futenma Air Station continues unsolved at the time of writing, and it is likely that a combination of new political actors will result in new centre–local tensions. In fact, it seems that some civic groups are likely to build a strategy against the national government and the US bases, and continue with a political challenge to base relocation. This, in fact, was manifested by anti-bases protests during the 2000 G8 summit. While the national government promoted its greater concern for (or benevolence toward) Okinawa, the existence of multiple stakeholders, including those who argued on local human security and environmental grounds among the local society, also increased.

In sum, given the increasingly dynamic nature of governmental and nongovernmental relations at different levels, and uncertainty of the direction of change in global geopolitics, it is necessary for national and local actors to create more inclusive mechanisms in Okinawa that can promote wider participation and increase the level of capacity to under-stand external changes and make public policies for building a more self-reliant region. A possible project the local society should consider is the development of stronger (and multiple) human and organizational networks with external counterparts, especially given the fact that external actors are playing important roles in the locality, and the issue of the presence of US bases is still being localized rather than shared with the nationals and non-Japanese, in particular Americans.

Notes

*   I would like to thank Dr David W. Edgington, the Director of the Center for Japanese Research, and Dr Masao Nakamura, the former Director of the Center, for comments on the draft of this essay. I am also grateful for the Center for its financial support of my research.

1   For example, Futenma Air Station is home to US Marine aircraft and occupies 33 per cent of the jurisdiction of Ginowan City (see Figure 5.3). It was, and remains, a focal point of possible base conversion to non-military use because of the magnitude of its negative impact on local communities (for example, plane crashes, vehicle accidents, noise, pollution and other issues). Ginowan City conducted workshops between 1990 and 1992 to draft a redevelopment plan. In 1994, the City generated many ideas for non-military uses, arising out of further workshop discussions, to develop the first municipal plan for reuse of the Futenma Air Station site (*Futenma Hikojo Atochi Riyo Keikaku Kihon Koso*). Although the municipal assembly did not approve the plan, for various procedural reasons, the Ginowan City initiative, despite being *ad hoc*, represented an increased desire at the local level for the return of bases (Furushiro, 2001). The urgency of preparation for planning the reuse of US military sites was also articulated in a 1993 report stating the opinions of local landowners whose property was occupied by Futenma Air Station (Ginowan City, 1993).

2   The translation of this English title is the author's own.

3   The translation of this English title is the author's own.

4   It should be noted that the SACO Final Report included agreements to adjust training and operational procedures, implement noise reduction initiatives, and improve the status of forces agreement procedures in addition to the return of land.

5   The Murayama administration was formed when the Liberal Democratic Party, which had originally established the Japan–US Security Treaty, lost its dominant power in 1992 and had to work in coalition with its historical opponent, the Japan Socialist Party and a newly established small party, Sakigake.

6   Phase 1 covered the period of the program's inception (1996 to 2001), Phase 2 runs from 2002 to 2010, and Phase 3 will cover 2011 to 2015.

7   The relocation of an air refuelling force consisting of twelve planes from Futenma Air Station to the existing US Iwakuni Base in Yamaguchi Prefecture was permitted by the governor of Yamaguchi Prefecture, the Iwakuni city mayor and a Yu-cho town leader in 1997.

8   The coalition included members from the Liberal Democratic Party, the Social Democratic Party and the Sakigake New Harbinger Party.

9   See a report issued by the national government on 31 May 2000 entitled '*Okinawa Beigun Kichi Shozai Shichoson ni Kansuru Kondankai Teigen no Jisshi ni Kakaru Yushikisha Kondankai Houkokusho*', <http://www.kantei.go.jp/jp/singi/okinawa/review/report.html>.

10   The purpose of the 1996 prefectural referendum was merely to demonstrate a collective will among the Okinawa public against the presence of US bases and did not require Governor Ota to take any specific action.

11 After Higa resigned, the Defense Agency chief, Yoshinari Norota, presented Higa with a letter of appreciation for the mayor's contribution to the stability of defence facilities and the promotion of a firm foundation of security (*Ryukyu Shimpo*, 15 January 1999).

12 On the other hand, this enormous expense brought criticism from Oxfam International, a British non-governmental agency (NGO), which claimed that the conference budget could have written off the debt of Gambia or the Republic of Equatorial Guinea (*Okinawa Times*, 22 July 2000).

References

Accordino, John J. (2000) *Captives of the Cold War Economy: The Struggle for Defense Conversion in American Communities* (Westport, Conn.: Praeger).

Arasaki, Moriteru (1999) *Seiji o Minshu no Te ni* (Tokyo: Gaifu-sha).

Broad National Combination for Independence, Peace and Democracy (1997) *Okinawa no Kokusai Toshi Keisei Koso: Kichi Henkan Action Program wo Shiji Shiyo: Kokumin he no Appeal* (Tokyo: Nihon no Shinro).

Castells, Manuel (1996) *The Rise of the Network Society* (Malden: Bazil Blackwell).

Castells, Manuel (1997) *The Power of Identity* (Malden: Bazil Blackwell).

Cox, Kevin R. (ed.) (1997) *Spaces of Globalization: Reasserting the Power of the Local* (New York: Guilford).

Douglass, Mike and John Friedmann (eds) (1998) *Cities for Citizens: Planning and the Rise of Civil Society in a Global Age* (Chichester, Sussex: John Wiley).

Edgington, David W., Fernandez, Antonio L., and Hoshino, Claudia (eds) (2001) *New Regional Development Paradigms. Vol. 2: New Regions – Concepts, Issues, and Practices* (Westport, Conn. and London: Greenwood), published in cooperation with the United Nations and the United Nations Centre for Regional Development.

Furushiro, Toshiaki (2001) 'Ginowan-shi no Kichi Iten to Atochi Keikaku', in Akiyoshi Takahashi (ed.), *The Return, Transfer and Reutilization of the Military Bases and Okinawa Development* (Kawagoe, Japan: Tokyo Kokusai Daigaku).

Gabe, Masaaki, (1993) '90 nendai saihen no naka no zaioki beigun kichi', in Masaaki Gabe and Soko Shimabukuro (eds), *Post Reisen to Okinawa* (Naha: Hirugi-Sha), pp. 69–127.

Ginowan City Department of Urban Development, Urban Redevelopment Section (Toshi Kaihatsu-bu Toshi Saikaihatsu-ka) (1993) *Futenma Hikojo Atochi Riyo Keikaku Jinushi Iko Shosa Houkokusyo*.

Hirst, Paul and Thompsion, Grahame (1999) *Globalization in Question: The International Economy and the Possibilities of Governance*, 2nd edn (Malden: Polity Press).

Japan Defense Agency (2002) *Boei Hakusho, Heisei 14 nen ban* (Tokyo: Printing Bureau, Ministry of Finance, Japan).

Johnson, Chalmers (1999) 'The 1995 Rape Incident and the Rekindling of Okinawa Protest against the American Bases', in Chalmers Johnson (ed.), *Okinawa: Cold War Island* (Cardiff: Japan Policy Research Institute).

Johnson, Chalmers (2000) *Blowback: The Costs and Consequences of American Empire* (New York: Metropolitan).

Johnson, Chalmers (2001) 'Okinawa Between the United States and Japan', in Josef Kreier (ed.), *Ryukyu in World History* (Bonn: Bier'sche Verlagsanstalt).

Kurima, Yasuo (1998) *Okinawa Keizai no Gensou to Genjitsu* (Tokyo: Nihon Keizai Hyouron-Sha).

Markusen, Ann R., Hall, Peter, Campbell, Scott and Deitrick, Sabina (1991) *The Rise of the Gunbelt: The Military Remapping of Industrial America* (New York: Oxford University Press).

Morris-Suzuki, Tessa (1998) *Re-inventing Japan: Time, Space, Nation* (Armonk, NY: M. E. Sharpe).

Nagata, Naohisa (1996) 'The Roles of Central Government and Local Government in Japan's Regional Development Policies', in Jong S. Jun and Deil S. Wright (eds), *Globalization and Decentralization: Institutional Contexts, Policy Issues, and Intergovernmental Relations in Japan and the United States.* (Washington, DC: Georgetown University Press).

Okinawa Prefecture, Cosmopolitan City Development Promotion Office (1997) *Summary Report of International Workshop on Regional Development* (Naha: Okinawa Prefecture).

Okinawa Prefecture, General Affairs Department (1998) *Okinawa no Beigun Kichi* (Naha: Okinawa Prefecture).

Okinawa Prefecture, General Affairs Department (2001) *Okinawa no Beigun oyobi Jieitai Kichi* (Statistical Report) (Naha: Okinawa Prefecture).

Okinawa Times (various dates).

Ota, Masahide (1996) *Okinawa, Heiwa no Ishiji* (Tokyo: Iwanami Shuppan).

Ryukyu Shimpo (various dates).

Smith, Sheila A. (2000) 'Challenging National Authority: Okinawa Prefecture and the U.S. Military Bases', in Sheila A. Smith (ed.), *Local Voices, National Issues: The Impact of Local Initiative in Japanese Policy-Making* (Ann Arbor, Mich.: The Center for Japanese Studies, University of Michigan).

Stöhr, Walter B. (ed.) (1990) *Global Challenge and Local Response: Initiatives for Economic Regeneration in Contemporary Europe* (London and New York: Mansell), published for the United Nations University.

Stöhr, Walter B., Edralin, Josefa S. and Mani, Devyani (eds) (2001) *New Regional Development Paradigms. Vol. 3: Decentralization, Governance, and the New Planning for Local-Level Development* (Westport, Conn. and London: Greenwood), published in cooperation with the United Nations and the United Nations Centre for Regional Development.

Tamamori, Terunobu and James, John C. (eds) (1995) *A Minute Guide to Okinawa: Society and Economy* (Naha: Bank of the Ryukyus International Foundation).

Wakaizumi, Kei (2002) (ed. John Swenson-Wright) *The Best Course Available: A Personal Account of the Secret U.S.–Japan Okinawa Reversion Negotiations* (Honolulu: University of Hawaii Press).

Part II

A Changing Business Environment: Individual Rights and Globalization

6

Aging, Female and Foreign Workers, and Japanese Labor Markets: An International Perspective

Alice Nakamura, Masao Nakamura and Atsushi Seike

The Japanese economy has been in a prolonged recession since the bursting of the financial bubble in 1990, and at the time of writing unemployment rates have reached historical highs even for men in their prime. The causes of the recession are long-term imbalances and fundamental changes in the environment and the structure of the Japanese economy. In the late 1980s, when this financial bubble was forming, firms, households and all levels of government made massive amounts of inefficient investments, both real and financial. (Real investments such as firms' investments in plant and equipment are often distinguished from financial investments such as investments in stocks, bonds and other financial securities.) In the aftermath of the bursting bubble, Japan has been suffering from non-performing loans of all kinds and has been unable to direct new capital into productive areas of the economy. Globalization has also contributed to the country's unemployment woes.

Japan has been struggling to recover from its financial troubles in the context of a globalizing world economy that has been relentlessly forcing Japanese manufacturers to cut their costs. This has led many manufacturers to move large portions of their operations overseas, particularly to China and other countries in Asia. It is believed that at least 2 million jobs were moved out of Japan to overseas locations in the 1990s. This massive exodus of jobs came at the same time as Japanese companies were restructuring and reducing their workforces to cope with the economic downturn. In the post-Second World War Japanese way of thinking, employment security has been a priority issue for both government and private-sector decision-makers. Unemployment was viewed as depriving workers of their dignity, and unemployed workers were feared as a potential source of political and social instability. Post-Second World War employment practices virtually guaranteed permanent employment for regular full-time workers. These practices were possible because, from the end of the war until the 1980s, Japan's growing economy generated enough private- and public-sector permanent employment opportunities to meet the needs of at least the traditional male Japanese workers. The recent serious threat of unemployment has now hit even the two types of workers for whom employment used to be guaranteed – male workers in their prime, and new graduates. Because of this, the new wave of less than full employment has the potential to undermine the cohesion of Japanese society and has generated serious policy concerns.

To make matters more complicated, Japan also has a rapidly aging population. This aging of the population will reduce the number of potential labor force participants and hence, of itself, should reduce the number of the unemployed. However, the aging of the population will also reduce the number of tax-paying workers, and the number of retired people each worker must support in terms of public expenditure is already increasing.[1] This trend is expected to put pressure on the public purse, and to make it harder to find funds for retraining and income assistance for unemployed workers. By now there is serious public concern that the promised levels of social security for Japan's growing retired population will not be sustainable.

The past successes of the Japanese economy were intricately tied in with tailored risk-sharing arrangements that spread employment, income and other business risks across all sectors of industry and all households. For example, the lifetime (or long-term) employment arrangements that many male workers have enjoyed historically in Japan meant that firms absorbed some of the risks from downturns in demand by continuing to employ a large core of workers, even though what they were paid would decrease through a contraction of bonus payments. At the same time, reductions in bonus payments and annual contract wage adjustments, as well as reductions in overtime and the use of casual labor, allowed employers to contract their labour expenditure in response to business downturns without laying off any of their regular workers. In return for this job security, workers in Japan have tended to cooperate to help hold down firms' costs of adjusting to new technologies by not resisting these innovations or the resulting changes in working practices. In Japan, business risks caused by macro-economic fluctuations (including foreign exchange risks and the uncertainty involved in new product development) have also typically been shared between the assembler firms (the core) and the suppliers within vertical *keiretsu* groups.

However, many Japanese business practices do not conform to the standard practices of the country's main international competitors. Japanese firms have provided large portions of their workforces with long-term employment stability and have also relied heavily on Japanese in-house (often expensive) *keiretsu* suppliers. How can firms operating in this way compete against US counterparts that use layoffs on an ongoing basis to minimize labour costs, and that are taking advantage increasingly of new information technologies and trade liberalization to procure materials globally from the lowest-cost suppliers? With many Japanese firms now struggling rather than growing, and facing intense competitive pressures to reduce costs, it is proving increasingly difficult for Japanese employers to continue to guarantee employment security for a large core of workers, or the traditional tenure-based wage arrangements. In this chapter, we discuss below public policy problems associated with these issues seen from an international perspective. Special attention is devoted to issues connected with female and foreign labor since Canadian, US and European policies toward these groups of workers is helping to counteract the effects of an aging workforce, but this has not been the case in Japan.

Japanese industrial relations and employment practices

Japan was not always blessed with cooperative labor–management relations. In the pre-Second World War period, even though the rights of organized labor were not fully guaranteed, there were many large-scale labour disputes.[2] The military government responded in the 1930s by trying to suppress labor demands and unrest. During the war the unions were reorganized into the Sangyo Hokoku Kai (The Wartime Association of Industry). In the years immediately following the war, there were many labour disputes, including strike action against Toyota, Nissan and other major corporations. The primary reason for these disputes was the poverty of the vast numbers of Japanese workers, especially in the postwar reconstruction period. Radical union leadership gained support in these conditions.

However, by the early 1960s the Japanese economy had recovered fully, and workers began to reap the benefits of, and take pride in, the competitiveness of Japanese firms in world markets. During this period, workers were willing to cooperate with their employers to improve productivity. The labour unions in Japanese steel, shipbuilding, automobile and certain other major industries shifted their focus from militant confrontation to more business-orientated and pragmatic approaches.

Employers reciprocated by becoming more generous in raising worker wages. There is scholarly disagreement regarding precisely when the shift to more harmonious labour relations took place in Japan. Nevertheless, we can safely say that harmonious relations were firmly established, in the private sector at least, sometime during the high growth era of the 1960s. Japan's achievement of a relatively stable and harmonious industrial and labour relations system during this period was unusual by international standards. This Japanese system involved some unusual features too, including complex coordination of the incentives of various participants in labour markets and innovative risk-sharing arrangements.

Japanese industrial relations

Three key features characterize modern-day Japanese industrial relations: lifetime (or long-term) employment, the *nenko* (seniority-based) wage system, and enterprise-based unionism. It should be noted that these three features are far more typical of the sorts of jobs that have traditionally been filled by younger men. Many older workers and most female and foreign workers are in jobs that lack one or more of these features. It has been found too that the degree to which these practices have been followed is related inversely to firm size.[3] Certain benefits are commonly associated with each of the three distinguishing features of Japanese industrial relations practices. These are summarized below.

Lifetime employment

(i)   Because firms and employees can count on long-term employment relationships, both sides are willing to invest in employees' human capital. More is spent in Japan on on-the-job training and on formal job-related education programs than in North America.

(ii) Long-term employment allows firms to use job rotation to develop workers' multi-task skills and to expose workers to different aspects of business and production operations. There are few job classifications. Firms can deploy personnel flexibly and effectively in times when technologies and market conditions are in flux.

(iii) New productivity enhancing technologies can be introduced with minimal worker concern about job losses.

Nenko *(seniority-based) reward wage system*

(i)   Workers are assessed on their achievements over substantial periods of time. Hence workers are more motivated to keep the long-run consequences in mind when carrying out their jobs.

(ii)   Workers are assessed by many supervisors. This, combined with the lengthy time-frames for career assessments, leaves less room for erroneous judgments in employer personnel policies, including the allocation of employer-sponsored training opportunities and promotion decisions.

Enterprise-based unionism

(i)   Because of the long-term commitments employees have to the firms they work for, their unions are in a better position to demand a fair share of firm profits. This may also be part of the explanation why enterprise unions have become so important in Japan.

(ii)   Firms are able to share information on firm performance, problems and opportunities with enterprise unions. Indeed, full-time positions in enterprise unions are sometimes part of the career track for potential future managers of firms in Japan.

(iii)   Because of the trust and sharing of information, and the common objectives fostered by enterprise unions, workers and managers alike accept rollbacks of bonus payments in difficult times without making threats to leave or suffering a deterioration in morale of the sort that endangers production efficiency and product quality in many Canadian and US firms.

Mechanisms for adjusting the wages bill

Of course, Japanese firms, like the firms of other nations, must deal with business cycle fluctuations. In downturns, Japanese firms have needed to find ways of adjusting the total wage bill, but the lifetime employment practices in Japan have meant that this total wage bill flexibility had to be accomplished without layoffs. The methods adopted included wage adjustments, flexible deployment of the core workforce, adjustments of hours through changes in overtime work, and adjustments in the hours and employment of workers not treated as part of the core workforce.

Wage adjustments

Japanese workers are paid regular monthly (fixed contract) earnings as well as bonus payments. Thus workers have an assured level of monthly earnings, plus a bonus that fluctuates with the business fortunes of their employer. The amounts of the bonuses are not specified in advance, and fluctuate with economic conditions, but in normal economic times they generally range between four to six months' worth of regular contract earnings. The amounts of both the regular wages and the bonus payments are decided in negotiations between firms and labor unions. The Japanese labor code prohibits labor contracts from extending beyond one year, and the annual wage adjustments in Japan reflect this labor law. (In contrast, union wage contracts in Canada and the USA are often for considerably longer than one year.) Regular wages are settled in the spring labour negotiations. Bonus payments are negotiated somewhat later, but before the summer. At the firm level, both regular wages and bonus pay settlements reflect general economic conditions as well as the firm's performance over the previous twelve months. Because of this, a firm's total wage bill adjusts in a timely manner to changing economic fortunes.

In North America, bonuses are mostly paid to managers and executives. In contrast, in Japan, bonuses are part of the compensation package for most workers, regardless of their rank. However, the proportion of total annual pay a worker receives in the form of bonus payments tends to rise as qualifications rise. This pattern is consistent with the hypothesis that the bonus fractions reflect the amounts of managerial and other hard-to-observe tasks involved in workers' jobs (Nakamura and Hübler, 1998). Year-to-year changes are much greater for bonuses than for regular wages. This provides a mechanism other than employment layoffs to share between firms and workers risk caused by business fluctuations. (Nakamura and Nakamura (1991) discuss the risk sharing aspects of bonus payments.) Firms also use bonuses as short-run incentive schemes for individuals and groups of workers. Other incentive mechanisms in common use in Japan include regular salary raises, promotion, and better job assignments. Japanese employers typically have much more latitude than their North American counterparts when it comes to job assignments.

Adjustments of overtime hours and non-regular worker employment

More so than in North American firms, overtime hours for regular workers are used as a means of meeting changes in demand conditions. This may be partly because the legal overtime wage premiums in Japan are about 25 per cent: half of the North American rate. Though regular workers' employment is protected to a large extent, in difficult times it has been considered acceptable for firms to reduce their wage bills through layoffs of non-regular workers, including part-timers. Moreover, when demand conditions improve, firms in Japan have first tended to use more overtime and part-time worker hours to meet the increased demand. Usually, new regular workers have only been hired when additional increases in overtime and part-time hours were not feasible or were not deemed to be in accordance with longer-run strategic plans.

Flexible deployment of the workforce

When facing business downturns, Japanese firms deploy workers in the areas where they are needed most, sometimes involving geographical relocation and changes in work tasks. The deployment of a firm's workers across production and sales jobs, and even in other related (or sometimes unrelated) firms, is not unusual during serious business downturns.

One enabling factor for the flexible deployment of the Japanese workforce is that wages are usually assigned to individual workers rather than being job-specific. This explains why wage differentials by job task at the time of initial appointment are small in Japan compared to the USA (Shimada, 1981). However, wages rise steeply in Japan with increasing tenure.

Assessing Japan's post-Second World War industrial relations practices

Good things

There is considerable evidence[4] that post-Second World War Japanese industrial relations practices served Japanese manufacturers well until the 1980s. These practices, together with the production *keiretsu* groups, are often credited with allowing Japanese manufacturers in areas such as electronics, auto, precision and general machinery industries to achieve their global competitiveness goals with high standards of quality control and efficient just-in-time operations.[5] These characteristics of the Japanese industrial relations practices continue to enable high quality standards and operational efficiency.[6]

Problems

The main problems associated with these practices include: (i) the high cost of maintaining them, especially when the returns are measured by short-term financial criteria; and (ii) the growing disparities between these practices and the economic competitiveness practices and individualism of liberal democracy, which has been gaining a hold as the global ideal.[7]

Indeed, the short-run expense of Japanese business practices, and ongoing global cost-cutting pressures, have forced many Japanese firms to reconsider their systems. For example, many firms have been forced to reduce the amount of internal training they provide for their workers, and many also have scaled down their once-generous seniority-based salary increases. Now, the globally popular notion that a competitive market mechanism and individual rights are the appropriate basis for a national economic system, as in the USA, has come to permeate the thinking of Japanese firm managers, politicians and bureaucrats alike. Some of the changes that have taken place, or are being contemplated, in Japanese business and education practices reflect these influences. This includes reforms of Japan's corporate governance system, the introduction of US-style law schools, and the significant increases that have taken place in the number of practicing lawyers in Japan.

Japanese private and public policy-makers, however, have been slow to set up US-style market mechanisms and protection for individual rights. One area where this is evident is in the employers' treatment of female and foreign workers, the topic of the next section.

Globalization, the bubble and the Japanese labor market: policy issues

Since the late 1980s, and especially since the bursting of the bubble in 1990, Japanese post-Second World War industrial relations and employment practices have been under pressure to change.

Globalization

Rapid liberalization of foreign trade and deregulation took place in the late 1980s in the economies of North America and Europe. There seems to be no doubt that the Canada–US Free Trade Agreement, the North American Free Trade Agreement and the massive deregulation of the US economy prompted economic growth in North America in the 1990s. Similar economic integration and deregulation also took place in Europe.

These changes to the business environment allowed corporations in both North America and Europe to cut the costs of both production and other business activities significantly. Businesses gained the ability to procure from the globally lowest-cost suppliers, and this enabled large cost reductions. This global procurement has been facilitated by the growth of low-cost electronic communications. Many Japanese companies lagged behind their global competitors in their competitiveness during the bubble era of the late 1980s and the deep recession of the 1990s, and the continuing high value of Japanese yen did not help the global competitiveness of Japanese corporations. Facing these realities, Japanese firms have been forced to look at their postwar industrial relations practices and explore ways to respond to the new realities by revising these practices. One possible way for Japanese firms to gain competitiveness is to shift more of their production overseas, to countries where wages are lower than in Japan. This exporting of employment is already well under way. What remains to be discovered is how serious its long-run impact will be on the Japanese economy.

Hollowing out

The postwar Japanese industrial relations and employment practices described above evolved over a long period of time, and served Japan well in its high growth period up to the 1980s. However, rapid globalization since then has been accompanied by large shifts in the geographical distribution of manufacturing capacity. Japanese manufacturing technologies such as the just-in-time production system and its underlying quality management methods were transferred out successfully, albeit in modified forms, to foreign competitors, so the Japanese comparative advantage in manufacturing, which relied heavily on special industrial relations, employment and *keiretsu* practices, was eroded.

The continuing high value of the Japanese yen further damaged the Japanese competitive position. Many Japanese firms had to invest heavily in overseas facilities. This foreign direct investment (FDI) helped to reduce the Japanese firms' production costs, but led to the export of large numbers of production jobs. There has been a hollowing out of employment in Japan, with losses of well-paid manufacturing jobs but increases in demand for administrative functions including management and R&D,[8] while other societal changes have also created an increasing demand for some sorts of low-wage service sector jobs. The long-run net effects of this hollowing out of Japanese employment are not yet known, but it is already clear that this has led to increased unemployment and to significant losses of corporate and household income tax revenues. Also, the hollowing out has triggered other major changes in the industrial structure of the Japanese economy,[9] including changes in how the rights of individuals as workers, and as consumers and customers of social services, are dealt with in Japan. It is from this perspective that we now turn our attention to the situation and potential of female workers.

Female workers

Japan's postwar industrial relations practices emphasize the hiring of new graduates and life-long in-house training and career development. Table 6.1 shows that many Japanese firms do not even consider hiring mid-career workers who seek employment in secondary labour markets.

The absence of active secondary labor markets is a particularly serious problem for Japanese women who leave regular career positions to have children (see Table 6.2). When they feel ready to reenter the work force, these women have great difficulty in finding new jobs with pay

Table 6.1 Reasons for mid-career hiring: Japanese firms, 1998 (percentages)

Type of position	Firms hiring mid-career workers	Replacement for vacancies	Not enough new graduates	Securing experts	Revitalizing firm by diversified hiring	Expanding business	Other	No reply
Managerial	12.7	26.3	0.4	47.0	26.7	20.6	5.5	3.7
Clerical	31.8	71.3	3.8	13.5	9.1	13.3	3.8	3.5
Technical, R&D	18.2	41.8	8.0	54.0	14.3	23.9	3.6	2.3
Production (blue collar)	58.9	73.5	7.7	10.4	10.0	23.3	4.5	1.6

Source: Personnel Management Survey, Ministry of Labor, 1998.

Table 6.2 Obstacles to resuming work after having children, 1995 (percentages)

Low opinions of women's ability/work	Work positions scarce	Work environment difficult for combining home and work	Information on employment scarce	Little employment help	Few facilities for day care and nurseries	Little desire for work for pay on women's part	Other
26.5	50.2	77.3	28.2	28.4	62.3	19.7	1.9

Source: Survey of Help for Resuming Employment by Career-oriented Women, Nissei Research Institute, 1995.

and responsibilities commensurate with their qualifications. Moreover, even female graduates seeking their first jobs are believed to face serious discrimination. That is, these women do not have such job opportunities as otherwise similar male graduates, and this is believed to be partly because the life-cycle labour supply patterns that employers in Japan view as typical for women lead many employers to decide against investing in training and other career opportunities for their female workers even though some will turn out to be very committed to their jobs (see, for example, Nakamura and Nakamura, 1985; Jacobsen, 1998).

Compared with North America, in Japan there has been little improvement over time in the workplace situation of women. In response to the Japanese Equal Employment Opportunity Law enacted in 1986, some large Japanese firms did open their general managerial career paths to female university graduates. The workers on these career paths are typically required to organize their lives to suit their employers' business demands, including relocation and liberal overtime work. Prior to 1986, with rare exceptions, these career paths were open only to men. At the time of writing, however, few women have chosen to follow up the new opportunities for embarking on managerial career paths. They continue to choose career paths that do not require geographic relocation and that lead to positions as lower-ranking managers or specialists.[10] Table 6.3 shows Japanese women's choices among a number of alternatives.[11] Japanese firms' general managerial career paths are compatible with plan (A) and, to a lesser degree, with plan (B). However, most women do not choose either (A) or (B).

If this status quo is perpetuated, most of the upper level managerial positions in Japanese firms will continue to be filled by men, and the gap between male and female wages will not shrink, contrary to the stated objectives of supporters who helped to push through the Equal Employment Opportunity Law. Table 6.4 shows that the wage differential between men and women for Japan is quite large by international standards.[12] The Japanese Equal Employment Law has no enforcement provisions. The absence of equal employment enforcement provisions may explain why, in implementing major hiring cutbacks during the economic slowdown in 1992 and 1993, firms were very open about their decisions to offer reduced proportions of the available positions to women, in comparison with previous years. The cutbacks in the positions open to women were particularly severe for general managerial career paths. Many view this as evidence of the continuing marginal position of women in the Japanese workforce. Table 6.5 further demonstrates that few women occupy managerial and other administrative positions in Japan.

Table 6.3   Life-cycle plans: Japanese Single Women, 1987, 1992, 1997 (%)

	Ideal life-cycle plans			Planned life-cycle arrangements			Reality for married women
	1987	1992	1997	1987	1992	1997	1997
(A) No marriage, lifetime work	3.7	3.3	4.4	7.1	9.5	9.3	–
(B) Marriage, no children, lifetime work	2.5	4.1	4.4	1.4	2.6	3.0	2.3
(C) Marriage, children, lifetime work	18.5	19.3	27.2	15.3	14.7	15.5	21.9
(D) Marriage, work, children, give up work, resume work after rearing	31.3	29.7	34.3	42.2	45.8	42.9	38.8
(E) Marriage, work, children, give up work, housewife afterwards	33.6	32.5	20.6	23.9	19.2	17.7	27.7
(F) Other	10.7	11.1	9.2	10.1	8.2	11.6	9.2
Sample	2605 (100%)	3647 (100)	3612 (100)	2605 (100)	3647 (100)	3612 (100)	7354 (100)

Source: National Survey of Marriages and Births (Survey of Singles), National Institute of Social Security and Population, 1998a; 11th Survey of Births (Couples Married for 15–19 years), National Institute of Social Security and Population, 1998b.

Table 6.4 Male–female wage differential (female wages as a fraction of male wages; percentages)

Japan, 1998	USA, 1995	France, 1993	Germany, 1995	The Netherlands 1995	UK, 1996	Australia, 1995
63.1	74.0	80.8	74.2	79.3	79.4	90.0

Notes: Japanese wages used include regular contracted pay and do not include overtime or bonus pay. US wages are those for year-round, full-time workers.
Source: *Wage Structure Basic Survey*, 1998a, Ministry of Labor (Japan); *Year Book of Labor Statistics, 1996*, International Labor Organization (other countries).

The Japanese Equal Employment Laws are only applicable to men and women in the same job categories. Taking advantage of the lack of enforcement provisions in these laws, many employers proceeded to hire women as part-time workers, though their work requirements were often the same as regular full-time workers (Table 6.6). As Table 6.7 shows, part-time workers are paid significantly less per hour than full-time workers; therefore keeping women in the part-time categories allows employers to pay them less and give them fewer rights while remaining within the letter, if not the intent, of the equal employment laws. What has happened is that the proportion of women in part-time categories has increased, and the proportion of women in the full-time category has declined, in Japan since the enactment of the Japanese Equal Employment Laws in 1986.[13] One reality at the root of the disadvantages faced by working women in Japan is that the existing industrial relations system makes it costly for employers to accommodate periods of absence or reduced work effort for child-bearing and rearing, and many Japanese couples would like to have children. This is despite the fact that Japanese laws on maternity leave were enacted in both 1992 and 1995: laws that allowed both women and men to take maternity leave, and prohibiting the dismissal of employees who take such leave. In general, however, Japanese workers rarely make full use of even the paid vacations to which they are entitled (Table 6.8).[14] For many Western firms that have had more experience in dealing with women's issues and are set up to accommodate the needs of female workers, this problem area for Japanese firms and society is a potential window of opportunity.[15]

In Japan, little serious attention has been paid to the efficient use of female labor. Unlike the situation in North American, the Japanese Equal Employment Law, in both its original and revised forms, has

Table 6.5 Workers by type of occupation (percentages)

	Japan, 1998		Canada, 1996		USA, 1996		Germany, 1996		Sweden, 1995	
	Women	Men	Women	Men	Women	Men	Women	Men	Women	Men
Technical	15.3	12.1	37.2	29.1	20.6	15.6	36.5	27.9	47.3	24.7
Administrative	1.0	6.1	–	–	13.3	14.6	3.6	7.2	–	–
Clerical	34.1	15.0	25.0	5.3	24.8	5.6	20.5	7.0	20.8	12.7
Sales	12.1	14.9	10.2	9.9	13.0	11.4	19.5	5.1	9.3	9.6
Service	12.6	7.0	17.5	10.9	17.5	10.2	–	–	11.8	7.1
Farming, forestry, fishing, hunting	0.6	0.8	2.1	6.5	1.2	4.2	1.7	2.5	1.6	4.7
Production, transportation, laborer	24.1	37.3	7.9	38.3	9.7	38.3	7.3	41.1	9.2	41.1
Military, other	–	–	–	–	–	–	11.6	9.3	0.1	0.0
Total workers (10,000)	2127	3264	620	748	5850	6821	1528	2071	193	206

Notes: Workers 15 years of age or older for Canada and Germany; workers 16 years of age or older for the USA; workers in the age bracket 16–64 for Sweden.

Source: *Labor Force Survey, 2000,* Cabinet Statistical Agency; *Year Book of Labor Statistics, 1996,* International Labor Organization.

Table 6.6 Japanese workers by type of employment (as at February 2002) (Sample 10,000 workers)

	Total	Women	Men
Employed (excl. company directors)	4999 (100%)	2076 (100%)	2923 (100%)
regular employees	3640 (72.8%)	1083 (52.2%)	2557 (87.5%)
part-time workers	1152 (23.0%)	891 (42.9%)	261 (8.9%)
Workers on temp. contracts	208 (4.2%)	103 (5.0%)	105 (3.6%)

Source: *Special Labor Force Survey*, Ministry of Health, Labor and Welfare, February 2002.

Table 6.7 Wages per hour: full-time and part-time workers (¥)

	Female workers		Male workers	
	Full-time	Part-time	Full-time	Part-time
1990	989	712	1632	944
1992	1127	809	1812	1053
1994	1201	848	1915	1037
1996	1255	870	1976	1071
1998	1295	886	2002	1040
2000	1329	889	2005	1026

Source: *Wage Structure Basic Survey*, Ministry of Health, Labor and Welfare, 2001.

Table 6.8 Annual paid vacations (in days per year)

	Days of annual paid vacation per worker[a]	Days of annual paid vacation taken (%)
1996	17.4	9.4 (54.1)
1997	17.4	9.4 (53.8)
1998	17.5	9.1 (51.8)
1999	17.8	9.0 (50.5)
2000	18.0	8.9 (49.5)

Note: (a) Vacation days carried over from previous years not included.
Source: *Unified Survey of Working Conditions*, Ministry of Health, Labor and Welfare, 2001.

delivered relatively little to female workers in terms of helping them to secure real employment and promotion opportunities. This is seen, for example, in the difference between Japan versus Canada and the USA in female workers' probabilities of achieving successful private-sector professional careers. At the time of writing, it is inconceivable that a woman would be appointed as the CEO of a Japanese publicly held company as large as, say, Hewlett-Packard. In contrast, in the USA, prospects for female executives continue to improve.

Globalization has forced Japanese firms operating overseas to face the social reality of the host countries. These host country realities include equal opportunities for employment, and the protection of pay equity for females and disabled workers, plus the protection of a variety of other individual rights. Unlike the rapid and massive transfer to the West of Japanese production technologies that took place in the 1980s and 1990s, there is little evidence of rapid or massive transfer from the West to Japanese corporations of managerial practices to enable them to conform with the emerging global standards on aspects such as the safeguarding of basic individual rights for women and other groups of workers, as well as for consumers. This gap in the level of understanding between Japanese firms and other societies has caused serious management problems and subsequent financial losses for the foreign direct investment (FDI) operations of many Japanese firms.

For example, the US Equal Employment Opportunity Commission (EEOC) filed a lawsuit on 9 April 1996, on behalf of a group of current and former employees of Mitsubishi Motor Manufacturing of America (MMMA), who claimed to have been subjected to systematic sexual harassment since 1990 in MMMA's manufacturing plant at Normal, Illinois. MMMA subsequently had to settle the case with the EEOC by agreeing to pay a sum of $34 million. Lawsuits such as this are unlikely to be initiated or supported by Japanese government agencies even in the face of clear evidence of discrimination in private-sector firms in Japan, and there is little in the way of any other sort of enforcement mechanisms.

In contrast to the situation in Canada and the USA, where discrimination against female and minority workers (including those who are disabled or older) became a social issue challenging the cohesion of society,[16] there is little evidence of this sort of social concern in Japan, at least up to the time of writing. Viewed from the perspective of economic efficiency, however, more forceful laws to help realize a fuller utilization of Japan's female labor force seems justified.

Foreign labor

Although Japanese labor markets have been slow to develop for mid-career job seekers and female workers, and unemployment rates have been rising, nevertheless many jobs remain vacant. The vacant positions range from menial jobs that few Japanese want, to highly-paid scientific, technical, managerial and professional positions. Especially at the lowly-paid end of the spectrum, openings are often filled by foreign workers, including some who are working legally, and others illegally. Many agree that this need for foreign labour will increase as Japan's population begins to both shrink and age. We consider policy issues related to foreign workers and immigration below, and aging will be discussed after that.

Foreign workers in Japan

Official Japanese government policy towards foreign workers is that Japan has no compelling reasons to have them. The Japanese Cabinet endorsed this policy for the first time in March 1967, again in January 1973 and then again in June 1976. Post-Second World War immigration laws reflected official policy statements on foreign workers; foreigners have been prohibited from working in Japan since the war, with the exception of small numbers who are needed to perform special tasks, such as teaching English. This policy was adopted when Japan was able to recruit the required number of new workers for modernizing and expanding its manufacturing industries from its own growing population, and from relocations of workers from agricultural to the growing industrial areas. However, the era of abundant labor has now come to an end. At the same time, globalization of the Japanese economy has forced many Japanese firms to search outside the country for skills in short supply among Japanese workers. The Japanese public began to recognize the changing nature of the demand for labour. In 1981, the Seibu Group of companies asked for (and were granted) government permits to hire foreign workers on a long-term basis to fill certain positions for which insufficient numbers of Japanese workers had the necessary skills. Seibu Group of companies were the first in the Japanese corporate sector to seek this sort of permission (from the Minister of Justice) to hire foreign workers. The number of foreigners working for various Japanese firms increased to 3,004 by 1984 and increased further to 6,242 by 1986.

It was also in the early 1980s that the number of illegal aliens in Japan began to increase massively. These foreigners typically entered on tourist visas and then remained after their visas expired and took paid work. Though the figures are very uncertain, the Japanese government estimates the number of illegal foreign workers in the 1980s was approximately 50,000 as of December 1987, and 70,000 by July 1988, while private-sector estimates are higher, ranging from 100,000 to 200,000. A variety of factors contributed to the rapid increase of illegal foreign workers during the 1980s. These are believed to include Japan's continuing strong economy and currency; the demand for workers willing to undertake tasks many Japanese workers were unwilling to accept for the going wages; the deteriorating economic situations in some of the Middle Eastern oil-producing countries which used to employ many workers from Asia; and the deteriorating economic conditions in some of the Asian countries.[17] Certainly, it has been reported widely that the demand for illegal foreign workers who are willing to do 'dirty, dangerous and demanding' tasks for low wages has been increasing among Japanese medium-sized and small firms. It is believed that the wages of illegal workers are generally in the range of 50–80 per cent of the those of Japanese workers performing similar tasks, and illegal aliens in Japan are not eligible for Japan's national health insurance. Hypothetically, through their employers these workers could be eligible for company medical insurance, and the workers' compensation public disability insurance. Nevertheless, it is viewed as unlikely that employers would be extending these benefits to their illegal alien workers because of the fear on the part of the employers that they would be prosecuted if the Japanese government discovered their employment of illegal aliens. Thus the disparity between what the Japanese and the foreign workers receive is believed to be greater than just the wage disparity in the case of the illegal workers.

At the time of writing, foreign workers, including those employed illegally, are believed to comprise about 1 per cent of the Japanese workforce, and this percentage is expected to increase as the size of the Japanese workforce begins to decline as a result of a combination of low birth rates and aging (Table 6.9).

Foreign workers: the Canadian experience

Unfortunately, Japan lacks reliable data on the behavior of immigrants, since there are very few legal immigrants in Japan. This shortcoming severely limits the scope of economic analysis regarding the economic contributions of immigrants. Below we show briefly how the legal immigrants in Canada fare in an economic sense versus their indigenous Canada-born counterparts. We explain briefly the current status of immigration in Canada, and then discuss how immigrants perform in the Canadian economy.[18]

Table 6.9 Foreign workers in Japan, 1990–8 (Sample 10,000 workers)

	1990	1992	1993	1994	1995	1996	1997	1998
(1) Foreign workers (all included)	26	58	61	62	61	63	66	67
(1x) Illegal workers (estimated lower bound)	10.6	29.2	29.7	28.8	28.5	28.3	27.7	27.1
(2) All workers	6384	6578	6615	6645	6666	6711	6787	6793
(2x) Employed workers	4835	5119	5202	5236	5263	5322	5391	5368
(3) Foreign workers ratio: (1)/(2)	0.4%	0.9%	0.9%	0.9%	0.9%	0.9%	1.0%	1.0%

Notes: Figures for illegal workers (1x) are figures estimated by the Japanese government. It is generally agreed that the actual numbers are much higher than those given here.
Source: Cabinet Statistical Agency (2000).

Immigration has been an important source of population and labour force growth for Canada. Beaujot (2000) finds that, over the period 1901–96,[19] the total immigration of some 12 million persons and the estimated emigration of some 6 million produced a net population gain of 6 million. This represents a fifth of Canada's population growth over that period. By historical standards, immigration levels have been especially high in more recent years. For the 1951–91 period, net migration accounted for about a quarter of population growth, and this proportion rose to 51 per cent for the years 1991–6.

In many respects, Canadians seem to prefer immigrants who mirror their own behavior patterns. Certainly, some past immigration policies reflected this preference.[20] Table 6.10 shows that immigrants from the UK and other European countries, the traditional source countries for most of the incumbent Canadian population, made up the overwhelming majority of immigrants to Canada before 1971. As Canadian policies on immigration relaxed during the 1970s, the rules and policies that had constrained immigration from other parts of the world were revised and the primary source countries for immigration to Canada shifted dramatically: from that time, the majority of immigrants came from Asia and Africa. By the 1990s, the UK and other European countries provided only a quarter of immigrants to Canada. One policy concern resulting from the drastic change in the composition of immigrants to Canada was how these new types of immigrants, mainly from developing and often extremely poor countries, might contribute to economic activities in Canada.

Table 6.10   Percentage distribution of foreign-born individuals by country of birth for three periods of immigration

Country of birth	Period of immigration		
	Before 1971	1971–80	1981–91
United States (USA)	5.4	6.7	4.3
Europe			
United Kingdom (UK)	24.2	13.3	5.5
Federal Republic of Germany	7.2	1.6	1.3
Italy	15.3	2.8	0.7
Portugal	3.0	6.2	2.7
Poland	4.6	1.1	6.3
USSR	3.9	0.8	0.9
Other Europe	23.8	9.9	7.1
Asia			
Middle East and Western Asia	0.9	3.0	8.1
Southern Asia	1.6	8.4	9.1
Hong Kong	0.6	4.0	7.8
Peoples' Republic of China	1.9	4.0	5.8
Philippines	0.5	4.6	5.4
Vietnam	0.0	4.5	5.5
Other East/South East Asia	0.8	4.9	6.3
Africa	1.6	5.9	6.1
Central and South America, Caribbean and Bermuda	4.0	16.8	16.2
Other	0.6	1.4	1.0
Total	100.0	100.0	100.0

Source: Nakamura *et al*. (2003). Based on the 1991 Census Public Use Sample data for individuals available from Statistics Canada.

Earlier waves of immigrants to Canada achieved higher average earnings than those born in Canada. It is widely believed in Canada that this is because they contributed skills and knowledge in scarce supply at that time, and were unusually hard-working. Many Canadians would like this immigration program to continue to make a similar contribution to Canadian economic development.

Table 6.11 compares the annual earnings and level of education (years of schooling) for male and female individuals in Canada who were working in 1990. We are particularly interested in comparisons among those who were Canadian-born, those who immigrated from the traditional source countries (proxied here by birth in the USA and the UK), and those

Table 6.11 All Industries mean values: men and women, 25–64 who were working in 1990

		USA/UK born		Born elsewhere	
	Native born	Came before 1981	Came in 1981–90	Came before 1981	Came in 1981–90
Annual earnings (1990$), Men					
1 Non-minority	35 287	47 566	43 624	36 056	28 041
2 Minority	34 266	41 741	30 597	35 752	23 105
Years of schooling, Men					
3 Non-minority	12.7	14.6	15.2	11.0	13.6
4 Minority	14.1	14.7	14.8	13.8	13.6
Sample size, Men					
5 Non-minority	133 321	4 074	595	9 700	1 937
6 Minority	1 543	79	44	6 402	4 802
Annual earnings (1990$), Women					
7 Non-minority	20 978	23 786	20 100	20 265	16 223
8 Minority	23 566	25 361	20 459	22 696	15 663
Years of schooling, Women					
9 Non-minority	13.0	13.9	14.5	10.7	13.7
10 Minority	13.8	14.7	14.1	13.1	13.2
Sample size, Women					
11 Non-minority	110 351	3 755	698	6 201	1 516
12 Minority	1 413	77	34	5 799	4 156

Source: Nakamura *et al.* (2003). Based on the 1991 Census Public Use Sample data for individuals available from Statistics Canada.

from other countries, including developing countries in Asia and Africa. We see from Table 6.11 that male and female immigrants who came from the USA and the UK prior to 1981 clearly have higher levels of education and earn more than their Canadian-born counterparts. The same patterns are observed for immigrants from countries other than the USA and the UK, except that their levels of earnings are considerably lower than for the corresponding immigrants who came from the USA and the UK prior to 1981. In fact, the immigrants from countries other than the USA and the UK have generally lower levels of education and earn less than their counterparts born in Canada.

We can see that more recent immigrants from the USA and UK have continued to enjoy relatively high earnings compared with the those born in Canada. However, more recent immigrants born outside the

USA and UK seem not to have done as well on average. Moreover, the proportion of immigrants born outside the USA and UK has risen over time, so their experiences have come to dominate the overall immigrant results.[21] Some Canadians fear that the lower earnings of more recent immigrants mean that they are less welcomed by employers because their skills or work habits are less well suited to Canada.[22]

Policy implications for Japan

We have seen above that, as globalization has an impact on Canadian immigration policies, more immigrants are beginning to be accepted from countries other than the traditional source countries such as the USA and Europe. Perhaps because of a less good match of workers to the skill needs of employers, immigrants' economic contributions seem to have declined over time. It is possible that a similar situation will develop in Japan.

The primary source countries for foreign workers in Japan (both legal and illegal) include Asian countries and a few South American countries (for example, Brazil); indeed, the latter countries provide legal foreign workers who are of Japanese origin. How to assess these foreign workers' economic contributions to the Japanese economy relative to indigenous Japanese workers is a difficult problem so long as so many of the foreign workers continue to be illegal. Analysis prospects are also complicated by claims that many foreign workers are performing tasks that Japanese workers are unwilling to perform for the wages offered; that is, it is claimed that many foreign workers are segregated into occupational sub-categories where there are few, if any, Japanese workers, thereby limiting the possibilities of making meaningful wage comparisons.

However, it is becoming increasingly important to know more about the situation of immigrant workers in Japan, particularly regarding illegal aliens. It seems clear that if Japan continues its current immigration policies and illegal foreign workers continue to increase in number as predicted by many as a result of the expected labour shortages in Japan, this could lead to the formation of a permanent low-status group. Developments of this kind could threaten Japan's social stability.

Aging of the Japanese population: related policy issues

Japanese demographic development is characterized by two factors. The first is prolonged longevity and the second a substantially reduced birth rate. Both of these are found, to varying degrees, in most developed countries in the West. Japan is distinguishable from other developed countries in that the aging of the population is taking place more rapidly and there is little immigration. The issues associated with the rapidly aging Japanese population will be discussed in this section.

The aging population and labor market supply and demand

Aging

In the year 2000, 17.4 per cent of the Japanese population was over 65 years of age. It is estimated that this figure will increase to 25 per cent by 2015, and further to 35.7 per cent by 2050. At the same time, the number of people in their twenties will decline, not only in proportionate terms but also in absolute number, from 19 million in the year 2000 to 12.5 million by 2015.[23]

Industrial structure

Japanese firms have been forced to internationalize their operations significantly since the early 1980s, and this has had a serious impact on the types of employment available in Japan. The numbers of workers in primary industries such as agriculture, forestry and fishing have been declining since the late 1970s. Also, the manufacturing sector, which traditionally had provided the largest share of Japanese employment, had begun to shrink by the mid-1990s. At the time of writing, professionals, technical specialists and clerical workers represent the bulk of domestic employment. In fact, the largest increase in employment has been for professional and technical workers, who are generally highly educated and trained.

Unemployment

Inadequate employment has traditionally been thought to cause social problems in Japan, perhaps more so than in the West because of the way the labour market, employment practices and employment insurance (called unemployment insurance in Japan) function. As we have argued above, the labour market associated with the post-Second World War employment practices has focused on new graduates and is not well suited to meet the job-matching needs of mid-career workers who quit work by choice or who try to reenter the workforce after absences caused by child-bearing, illness, disability or job loss. (See Figure 6.1.)

The bursting of the financial bubble in 1990 and the ensuing recession forced many Japanese firms to lay off workers in unprecedented numbers, and seriously challenged and tested the ability of the Japanese labour market to match the unemployed workers with appropriate employers.

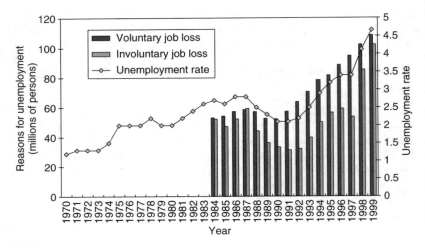

Figure 6.1   Reasons for unemployment
Source: Management and Coordination Agency, *Annual Report on the Labor Force Survey*, Tokyo: 1970–99.

Despite certain government measures aimed at encouraging the reemployment of these workers, Japanese firms so far have not been able to absorb many of them, and this is especially so for those who are older (that is, those above fifty years of age).

Necessary changes in the Japanese labor market for securing employment

Given the aging of the Japanese workforce and anticipated high levels of unemployment, Japan must make changes in its institutions, and public and corporate labour policies, in order to regain its higher employment rates. We discuss these suggested changes in this section.

The current demographic estimates suggest that, by 2013 or so, the Japanese workforce will have significantly more older workers than ever before relative to the size of the younger cohort of workers. The accounting identity for life-cycle calculations of income and expenditure for the population as a whole implies that older workers must work longer and retire later than what is now the standard retirement age. Even now, many older workers opt to work after their first retirement at the age of sixty to sixty-three. Can firms change their current mandatory age of first retirement from sixty-three to, say, sixty-five?

We have already argued above that many Japanese firms face keen global competition. This may mean that these firms will decide they cannot afford to extend their mandatory retirement age, fearing this would make their operations more inflexible and costly. Rather, the trend in contemporary employment practices in Japan is that firms are hiring more workers on employment contracts for limited periods of time. It is likely that the Japanese firms, while maintaining secure employment for a core of regular workers, will employ increasing proportions of workers on short-term appointments; that is, it is likely that they will expand 'non-regular' employment. Short-term appointments may have certain desirable characteristics for professional workers and technical specialists who are in strong demand.

As more firms become reluctant (or unable) to provide life-long (long-term) employment for large numbers of their employees, many workers will be motivated, or indeed forced, to look for new jobs in the labor market in mid-career. Thus it has become essential for Japan to develop effective labour market mechanisms that can help unemployed workers locate new employment commensurate with their qualifications.

In the past, reallocation of labour from declining to new industries in the Japanese economy was typically accomplished through the means of the growing industries absorbing increasing proportions of young graduates as new employees. Given that fewer young workers are expected to enter the labor market in the future, this system of reallocation of workers is not expected to work as well in the years to come. Japan needs labor market mechanisms that can help experienced workers and professionals move from declining to new industries. The current Japanese labor market does not function efficiently in this regard.

Necessary changes in Japanese employment practices

We have described the post-Second World War employment practices that still reign in Japan. In order to accommodate the types of changes required to improve employment prospects for many Japanese, some of these practices must change.

First, seniority-based (*nenko*) wages cannot continue. The rationale underlying the *nenko* wage system is best illustrated in Figure 6.2. For carefully selected regular workers under the traditional Japanese life-time employment system, a simple wage determination system where wage rates increase with the age of a worker (*EFGH* in Figure 6.2) makes economic sense for both the employers and the workers. A newly employed worker with low marginal productivity gets paid more than the productivity warrants (*EF* versus *ABF*), but the situation reverses as

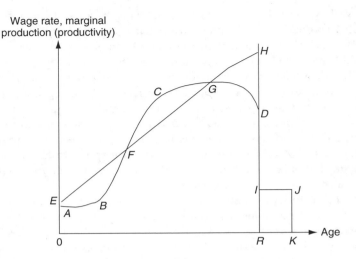

Figure 6.2   Workers' productivity and wage rates
Notes: *A, B, F, C, G* and *D* represent workers' productivity levels at different points in time over their life cycles (between age 0 and age *R*); *E, F, G* and *H* represent the wages firms pay to the workers; the workers retire at age *R* and receive retirement pay *IJ* until age *K*.

the worker's skill level increases (*FCG* versus *FG*). The situation reverses again as the worker's productivity declines with age (*GD* versus *GH*). Under this kind of wage system, mandatory retirement (at age *R*) is a necessity. At age *R* the worker retires and begins receiving his/her company pension (*IJ*) that ends at age *K*. The parameters of this wage system, including the slope of the wage rate, the mandatory retirement age and the amount and the pay period of the pension, are set for each type of worker to try to ensure that worker contributions to the firm over the worker's total years of services are at least as great as the total wages the worker receives. There are two basic assumptions that underlie this argument. One is that workers' productivity increases with age up to a point, stays at that point for some years, and then begins to decline as retirement age approaches. There is some evidence that seems to backup this assumption. Figure 6.3 shows Japanese firms' views about worker productivity versus wages for workers over the ages of 25–55. These survey results are consistent with Figure 6.2. The second basic assumption is the long-term employment practice itself that was the norm for the large majority of male workers for many years in post-Second World War Japan. However, it now seems almost certain that there will be far fewer workers who have long-term job security in Japan

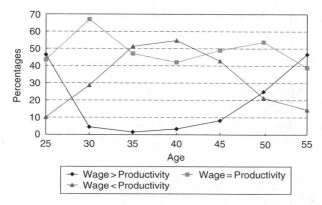

Figure 6.3. Employers' perception of the relationship between workers' wages and productivity as a function of workers' ages
Source: Association of Employment Development for Senior Citizens (1995).

in the years to come. This proportion has already been falling for some time now.

With the new reality of term employment arrangements for large numbers of workers, a more realistic wage system would be the one that attempts to gear current levels of worker pay to workers' current contributions to the employer. This is the type of wage system we commonly observe, for example, in North America. It is our view that a wage system similar to the North American one will become dominant for professionals and specialists, while a relatively small proportion of company personnel, including senior management and a small core of regular workers, will continue to enjoy the benefits of the traditional Japanese postwar long-term employment and pay practices.

A second change required in Japanese employment practices is to abolish the promotion system by which most, if not all, of the regular employees gain promotion to higher managerial positions. This has been an expectation shared by both employers and employees. As Figure 6.4 (a) shows, this promotion practice presumes an ever-growing workforce, which is not a reasonable assumption any more. The reality has been that many firms have had to carry older workers with quasi-management titles and no work responsibilities. Many of these redundant managerial workers are likely now to end up being restructured out. Given that the present low (to no) growth employment situation is likely to persist for some years to come, it is more realistic for firms to eliminate any

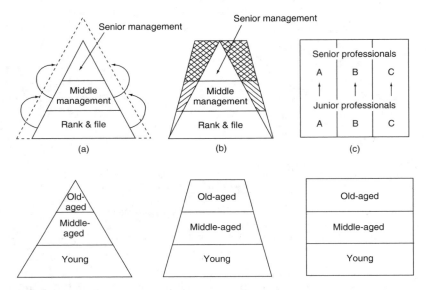

Figure 6.4   Changing forms of the personnel management system
Source: Seike (1993).

promise of promotion to a managerial position for workers as they get older and accumulate more seniority. In this new system, as workers develop specialized skills over time, they would come to be treated as specialists in their own fields.

The third change required is to abolish mandatory retirement at Japanese firms. We should note that many Japanese workers continue doing paid work following their first mandatory retirements. Nevertheless, mandatory retirements tend to encourage workers to withdraw from the labor market, with this being especially so for those who have been more successful and hence can better afford to retire. Figure 6.5 shows that older workers who have withdrawn from the workforce following mandatory retirements tend to enjoy higher wages (and hence, presumably, were higher productivity workers). This is an adverse selection problem. Retaining older workers like these who might otherwise have stayed on in the labor market seems to be an effective way to deal with the shrinking Japanese workforce. As Table 6.12 shows, some Japanese firms did, in fact, begin to modify their industrial relations practices along these lines in the 1990s.

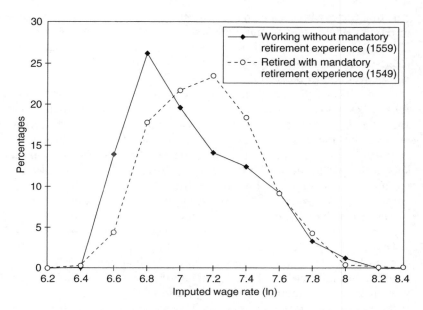

Figure 6.5 The distribution of wages for older workers with and without mandatory retirement experience: men, aged 60–69

Table 6.12   Changing labor management policies: Japanese firms, 1996 and 1993 (percentages)

Permanent employment policy

Important	Unimportant	Neither	No reply
18.9 (31.8)	50.5 (41.5)	29.0 (22.1)	1.5 (4.5)

Promotion policy: which is more important, seniority or merit?

Seniority	Merit	Both	Neither	No reply
3.6 (11.0)	48.4 (37.8)	41.7 (30.3)	5.5 (18.2)	0.8 (2.7)

Note: Numbers in parentheses are for 1993.
Source: *Personnel Management Survey*, Ministry of Labor, 1996.

Necessary changes in the relationship between employers and workers

The types of changes required for the development of a more suitable employment system cannot be implemented unless the relationship between the employer and the union (or its proxy) is also changed.

Equating wages with each worker's contribution to the firm at every point in time inevitably encourages worker-specific determination of working conditions. Some Japanese firms have already begun paying wages that reflect individual worker performance more than before. This is happening to some workers who are union members.

Given that employers usually have much more information than the workers about emerging business conditions, and an overwhelming amount of bargaining power over workers in wage negotiations, particularly on a one-to-one basis, it seems quite appropriate for labour unions to continue to play an active role in work negotiations. At least the union should negotiate with the employer for a reasonable framework of rules for merit-based wage determination. This would be beneficial to the employer as well, since the cost to the employer of dealing directly with matters such as wage-related worker grievances would be substantial.

Japanese labor unions in their post-Second World War practices have refused explicitly to accept policies that treat workers differently depending on their ability, and yet have been successful in securing employment for their members. Union efforts to achieve numerical target wage increases for model workers have also been successful. However, this union behavior must now change. It is especially critical for unions to recognize individual differences in ability and capacity to learn on the job. In this context, the most important role labor unions can play in the new system of industrial relations is to ensure that all workers are given the opportunities to undertake training, and opportunities to do tasks that suit their abilities and experience. Japanese labor unions have an important role to play in formulating rules for an individual-specific, merit-based wage determination process, and processes for ensuring equal opportunities for training and productive task assignment for all workers.

Necessary changes in the annual wage round (*shunto*)

The Japanese annual round of wage determination in the postwar era has allowed firms from many industries to adjust their wages regularly, thus providing opportunities for both firms and workers to bring wages into line with the performance of workers in aggregate. As Japanese wages become more individual-specific, and the slow-growing Japanese economy no longer serves to justify significant wage increases, the role of the annual wage round may be called into question. Two of the roles the annual wage round has played in postwar practices will still continue to be important. The first of these is a role of information provision. The information content of the wage-setting processes in large corporations takes place every spring, and is especially significant for medium-sized and small firms. The information provided by negotiations at major corporations is placed in the public domain and provides a positive framework for negotiations to follow at medium-sized and, especially, smaller firms. This sharing of information seems useful in many ways and is believed to result in faster resolution of the wage-setting processes.

Second, the annual wage round has often played an important role in the determination of surplus-sharing rules (as a result of increased productivity) between the firms and their workers. For example, the primary reason that the Japanese economy was able to recover as fast as it did from the hyper-inflation caused by the oil crises (particularly the second of these) in the 1970s, was that the workers agreed to restrain their demands for wage increases in the annual wage round. There will certainly be situations in the very near future in Japan's aging society where issues of how to allocate surpluses generated by increased productivity are pressing, particularly given the likely problems to be faced in meeting the expected levels of support for older people, and the likelihood of emerging conflict between older and younger people concerning benefits, plus premium levels for public and private pensions. The annual wage round in some revised form may be an appropriate place where policy issues such as these can be debated and dealt with.

Government policy measures that would facilitate the above changes

In order to facilitate the types of changes discussed above in the Japanese labor market, employment practices and industrial relations, many Japanese government policies must also change. The primary policy objective must be to ensure the employment security of workers in the labor market as a whole, including the development of mechanisms to help workers change jobs, and compensation practices that produce a greater alignment between the current wages and workers' contributions to the profits of their employers. Lifetime employment security traditionally provided by a single employer is no longer possible for many workers. We consider two policy initiatives that we feel would contribute to the realization of a different labor market.

First, mechanisms are needed to increase the availability of information about the labour market itself. In particular, workers should be able to access information about available jobs conveniently on an ongoing basis. Even employers would benefit from having access to information about job openings at other firms. Deregulation of the operations of private-sector employment agencies seems to be essential; these agencies help to match professionals and specialists seeking employment to suitable available jobs.[24] Facilitating placements of mid-career professionals and specialists, which usually take a long time to complete, is one of the most urgent challenges facing the Japanese labor market.

Second, a policy is needed to develop a more comprehensive social safety-net for unemployed workers. For example, extending the period of employment insurance for redundant middle-aged workers seems to be appropriate. On the other hand, employment credits (subsidies) which encourage declining industries to continue to operate should be eliminated.

It also seems essential for the government to promote new responsibilities on the part of individuals and households that are more in line with the new realities of the labour market and business conditions. For example, elimination of the seniority-based wage system may imply that workers themselves must save from the higher income they earn in their thirties for their future expenditure in their fifties and later years. Life-cycle savings considerations must also be reflected in policies for company and private pension plans.

Another important policy issue concerns how to encourage workers to develop skills during their life. Traditionally, this task has been one of the main responsibilities of Japanese firms. However, as workers' wages begin to reflect primarily their contemporary contributions to firms' profits, it is likely that employers will be less motivated to train their workers. To the extent that public and private (including household) investment in the human capital of workers is thought to be profitable for society, efforts to increase this kind of investment may also be necessary. For example, long-term government loans for skill development should be encouraged. For practical reasons, these loans would need to have long repayment periods. (Mandatory retirement or age discrimination may be obstacles to the implementation of measures of this kind.)

Government policies toward employer–labor relations must also change. We speculate that there will be many wage dispute cases as more employers start to implement person-specific, merit-based wages. In addition to a substantial revision of the labor offices of the Japanese and prefectural governments, we need to consider expanding the authority of the management–labor committees at the company level so that they can deal more effectively with the resolution of wage disputes in their own companies.

Conclusion

In this chapter we have argued that an aging population combined with the impacts of globalization, the after-effects of the bursting of the financial bubble in 1990 and changing work preferences, are likely to keep unemployment levels high in Japan well into the twenty-first century. To enable the reinstatement of lower unemployment rates, the Japanese labor market must change in fundamental ways. Such changes would require all market participants, including workers, employers and governments, to change their postwar employment practices drastically. New industrial relations practices and government policies must encourage appropriate matching between all types of job applicants (including females and other mid-career job seekers, as well as foreign workers) and available job opportunities. This matching needs to be compatible with the incentives of workers and employers. In so doing, the role of foreign workers in the Japanese labor market, together with possible changes in the immigration laws, must be addressed. Without these fundamental changes in the functioning of Japanese labor markets, employment security for most workers, which has been the cornerstone of the Japanese government's labor policy since the end of the Second World War, may be jeopardized and serious social instability might arise.

Notes

1   This is seen by the ratio between the number of people above 65 years of age and the number between 15 and 64 years of age. This ratio for Japan was 0.26 in 2002 (that is, 3.9 workers support one retired person) but is expected to increase to the 0.50 range by 2030 (2 workers to support one retired person) and further to about 0.67 by 2050 (1.5 workers to support one retired person).
2   These include the famous Kikkoman dispute that Fruin (1983) has written about.
3   See, for example, Nakamura (1993) and Nakamura and Vertinsky (1994).
4   See Chapter 11 and the references cited there.
5   See, for example, the publications by Krafcik (1988) and the US General Accounting Office (1988). Toyota developed a special production system (often termed the Toyota production system) in the 1960s and shared it with other Japanese firms in the auto as well as other manufacturing industries.
6   Japanese cars still enjoy quality advantages compared to cars sold by the firms of other nations in the US market.
7   See, for example, Fukuyama (1992).
8   See, for example, Head and Ries (2001).
9   What has been happening could be consistent with the notion that hollowing out assists a national economy in moving towards higher value-added industries and away from older, lower value-added ones. This process succeeds if the workers and capital that get structured out of the declining industries are smoothly channeled into the higher value-added ones.

10 According to a survey conducted in February 2000 by The Japan Institute of Workers' Evolution, only 54 per cent of women who were offered regular career positions as new graduates in 1986 were still working in 2000. The figure was 44 per cent for those who started work in 1991.

11 Although divorce does not play any prominent role in these scenarios, the probability of divorce has been increasing for Japanese couples.

12 Many factors contribute to observed male–female wage differentials in Japan. One factor is that women in Japan work outside the home much less than women in North America and Europe during their child-bearing and rearing years, and hence accumulate much less human capital than men, which partially explains their lower wages in comparison with men. See, for example, Jacobsen (1998).

13 Another likely reason is the scarcity of full-time positions relative to part-time positions for women, which fits in with employer preferences to move female workers to part-time categories.

14 Workers are often reluctant to ask for, or take, maternity and holiday leave to which they are contractually entitled because of feared adverse effects on their career advancement, or on the business operations of their employers. Moreover, many employers are, in fact, reluctant to allow their employees to take the full amount of personal leave to which they are contractually entitled.

15 For example, IBM Japan often uses the excellent promotion opportunities they provide for their female employees to promote their public image and attract capable workers.

16 For example, Nakamura and Nakamura (1989).

17 The primary sourcing countries of Japan's legal and illegal foreign workers include China, South Korea, Thailand and the Philippines.

18 For further details see Nakamura *et al.* (2003).

19 Information on the immigrant population and the Canadian immigration program can be found in Citizenship and Immigration Canada (1994, 2000, 2001) and in Informetrica (2000).

20 See Green (1995).

21 Other studies include Nakamura and Nakamura (1992), Baker and Benjamin (1994), Beach and Worswick (1994), Grant (1999), Nakamura *et al.* (1999), and Li (2001).

22 See Nakamura *et al.* (2003) for the implications of empirical facts and alternative measures of labor input and productivity growth that are relevant to assessing these concerns.

23 Japan's birth rate (the expected number of children a woman will have over her lifetime) was relatively constant at around 2.1 until the early 1970s, and then began to decline persistently, falling to about 1.35 in the late 1990s. At the time of writing, Japan's population replacement birth rate is 2.08. The current birth rate is considerably below its replacement level but by no means unique, given the birth rates for the following European countries: Germany (1.36 in 1999), Italy (1.19 in 1999) and Spain (1.16 in 1996). Relatively few developed countries have birth rates above 2.0. Another country that is experiencing rapidly declining birth rates is South Korea, where the birth rate declined from 4.54 in 1970 to 1.17 in 2002. Exceptions are: the USA (2.13 in 2000) and Iceland (2.04 in 1997).

24   Economy-wide electronic job matching information systems such as the Career Owl system (2003) facilitate this matching process.

References

Association of Employment Development for Senior Citizens (1995) *Roreika shakai ni okeru model chingin* (Report on Wage Models for an Aging Society) in Japanese (Tokyo).

Baker, M. and Benjamin, D. (1994) 'The Performance of Immigrants in the Canadian Labor Market', *Journal of Labor Economics*, vol. 12, pp. 369–405.

Beach, C. M. and Worswick, C. (1994) 'Is There a Double Negative Effect on the Earnings of Immigrant Women?', *Canadian Public Policy*, vol. 19, pp. 36–53.

Beaujot, R. (2000) 'Immigration and Canadian Demographics: State of the Research, Citizenship and Immigration Canada', www.cic.gc.ca, Cat. No. MP22–16/2–2000E.

Cabinet Statistical Agency (2000), *Labor Force Survey*, Tokyo.

Career Owl Electronic Job Matching Information System, www.CareerOwl.com, 2003.

Citizenship and Immigration Canada (1994) *Canada 2005: A Strategy for Citizenship and Immigration. A background document*, Ottawa.

Citizenship and Immigration Canada (2000) *The Economic Performance of Immigrants: Immigration Category Perspective*, IMDB Profile Series, www.cic.gc.ca, Cat. No. MP22–18/2–2000E.

Citizenship and Immigration Canada (2001) *Facts and Figures 2000: Immigration Overview*, www.cic.gc.ca, Cat. No. MP43–333/2001E.

Fruin, W. M. (1983) *Kikkoman: Company, Clan, and Community* (Cambridge, MA: Harvard University Press).

Fukuyama, F. (1992) *The End of History and the Last Man* (New York: Free Press).

Fuss, M. and Waverman, L. (1990) 'The Extent and Sources of Cost and Efficiency Between U.S. and Japanese Motor Vehicle Producers', *Journal of the Japanese and International Economies* vol. 4.

Grant, M. L. (1999) 'Evidence of New Immigrant Assimilation in Canada', *Canadian Journal of Economics*, vol. 32, no. 4, August, pp. 930–55.

Green, A. G. (1995) 'A Comparison of Canadian and U.S. Immigration Policy in the Twentieth Century', in D. DeVoretz (ed.), *Diminishing Returns: The Economics of Canada's Recent Immigration Policy*, Policy Study 24 (Toronto: C. D. Howe Institute and The Laurier Institution), pp. 31–64.

Head, K. and Ries, J. (2001) 'Kudoka and the Japanese Worker', in M. Nakamura (ed.), *The Japanese Business and Economic System: History and Prospects for the 21st Century* (Basingstoke: Palgrave/Macmillan).

Informetrica (2000) *Recent Immigrants in Metropolitan Areas*, www.cic.gc.ca, May, Cat. Nos. MP22–20/2–2000E, MP22–20/3–2000E, MP22–20/4–2000E.

International Labor Organization (1996) *Year Book of Labor Statistics*, Geneva.

Jacobsen J. P. (1998) *The Economics of Gender*, 2nd edn (Malden: Basil Blackwell).

Japan Institute of Workers' Evolution, The Tokyo, Japan, http://www.jiwe.or.jp/english/situation/index.html.

Krafcik, J. F. (1988) 'Triumph of the Lean Production System', *Sloan Management Review*, Fall.

Lazear, E. P. (1979) 'Why Is There a Mandatory Retirement?', *Journal of Political Economy*, vol. 87.

Li, P. S. (2001) 'The Market Worth of Immigrants' Educational Credentials', *Canadian Public Policy*, vol. XXVII, no. 1, March, pp. 77–94.

Management and Coordination Agency (1970–99) *Annual Report on the Labor Force Survey*, Tokyo.

Ministry of Health, Labor, and Welfare (2001) *Wage Structure Basic Survey*, Tokyo.

Ministry of Health, Labor and Welfare (2001) *Unified Survey of Working Conditions*, Tokyo.

Ministry of Health, Labor and Welfare (2002) *Special Labor Force Survey*, February, Tokyo.

Ministry of Labor (1996) *Personnel Management Survey*, Tokyo.

Ministry of Labor (1998) *Personnel Management Survey*, Tokyo.

Ministry of Labor (1998a) *Wage Structure Basic Survey*, Tokyo.

Nakamura, A. and Nakamura, M. (1985) *The Second Paycheck: A Socio-economic Analysis of Earnings*, (New York: Academic Press).

Nakamura, A. and Nakamura, M. (1989) 'Predicting the Effects of Comparable Worth Programs on Female Labor Supply', *Journal of Social Issues*, vol. 45, pp. 191–208.

Nakamura, A. and Nakamura, M. (1992) 'Wage Rates of Immigrant and Native Men in Canada and the U.S.', in B. R. Chiswick, *Immigration, Language and Ethnicity: Canada and the United States*, Monograph Series (Washington, DC: The AEI Press) pp. 145–66.

Nakamura, A., Nakamura, M. and Diewert, W. E. (2003) 'The Potential Impacts of Immigration on Canada', in C. Beach, A. G. Green and J. G. Reitz (eds), *Canada's Immigration Policy for the 21st Century* (Montreal: John Deutsch Institute, McGill-Queen's University Press).

Nakamura, A., Nakamura, M., Nicol, C. J. and Diewert, W. E. (1999) 'Labour Market Outcomes and the Recruitment Information Needs of Immigrant and Other Job Seekers', Paper presented at the Conference 'Shaping the Future: Qualification Recognition in the 21st Century', 14 October, Toronto.

Nakamura, M. (1993) 'Japanese Industrial Relations in an International Business Environment', *North American Journal of Economics and Finance* vol. 4, pp. 225–51.

Nakamura, M. and Hübler, O. (1998) 'The Bonus Shares of Flexible Pay in Germany, Japan and the U.S.: Some Empirical Regularities', *Japan and the World Economy*, 10, pp. 221–32.

Nakamura, M. and Nakamura, A. (1989) 'Inventory Management Behavior of American and Japanese Firms', *Journal of the Japanese and International Economies* vol. 3, pp. 270–91.

Nakamura, M. and Nakamura, A. (1991) 'Risk Behavior and the Determinants of Bonus versus Regular Pay in Japan', *Journal of the Japanese and International Economies*, vol. 5, pp. 140–59.

Nakamura, M. and Vertinsky, I. (1994) *Japanese Economic Policies and Growth: Implications for Businesses in Canada and North America* (Edmonton, Alberta: University of Alberta Press).

National Institute of Social Security and Population (1998a) *National Survey of Marriages and Births (Survey of Singles)*, Tokyo.

National Institute of Social Security and Population (1998b) *11th Survey of Births (Couples Married for 15–19 years)*, Tokyo.

Nissei Research Institute (1995) *Survey of Help for Resuming Employment by Career-oriented Women*, Tokyo.

Seike, A. (1992) (The labour economics of the old), *Koreisha no roudou keizaigaku* in Japanese (Tokyo: Nihon Keizai).

Seike, A. (1993) (The labour market in an aging society: work behavior and public pensions), *Koreika shakaino rodo shijo* in Japanese (Tokyo: Toyo Keizai).

Seike, A. (1993) 'Utilization of Older Workers', in K. Hori (ed.), *21 seiki no shinkeiei* (New Management for the 21st Century), in Japanese (Tokyo: Sogohorei).

Seike, A. (1998a) *Shougai genekishakai no jouken* (Work for life without retirement), in Japanese, Chukou Shinsho Series (Tokyo: Chuo Koron).

Seike, A. (1998b) 'Teinen to kokyo nenkin no jinteki shihon sonshitsu eno eikyo' (The impact of mandatory retirement and the public pension system on human capital loss), in Japanese, *Keizai Bunseki*, October.

Shimada, H. (1981) *Earnings Structure and Human Investment*, Keio Economic Observatory Monograph No. 4 (Tokyo: Kogakusha).

U.S. Equal Employment Opportunity Commission (1998) *Joint Motion for Entry of Consent Decree between the Equal Employment Opportunity Commission vs. Mitsubishi Motor Manufacturing of America (Diamond-Star Motors Corporation)*, Washington, DC, 11 June.

U.S. General Accounting Office (1988) *Report to Congressional Requesters: Foreign Investment, Growing Japanese Presence in the U.S. Auto Industry*, Washington, DC.

7

Gaijin (Foreign) Sumo Wrestlers Help Japanese Tradition to March On: A Case Study of Foreigners in a Japanese Labor Market[1]

Takanobu Nakajima and Kazuhiro Harakawa

'The *Gaijin* sumo wrestlers can really focus when it comes to an important match. The Japanese sumo wrestlers need to learn something from them.' *Kitanoumi, President, Nihon Sumo Kyokai (Japan Grand Sumo Association)*

The New Year sumo tournament of 2003 came to an end with Mongolian-born Ozeki Asashoryu winning the Makuuchi championship. His splendid record of fourteen wins and only one loss in the tournament assured his becoming a Yokozuna, the highest rank in the world of the Grand Sumo. The brilliant achievement by Asashoryu also underscored a rare event that happened for the first time in sumo history. Believe it or not, except for the Jonidan division, one of the lower rank divisions in sumo, all division champions in this tournament were '*gaijin* sumo wrestlers'.

The above quote by the president of the Nihon Sumo Kyokai appeared in the *Yomiuri Shimbun* (newspaper) the day following the end of the 2003 New Year sumo tournament. In this tournament, Mongolian sumo wrestlers performed outstandingly. Mongolians took the Makuuchi division (the highest ranking division) championship, as well as the championships of the Juryo division (the second-highest ranking division) and the Sandanme division (see Table 7.1). Another newspaper, *Sankei Sports Shimbun*, described this phenomenon by saying: 'Mongolians are heading for the golden country, Zipangu (Japan)', which connects the Mongolian sumo wrestlers to the historical attempt by Mongolia to invade Japan in the twelfth century.

Table 7.1   Ranks for Grand Sumo wrestlers

East	Rank	West	Notes
	Sekitori: wrestlers in the Makuuchi and Juryo divisions		
Makuuchi division: ranks with special titles			No limit on the number of occupants in each rank
	Yokozuna		No demotion; only retirement for exit
	Ozeki		Demotion possible
	Sekiwake		Demotion possible
	Komusubi		Demotion possible
Makuuchi division: Maegashira numbered positions Maegashira #1 Maegashira #2 Maegashira #15			Demotion possible for all numbered positions
Juryo division: numbered positions			Demotion possible for all numbered positions
	Juryo #1 Juryo #2 Juryo #7		
Toriteki: wrestlers in the Makushita, Sandanme, Jonidan and Jonokuchi division			
	Makushita division		Demotion possible for all positions below
	Sandanme division		
	Jonidan division		
	Jonokuchi		

Notes: A few weeks before every Grand Sumo tournament begins, all Grand Sumo wrestlers are ranked and assigned to appropriate positions in the above ranking table (called Banzuke). All Grand Sumo wrestlers are first arbitrarily divided into east and west teams although they do not compete as teams nor is a wrestler from one team necessarily matched against one of the other.

A sumo bout is fought between two wrestlers. A bout is won by forcing the opponent out of the inner circle or throwing him in the dohyo. To lose the match it is not necessary to fall in the circle or to be pushed completely out. The wrestler who touches the ground with any part of his body, his knee or even the tip of his finger or his top-knot, loses the match. Or he need only put one toe or his heel over the straw bales marking the circle.

Striking with fists, hair pulling, eye gouging, choking and kicking in the stomach or chest are prohibited. It is also against the rules to sieze the part of the band covering the vital organs. As there are no weight limits as in boxing or western wrestling it is possible for a wrestler to find himself pitted against an opponent twice his own weight.

We are going to take a closer look at foreign sumo wrestlers in this chapter.

The flourishing of foreign sumo wrestlers in recent years

Foreign sumo wrestlers playing in Japan's Grand Sumo is not a new phenomenon. Before the Second World War, there were Nisei (second-generation Americans of Japanese descent) sumo wrestlers. There were also sumo wrestlers from places like Taiwan and Korea when these countries were Japanese colonies. While there were these foreign sumo wrestlers who were registered in the Grand Sumo Association (Kyokai) in those days, they did not become popular because they did not perform well.

There is no doubt that Daigoro Takamiyama, who came from Hawaii and joined the Takasago stable in 1964, was the one who made foreign sumo wrestlers popular in Japan. His career record was fabulous. Before his retirement at the age of 39, he appeared in 1,430 Makuuchi matches, rising to the Sekiwake rank, winning the Makuuchi championship once, defeating Yokozunas twelve times, and receiving the *sansho* award eleven times.[2] Not only was he physically strong, he was also sturdy and able to survive for a long time as an active sumo wrestler.

After Takamiyama's retirement in 1982, the famous Yasokichi Konishiki came from Hawaii. Only two years after his first appearance at a sumo tournament, Konishiki was promoted to the Makuuchi division, then to the Ozeki rank (the second-highest ranking position). The powerful push from his 200-kilogram (440-pound) body created a 'Konishiki sensation' in the sumo world.

Even though Konishiki had accumulated a great record, however, he was not able to become a Yokozuna. But Konishiki breached the barrier between the Sekiwake (the third-highest ranking position) and the Ozeki ranks for foreign wrestlers, and contributed to raising the public perception of how much '*Gaijin* sumo wrestlers' can achieve in the world of sumo. After the Konishiki sensation of the 1980s, Akebono and Musashimaru, both from Hawaii, successfully became Yokozuna in the 1990s.

In the twenty-first century the Mongolian sumo wrestlers began to appear. The two Mongolians, Kyokushuzan and Kyokutenhou, arrived in Japan in 1992. Both left good performance records and eventually occupied the third-highest ranking positions. And after the New Year sumo tournament of 2003, another Mongolian-born wrestler, Asashoryu was promoted to Yokozuna, as noted above. For Asashoryu, it took only four years from his first appearance in a Grand Sumo tournament to reach the Yokozuna rank. Also in the New Year tournament of 2003, the Mongolians became champions in three of the Grand Sumo divisions. As of the summer tournament of 2003, there were thirty-two Mongolian sumo wrestlers (four in the Makuuchi division, seven in the Makushita, fifteen in the Sandanme and six in the Jonidan).

As of the summer tournament of 2003, there were forty-nine foreign sumo wrestlers. There were also a few admitted sumo wrestlers from some East European countries. Such a phenomenon was previously unheard of, and reflects the globalization of the world of sumo.

Regulation of *gaijin* sumo wrestlers

Until quite recently the Kyokai had few restrictions on foreign sumo wrestlers, but in May 1992, when foreign sumo wrestlers began to rule the wrestling ring, the Kyokai declared they would set a limit on the number of foreign sumo wrestlers, at two per stable. The Kyokai also set a limit on the total number of foreign sumo wrestlers in the Kyokai at forty.

Three foreigners passed the entrance test for apprentices on the first day of the 2001 summer tournament. With the acceptance of these three new foreign sumo wrestlers, the total number of *gaijin* sumo wrestlers reached the set limit of forty, and the Kyokai froze the admission of new foreigners until the total number of foreign sumo wrestlers went below forty again. But limiting the total number of foreign sumo wrestlers to forty was criticized, because it was thought it might start a 'first come, first served' competition among the sumo stables. To prevent such competition for foreign sumo wrestlers, the Kyokai abolished the capacity limit of forty, and instead established a 'one foreign sumo wrestler per stable' rule.

As of the summer tournament of 2003 there were forty-eight stables, with twenty-seven registering foreign sumo wrestlers, which made it possible for twenty-one more foreign sumo wrestlers to enter the stables. There are many opinions about the desirable number of foreign sumo wrestlers in the Kyokai. Some people would like to see fewer foreign sumo wrestlers, while others wish for more. In Mongolia, there is a sport called *bufu* (Mongolian sumo) which is played by 1,500 wrestlers. For these wrestlers, gaining acceptance into to the Japan Grand Sumo Kyokai is still difficult and only possible for a few elite players.

Why did the number of *gaijin* sumo wrestlers increase?

A foreigner working in Japan is not a novelty in today's global world. In professional sports other than sumo there are many foreign players in Japan, who show impressive and outstanding achievements. The Grand Sumo has also gained many foreign players in recent years. What characterizes these foreign players in the world of sumo – Japan's only professional sport tied to its traditional culture? We suggest the following reasons as the cause of this recent rapid increase in the number of foreign sumo wrestlers.

First, it must be made clear that the sumo wrestlers from Hawaii who were a sensation in Japan were introduced via the scouting efforts of the Kyokai, and it was not always the case that prospective sumo wrestlers from Hawaii were looking forward to being in Japan. To make sumo a popular sport and increase the supply of apprentices were the main reasons for the Kyokai's establishment of a close relationship between it and Hawaii. The relationship was begun by the former Yokozuna Maedayama (Master Takasago) when he took wrestlers from his Takasago stable to a sumo tournament in Hawaii in 1951. Master Takasago continued organizing sumo tournaments in Hawaii regularly since then.

After the success of a sumo tournament in 1962, Master Takasago repeatedly asked Jesse Kuhaulua to join sumo and was finally able to gain his agreement in 1964. Jesse Kuhaulua was renamed Takamiyama, and was the first Hawaiian-born sumo wrestler after the Second World War. Takamiyama (later Master Azumazeki) scouted both Konishiki and Akebono, the very successful Hawaiian-born sumo wrestlers, because of their exceptionally high athletic capabilities. Subsequently, three more brilliant American sumo wrestlers – Sentoryu, Musashimaru and Yamato – went to Japan and became Makuuchi wrestlers.

The efforts of the Kyokai contributed to the increase in the number of foreign sumo wrestlers, but the circumstances in which foreign sumo wrestlers came to Japan also played an important part. For example, the key reason why Takamiyama came to Japan was a guarantee from his stable-master of five years' provision of food, clothing and accommodation in Japan. It was also reported that Konishiki, who wanted to go to college, was not able to do so because his family could not afford it, so he chose sumo. These two examples suggest that Takamiyama and Konishiki made a rational choice in becoming sumo wrestlers after considering the alternative career choices available to them.

Speaking of a rational choice, the recent rapid increase in the number of sumo wrestlers from Mongolia may also be attributable to economic reasons. According to the 'World Development Indicators' issued by the World Bank, per capita GDP in the year 2000 for Mongolia was one-ninetieth of that for Japan (US$390). It is understandable that young, talented boys in Mongolia wish to come to Japan and test their ability to earn ninety times what they can earn in their homeland.

When there is an income gap between countries, it is natural for some people in the low-income countries to leave and seek better economic conditions in high-income countries. This phenomenon has already been observed in many sports and jobs. But in case of the Grand Sumo, a massive infusion of foreign wrestlers has not yet taken place because of the strong barrier that still exists against foreigners.

Are *gaijin* sumo wrestlers strong?

According to *Banzuke* (the ranking order of all sumo wrestlers) at the summer tournament of 2003, the ranks of the forty-nine foreign sumo wrestlers were broken down as follows: 2 Yokozunas, 1 Komusubi, 3 Hiramakus, 1 Juryo, and the rest being Makushita – that is, one-seventh of the foreign sumo wrestlers are in the Sekitori ranks. Since, among all sumo wrestlers, only one-tenth is Sekitori, it may look as though the percentages of foreign sumo wrestlers who were promoted to Sekitori ranks are high. But we cannot be fooled by this number. We must remember that the foreign sumo wrestlers competing in sumo in Japan are the ones who have been specially selected. Because of such pre-selection mechanisms for foreign sumo wrestlers, there might be certain 'sample selection biases' that need to be taken into account in interpreting statistics about foreign sumo wrestlers. Such sample selection biases tend to make the probability of promotion for foreign sumo wrestlers look higher than the probability for Japanese-born sumo wrestlers, as discussed below.

First, we need to recognize that the foreign sumo wrestlers have a greater talent than the Japanese sumo wrestlers at the time of entering the world of sumo. For example, the Mongolians who enter Japanese sumo have certain characteristics. It is usually the case that the young people coming into the world of sumo from Mongolia either have already achieved remarkable records in Mongolian sumo, or have attended Japanese high schools as students studying sumo. Asashoryu, the Yokozuna from Mongolia, falls into the second category. The secretary-general of the Mongolian Sumo Association, an association led by Kyokushuzan, says 'Mongolians are equipped with the basic skills of sumo because the Mongolians start playing sumo at a young age. We want to send as many sumo wrestlers as possible to Japan' (*Sankei Sports Journal*, 25 July 2002). The organization is willing to send young, tough and talented Mongolians to Japan.

For these reasons it is very difficult to determine whether foreign sumo wrestlers are stronger than the average Japanese sumo wrestler, but it may follow logically that foreign sumo wrestlers appear to be promoted faster than their Japanese counterparts.

Why is the number of foreign sumo wrestlers restricted?

Why does the Sumo Kyokai limit the number of foreign sumo wrestlers? There can be many hypotheses that could be considered to explain this. The first is that a *gaijin* wrestler is an outsider to the Japanese national sport. In an island country like Japan, consisting of people with a shared set of values, an 'infection of society' by an outsider creates a friction cost. A friction cost is the cost that arises when differences in languages, traditions and other cultural factors must be dealt with. But these types of costs are costs that must be borne by the sumo stables, not the Sumo Kyokai, since it is the stables that employ foreign sumo wrestlers. It is then hard to think why the Kyokai would oppose the entrance of a foreigner for cost reasons.

The second hypothesis is that the citizens of Japan do not feel good about *gaijin* ruling in the world of sumo. But, beginning with Takamiyama, and then on to Konishiki, Akebono and Musashimaru, who are all from Hawaii, and Asashoryu, Kyokushuzan and Kyokutenhou from Mongolia, the popularity of foreign sumo wrestlers appears to be at least as high as that of Japanese sumo wrestlers. The applause for the foreign sumo wrestlers when they enter the sumo ring is very enthusiastic.

The third hypothesis is that the Kyokai worries about the threat of the national sport sumo being destroyed by *gaijin*. Konishiki once said, 'Sumo is a fight!', and his ignorance of sumo's traditional and cultural aspects brought disrepute from the executives of the Kyokai. But are the Kyokai concerned about how much of the unique virtue and cultural values in the world of sumo could be understood by a *gaijin*? For example, rituals such as 'starting the fight with a bow and ending with a bow' and 'the sumo is mind, technique and body' may be difficult for foreigners to understand.

Attitude problems are not only found among foreign sumo wrestlers, however sometimes, even the Japanese sumo wrestlers anger their masters and leave their sumo stable. Foreign sumo wrestlers are typically very well prepared for their ordeal when they enter sumo, as the cost to foreigner sumo wrestlers in the case of misconduct is far larger than that paid by Japanese sumo wrestlers. Also, because they are foreigners, the monitoring by their stable-masters is stronger for them than for Japanese sumo wrestlers.

The fourth and only convincing hypothesis is that foreigners have a much higher physical ability than the Japanese. Because of this physical ability, limitless acceptance of foreigners into sumo would result in the dominance of sumo, a national sport of Japan, by foreigners. There is serious concern among the Japanese public about this potential consequence of 'too many foreign sumo wrestlers'.

Will the *gaijin* sumo wrestlers 'dominate' the world of sumo?

When the 'Konishiki sensation' blew through Japan, it was likened to the coming of the 'Black Ships' led by Commodore Perry in 1853, and when the Mongolian sumo wrestlers swept through Japan, it was compared to the Mongolian invasions in the thirteenth century. When a foreign worker with superior talent comes to Japan, many ordinary Japanese see that worker as a threat.

On the ninth day of the 2003 New Year Grand Sumo tournament, one day after the Japanese Yokozuna Takanohana announced his retirement, the *Yomiuri Sports* Newspaper wrote, 'Come on! Japanese sumo wrestlers! Those who are going to carry the national sport are *gaijin*? It will be the first time in history, if both of the Yokozunas are *gaijin!*' The same newspaper also included several articles about the situation: as an old Japanese saying goes, 'we lent him space under our eaves, and he stole the whole house, which describes the current situation of sumo', (Hidetoshi Tanaka, Manager of the Nihon University sumo club); 'Japanese wrestlers, as the successors of the traditional sumo culture, should learn from the foreign wrestlers' (Kitanoumi, the director of the Sumo Kyokai); and 'Japanese are responsible for an outsider like Mongolian-born Asashoryu ruling in the world of sumo' (Akebono, a one-time Yokozuna from Hawaii). This is a wake-up call for Japanese sumo wrestlers.

If this situation continues, will the forty-eight foreign sumo wrestlers occupy all the Makuuchi ranks? Here we argue as economists that no problem would really occur even if the Sumo Kyokai does not limit the number of foreign sumo wrestlers. There are three main reasons for this, which we explain below.

Sumo wrestlers are not highly paid

The first reason is that sumo is not a sport where one can make a fortune. Even Yokozuna Asashoryu earns only about ¥40 m (about US$340,000) a year. Comparing his salary to the salaries of the stars of professional baseball and soccer, we see that his amounts to only one-tenth of the salaries of the star players of other professional sports. Even though sumo is a tough sport in which the wrestlers carry a high risk of being injured, their salaries are still low. After subtracting the risk premiums for their injuries, sumo wrestlers' salaries appear to be much lower than the salaries for players of other popular professional sports.

In the West, highly talented young boys play sports such as soccer, baseball and football, all of which offer players much higher salaries, compared to sumo. So foreign talents of the highest calibre do not go to Japan to become sumo wrestlers.

At present there are many Mongolian sumo wrestlers. But this is because Mongolia is a developing country where few sports other than sumo are available. The outlook for the Mongolian economy is not clear, but if the income level in Mongolia rises, other sports will most certainly become more popular, and the enthusiasm for sumo will decline over time.

Specialised body required for sumo wrestlers

From day one as a sumo wrestler, the wrestlers follow a traditional life-style that creates a huge physique.[3] This is an extremely specialized type of human capital, and such human capital cannot be used advantageously for the purposes of everyday life or in other sports.

This highly specialized asset presents a big risk for foreign sumo wrestlers. Former Japanese sumo wrestlers can open a *chanko nabe* (sumo food) restaurant, but it is not so easy for a foreigner to start up such a business. Considering the risk of failure in sumo, it seems more sensible for foreigners to build up human capital that can easily be used for other jobs as well.

Qualifications required to become a stable-masters

In order to really succeed in the world of sumo, to flourish as a wrestler during an active career is not enough. Becoming a stable-master after retirement and staying in the Sumo Kyokai is also part of a successful career in sumo. Those sumo wrestlers who know the way to really succeed in the sumo world do not complain that most of their salaries are taken away by their stable-masters. The sumo wrestlers strive in training every day, trying to become a master after retirement to remain in the Kyokai.

But to become a sumo stable-master requires certain qualifications. According to the Sumo Kyokai rules, stable-masters must have Japanese nationality, which rules out this possibility for *gaijin*. In fact, Takami-yama, Konishiki and Akebono, all from Hawaii, had adopted Japanese nationality by the time of their retirement. And in 1996 Musashimaru, also from Hawaii, was allowed to become naturalized. They are all now Japanese citizens, and because they are Japanese no one can complain about their becoming stable-masters. Most foreign sumo wrestlers who succeeded in the world of sumo chose to take Japanese nationality so that they can stay in the Sumo Kyokai as stable masters.[4,5]

Not interested in sumo? The youngsters of Japan

In contrast to the increase in the number of admissions of foreign wrestlers into sumo, the number of new admissions among Japanese wrestlers has been decreasing. In the spring tournament of 1992, when Takahanada had his brilliant debut and began the 'Takahanada boom', a record high of 151 new Japanese apprentices passed the entrance test and entered the world of sumo. But after Yokozuna Takanohana's older brother Wakanohana was promoted to Yokozuna in 1999, gen-erating the 'WakaTaka boom', the number of new apprentices began to decrease. Subsequently, at the spring tournament of 2002, the number of new apprentices was reduced to only a third of what it was ten years before, at forty-nine. An event that symbolizes this took place in the entrance test in the fall tournament of 2002: there was only one candidate for the test.

With fewer youngsters in Japan being interested in sumo, what will the future of sumo be? There are many reasons why young Japanese started to ignore sumo as an occupation. One reason is, as Yuji Genda says, 'the seniority wage system becoming an unattractive practice for the young, it is likely that Japanese Grand Sumo, the sport emphasizing the strongest elements of Japanese management practices, has put a distance between itself and Japanese youth'.[6]

The increase in the rate of job change by young people in Japan is attracting attention in the media. According to the labour surveys of the Ministry of General Affairs, the rate of job change for men in the age group 15–24 was over 10 per cent during the period 1997–2002. Given the rate for men of all ages being around 4 per cent, these rates for young Japanese seem very high.

Seen through the eyes of the youngsters, the world of sumo, forcing the wrestlers to be '*kaisha* (company) men' does not make it appear to be an attractive profession. The sumo stable-masters often attribute the reason for sumo's unpopularity to 'the lack of aggressive ambition among the young'. For example, Sadogatake, a stable-master, says, 'Young people have gotten used to living a rich and fulfilled life.'

Many young people in the 'good old days' of sumo were scouted with stable-masters' magic words, 'Be a sumo wrestler and you'll be able to eat until you're stuffed.' But thanks to economic growth, standards of living have risen, and people are now far better off than ever before. The magic words that used to be used successfully to recruit new sumo wrestlers, have lost their touch.

But blaming Japan's economic growth for sumo's unpopularity is a mistake, and it is not true that Japanese young people today do not have the spirit for improving themselves. How do these Grand Sumo's stable-masters interpret the excitement shown in the tournaments of high school baseball players in the Koshien Stadium twice a year, or high school soccer players during the New Year holiday season?

If the Sumo Kyokai wants to increase the potential pool of Japanese youth who apply for admission into Grand Sumo, which may reduce its dependence on the supply of foreign sumo wrestlers, the Kyokai must analyze why Japanese young people are no longer attracted to sumo as their career choice.

Appendix: a brief explanation about the Grand Sumo

The organization

Sumo is one of the traditional Japanese combative sports, played by two wrestlers in a circle called *dohyo*. *Ozumo* (Grand Sumo) means sumo performance played by professional sumo wrestlers of an incorporated foundation named the *Nihon Sumo Kyokai* (the Japan Sumo Association; the Sumo Kyokai, hereafter).

The Sumo Kyokai, or the Japan Grand Sumo Association, is a non-profit organization composed of about fifty sumo 'stables' that recruit and train newcomers. Although a newcomer is free to choose to be based any one of the stables at the time of his entrance into sumo, he will not be allowed to move to another stable afterwards. (This is, of course, the way most Japanese workers – that is, new graduates – choose their first employers, to whom they devote most of their careers.) Based on their cumulative performance in all recent sumo tournaments, the sumo wrestlers are given their ranks in the Banzuke, the ranking order of all sumo wrestlers.

A newcomer begins his career at the bottom of the Banzuke, in the Jonokuchi division. If the number of his wins is more than the number of his losses in a tournament, then he will be promoted, and demoted if the situation is reversed. The division above the Jonokuchi is the Jonidan, followed by the Sandanme and the Makushita. Wrestlers in these four divisions are called Toriteki (probationary wrestlers), who are not paid but live in sumo stables without change, but carry out housekeeping tasks such as cleaning and cooking. The two divisions above the Makushita division are the Juryo and the Makuuchi divisions. Wrestlers in these two divisions are called Sekitori (see Table 7.1).

The difference is enormous between the Toriteki and the Sekitori divisions in terms of how the wrestlers are treated. Sekitori wrestlers are paid, taken care of by Toriteki for almost everything in their stables, and are allowed to wear colorful loincloths. The highest division of the Grand Sumo, the Makuuchi, consists of forty wrestlers. They are sumo elite among the 600 wrestlers in the Sumo Kyokai. And highest position the of the Makuuchi division is held by Yokozuna. Immediately below the Yokozuna are the ranks of Ozeki, Sekiwake and Komusubi, collectively called the San-yaku.

The salary system

The salaries of a Sekitori wrestler are in two parts. One part is the monthly wage based on the job descriptions in terms of rank that is, where he is in the Banzuke. The other part is the salary award paid six times a year, named the *hoshokin*. Every wrestler starts with a nil amount of *hoshokin*. The amount increases when he performs well in a tournament, but never decreases. There are various ways in which the hoshokin is increased. The difference between the number of wins and losses in any tournament raises *hoshokin* by the equivalent of about US$20. Winning a Makuuchi championship (that is, a Grand Sumo championship) corresponds to approximately US$1,200. A non-San-yaku wrestler in the Makuuchi (Hiramaku wrestlers) gets the equivalent of around US $400 when he defeats a Yokozuna (this is called *kimboshi*, a golden win).

Because the Hoshokin is cumulative over all tournaments and does not decrease even after a period of poor performance, it gives an incentive for wrestlers to keep their Sekitori ranks as long as possible. The wrestlers who have shown good performance over time, such as winning a Makuuchi championship and a *kimboshi*, will continue to be paid sufficient amounts of the *hoshokin* even if their current rankings are not very high. In this sense, the *hoshokin* functions as do seniority-based wages in Japanese firms.

The human capital of wrestlers

Sumo wrestlers get up early in the morning and start training without breakfast. After the training ends around noon, they have lunch consisting of special sumo food, called *chanko*. In the afternoon, they have a break, take a nap, read books and so on. After dinner they go to bed. According to medical studies, this sumo life-style an efficient way of accumulating calories and adding bulk in a short period of time. However, large body size does not necessarily make for a strong sumo wrestler. While increasing their size, they have to reduce fat within their body by hard training. Those who achieve this difficult combination of body characteristics are qualified to become Sekitori.

Sumo wrestlers' special physical characteristics, which are developed over many years, make it difficult for them to change jobs successfully. About half of the Sekitori wrestlers will be able to acquire the right to stay in the Sumo Kyokai as stable-masters after their retirement. The others will have to find jobs outside the sumo world. Former wrestlers often work in show business as performers or as restaurant chefs, as noted already. The long-term recession of the Japanese economy since the bursting of the bubble in 1990, however, has made these former sumo wrestlers' transition to the outside world even more difficult.

Notes

1   This chapter is based on updated materials originally presented as Chapter 8 of Takanobu Nakajima (2003) *Ozumo no keizaigaku* (The Economics of the Grand Sumo) (in Japanese) (Tokyo: Toyo Keizai). A brief introduction to the world of Grand Sumo is provided in the Appendix. Current information on the Grand Sumo is available from its official website. See http://www.sumo.or.jp/eng/index.php.

2   The *sansho* prize awards are given to the wrestlers who have achieved the greatest performance in the tournament in the following three areas: outstanding performance, fighting spirit and technique. Not all prizes are necessarily given in each tournament.

3   See the Appendix for more details about sumo wrestlers' daily life.

4   In fact, the former Yokozuna, Akebono, announced in October 2003 that he was leaving the Grand Sumo to become an active wrestler in a new professional combat sport called K1. It is thought that the main reason for his departure from sumo was that he was unable to secure enough financial resources to buy into one of the available permanent stable-master positions. As an accomplished Yokozuna, he was allowed to stay in sumo as a temporary stable-master for five years following his retirement. If this becomes a typical pattern for foreign sumo wrestlers post-retirement careers, it might reduce the future supply of foreign sumo wrestlers. It is likely that, while raising enough funds to buy into a permanent position of stable-master is very difficult for native-born Japanese sumo wrestlers, it is much harder for foreign-born wrestlers to achieve. The only foreign-born wrestler who has obtained a permanent stable-master position to date is Takamiyama.

5   Musashimaru, another Yokozuna from Hawaii, also retired abruptly in the middle of the November 2003 Kyushu Grand Sumo tournament in Hakata.

Repeated injuries resulted in poor performance and forced his untimely retirement. Like Akebono, Musashimaru was an accomplished Yokozuna and was also granted by the Sumo Kyokai the special right to remain in Grand Sumo as a temporary stable-master for five years.

6 Genda, Yuji (2001) *Shigoto no nakano aimaina huan* (Vague Anxiety in Jobs) (Tokyo: Chuo-Koron-Shinsha).

8
Gender as Intersectionality: Multiple Discrimination against Minority Women in Japan

Jennifer Chan-Tiberghien

I am an indigenous Ainu woman from Hokkaido, the northern island in Japan. As a result of being forcibly assimilated and ruled over by the Japanese government and because of structural discrimination, the indigenous Ainu have continued to be invaded by the mainstream Japanese culture... In addition, among Ainu, the situation of Ainu women is even more serious because of the strong patriarchal ideology. Because the severe discrimination and poverty resulted in a lack of education, illiteracy among Ainu women aged over fifty is widespread, and these women are thus forced to pursue occupations with bad conditions of employment... Under this harsh discrimination, some Ainu women chose Japanese men as their spouses, because they wanted to dilute the Ainu blood as thin as they could. As a result, these women are harassed by their Japanese husbands with words of disdain for being Ainu. (*Testimony from Ryoko Tahara, Ainu Association of Hokkaido*)

I am a Buraku woman living in Aichi Prefecture in Japan. Some of the most serious problems for Buraku women are illiteracy, unemployment and marriage discrimination, which sometimes drives these women to commit suicide... The Japanese government does not conduct any surveys to identify the challenges that Buraku women face, and to take effective measures for the improvement of our situation. Therefore I would like the CEDAW committee members to recommend that the Japanese government conduct surveys and take effective measures for our betterment. Even though national and local governments established Councils for the promotion of equal participation between men and women, there is no seat reserved for Buraku women. Here, I would like to insist that these governments should appoint Buraku women to be council members in order to better reflect the Buraku women's reality and opinion regarding policy. (*Testimony from Reiko Yamazaki, Buraku Liberation league*)

On 7 July 2003, two women from Japan's minorities spoke to members of the Committee on the Elimination of Discrimination Against Women (CEDAW) at a lunchtime briefing during its 29th session when Japan's Fourth and Fifth Periodic Reports to CEDAW were scheduled to be examined. They were supported by a network of forty-three women's and human rights non-governmental organizations (NGOs) from Japan (See Appendix 8.1). Long ignored by the Japanese government, invisible at the intersection of CEDAW and the Committee on the Elimination of All Forms of Racial Discrimination (CERD), and marginalized within both the Japanese women's and minority movements, their personal testimonies of multiple discrimination represented a breakthrough in gender and racial politics, both at the UN level and within Japan. This chapter looks at the impact of the globalization of human rights norms on Japan through the perspectives of women ethnic minorities in Japan.[1] I argue that an intersectional framework regarding multiple discrimination that emerged at the World Conference Against Racism (WCAR) in Durban in 2001 has enabled Japanese social movement organizations to put the issue of minority women in Japan on the Japanese political agenda through the UN. While it is commonly believed that the events of September 11 in the immediate aftermath of Durban have clouded much of the gains of WCAR, this research aims to show the impact of the racism conference on grassroots mobilization in Japan. I do not intend to argue that the new 'multiple discrimination' approach has brought about concrete legal or political change, though Japanese NGOs have been lobbying actively for an anti-discrimination law, which as yet still does not exist in Japan. Instead, the purpose of this chapter is to link the participation of minority women in Japan at WCAR to their newfound political visibility, both at the UN level and within Japan.

This chapter is in three parts. Part I looks the issue of women of ethnic minorities within Japanese feminism from three angles: the identity of Japanese feminism, the sex commodification debate, and the 'comfort women' redress movement. Part II provides a background on Japanese NGO mobilization at the World Conference against Racism in Durban in 2001, where a gender-as-intersectionality framework emerged. Finally, Part III discusses Japanese NGO mobilization at the 29th session of CEDAW in 2003, where minority women from Japan spoke out against the multiple discrimination they experience.

Where are Minority Women in Japanese Feminism?

The question 'what is "Japanese feminism?"' has been raised time and again by Japanese and non-Japanese feminists alike. As a veteran feminist, Chiyo Saito notes,

> How do we translate the term feminism into 'Japanese?' We are all used to the sound of the Japanese version of the English word *femini-zumu*, and yet every time I use the expression it seems increasingly vague...It is often said that northern European feminism is mature while American feminism is radical, and yet surely there are many feminisms in America. It is the social contexts and the sensitivities of the individuals involved that generate its various formations. Isn't it problematic to speak in terms of 'American feminism' or 'European feminism?' In this sense it is equally strange to speak of 'Japanese feminism'...For quite different reasons I have lately come to consider it very important to adhere to the concept of a 'Japanese feminism'.[2]

As Judith Butler critiques Western feminist theorizing, 'the urgency of feminism to establish a universal status for patriarchy in order to strengthen the appearance of feminism's own claims to be representative has occasionally motivated the shortcut to a categorical or fictive universality of the structure of domination, held to produce women's common subjugated experience'.[3] In the quest for an identity distinguished from 'Western feminism', 'Japanese feminism' has often been constructed/appropriated by Japanese feminists as a monolithic bloc, assuming uniform forms of gender oppression. Chizuko Ueno, for example, articulates household power, commonly known as *shufu* (housewife) power, and maternal values as two of the core characteristics of Japanese feminism. She explains:

> In any East Asian culture you will find that women have a very tangible power within the household. This is often rejected by non-Asian feminists who argue that it is not real power, but I would disagree. Asian women do have significant power, although it is not a form of power recognized by non-Asian feminists. I think that we need a far greater sensitivity to cultural differences. It is possible for Asian women to develop a feminism that is the product of their own cultural context and meaningful to them. To impose the goals of other feminisms onto those women or use foreign goals as a measure of the quality of the lives of Asian women is problematic.

I think there is another important area of difference...The question of maternal care is a low priority for many American feminists. There has been a devaluing of the maternal or nurturing role. The situation in Japan is quite different...Most Japanese women were opposed to the concept of equality and sameness. Equality with protection is an acceptable position here...Our primary goal is not to be like men but to value what it means to be a woman. This aspect of Japanese feminism is deeply rooted in the history of the women's movement in Japan as well as the individual experience of women. It's a double-edged sword, I admit, but it is also fundamental to the identity of Japanese feminism.[4]

This hegemonic representation of 'Japanese feminism' does not go unchallenged. As the late Yayori Matsui has consistently argued throughout her feminist career:

It is crucial for feminism to recognize and trace the complexity of the multiple contexts that generate gender politics. It is true that Japanese women are oppressed within their own society; it is also true that some Japanese women occupy positions of relative power, from which they oppress, or are implicated in the oppression of, other Japanese women. But it is not enough. We need to go one step further and look at the relationship of Japanese women to the women of countries that are economically dominated by Japan. What price do other Asian women pay for the prosperity and daily comfort of so many Japanese women? How do we as Japanese women stand in relation to the thousands of Filipino hostesses working in Japanese bars? Then there is the whole question of the Filipino, Korean, and Sri Lankan brides who are imported to Japan to overcome the shortage of women.[5]

Despite Matsui's personal crusade against sex tourism (the outflow of Japanese men to Asian destinations) since the 1970s and a mushrooming of 'ejaculation businesses' (*shasei sangyo*) (the inflow of Asian sex workers into Japan) since the 1980s, a sex commodification debate became mainstream within Japanese feminism in the early 1990s, largely over the issue of *enjo kosai* ('entertainment' offered by teenage schoolgirls in return for pocket money, an euphemistic expression for child prostitution). At one end of the spectrum is the 'freedom of expression' camp.[6] Daisaburo Hashizume, for example, argues that 'if prostitution is voluntary, it cannot be regarded as a human rights violation...The objectification and commodification of relations is a feature of contemporary society. We can't say that the commodification of women/their bodies is a violation of human rights'.[7] At the other end of the spectrum lie various feminist human rights perspectives. Chie Asano, for example, argues that it is impossible to distinguish between freedom and coercion, and that one cannot fully understand the commodification of sex without addressing its gender aspects – that is, how it affects women disproportionately.

What we call 'sex commodification' today is in fact the sex commodification of *women*. While it is urgent to consider the labor rights and human rights of those who sell their sexuality as a commodity from a sex work point of view, we need to address the issue of 'sex commodification' from the perspective of gender imbalance that is embedded in our society.[8]

Tomoko Kawabata, on the other hand, emphasizes that prostitution is not so much about a violation of the sex workers' human rights, but rather should be viewed as a sexual slavery system that concerns all women.[9] Though the discourse of *seiteki jiko ketteiken* (the right to sexual self-determination) from the 1994 Cairo Conference on Population and Development provided the conceptual underpinning and mobilization frame for the global campaign in the mid-1990s against the commercial sexual exploitation of children, and the subsequent passage of the Child Prostitution and Pornography Prohibition Act in Japan in 1999, the *enjo kosai* debate has been raised in almost complete isolation from both the issue of trafficking and wartime 'comfort women' redress movement which was raging at the time, not only in Japan, but in many other parts of Asia.

For more than three decades after the Second World War, the Japanese women's movement had been silent about the sexual crimes committed by the Japanese Army against forcibly drafted or recruited Korean and other Asian women. One cannot say that Japanese women were unaware of the issue. As Yoshimi argues, the wartime 'comfort station' system was widely known among the Japanese.[10] The 'comfort women' issue disappeared at the intersection of the Korean residents' movement in Japan and the Japanese women's movement. On the one hand, the postwar Korean residents' movement in Japan focused largely on issues of unification and democratization of the motherland, and nationality status within Japan. On the other hand, until the early 1990s, the Japanese women's movement was mainly concerned with sex roles issues, equal employment, and education. Despite the tremendous gains, an equality approach at the expense of differences within the Japanese women's movement is typified by the campaign work by the International Women's Year Liaison Group Japan, a network of fifty-two Japanese grassroots women's organizations formed in 1975 to lobby for Japan's ratification of CEDAW, which it did in 1985.[11]

The visit of a Korean 'comfort woman', Kim Hak Shun, in 1991 forced the Japanese women's movement to take action. While the then prime minister, Kiichi Miyazawa, made a public apology at the Japan–Korea Summit in 1992 and subsequently admitted the responsibility of the Japanese Army in setting up 'comfort stations', the government of Japan even now has not offered official compensation. An Asian Women's Fund, created in 1995 to deal with the issue, draws on 'private' donations. In December 2000, three Asian NGOs – the Violence Against Women in War Network Japan; the Korean Council for the Women Drafted for Military Sexual Slavery by Japan; and the Philippine-based Asian Center for Women's Human Rights – co-organized a 'Women's International War Crimes Tribunal on Japan's Military Sexual Slavery'. The Tribunal found that Emperor Hirohito was responsible for crimes against humanity. In addition, the final judgment emphasized the racial aspects of gender discrimination endured by the 'comfort women'.

The evidence demonstrates multiple violations of both the requirements for the protection of women as well as the prohibitions on race and sex discrimination. Most fundamentally the evidence shows that women were targeted for the provision of forced sexual services because they were women, thus denying them gender equality as well as their right to respect for their physical, mental and sexual integrity and human dignity. The creation of the 'comfort women' system reflects the intersection of extreme discrimination based on both gender and race/ethnicity. The ethnocentrism and racism of the Japanese military and government resulted in the prevailing philosophy that it was more acceptable to make colonized and conquered women into 'comfort women' than Japanese women.

If the quests for an identity for 'Japanese feminism' as well as the *enjo kosai* debate have largely left out the issue of minority women in Japan, the 'comfort women' redress movement pinpoints the racism within the Japanese women's movement. As Zenko Suzuki argues, it represents a paradigm shift in Japanese feminism, from its habitual 'victim' status (Japanese women being discriminated against within Japan) to its 'aggressor/victimizer' position (Japanese women being complicit in Japan's war crimes in Asia).[12] Even then, with the exception of a few works,[13] the voice of many other groups of minority women including Burakumin, Ainu, Okinawan and Korean residents, and migrant workers remain marginalized within mainstream Japanese feminism.[14] Let me now turn to their mobilization at the UN in the context of the World Conference against Racism in Durban in 2001.

Japanese NGO mobilization in the World Conference against Racism

Most studies of Japanese social movements have focused on domestic issues, whether the analysis is on the protracted Narita Airport struggle, a wide range of environmental issues, or 'housewife feminism'.[15] Little known is the globalization of Japanese social movements and, in particular, the development of advocacy NGOs and networks that target the usage of UN human rights instruments to lobby for domestic political change. The participation of Japanese NGOs in the Durban racism conference in 2001 needs to be contextualized in a long process of Japanese grassroots mobilization at the UN since 1975.

To name just a few examples, the International Women's Year Liaison Group was a pioneer in this regard. Created in 1975 to follow up on the First World Conference on Women in Mexico, this network has been credited with the successful lobbying of the Japanese government's signature of CEDAW.[16] However, it was not until the late 1980s and early 1990s that a number of advocacy NGO networks emerged within Japan, largely in preparation for various UN world conferences as well as alternative/'shadow' reports to various UN human rights committees. In 1986, the Japanese Teachers' Union, Nikkyoso, led the formation of a 60-NGO-strong *Kodomo no Jinken Ren* (the Federation for the Protection of Children's Human Rights, Japan) to lobby for Japan's ratification of the UN Convention of the Rights of the Child (CRC), which it did in 1994. In 1992, ECPAT (End Child Prostitution in Asian Tourism) Japan was formed as part of a global network to fight against child prostitution and pornography. The network played an indispensable role in the participation of the Japanese government at the First World Congress against Commercial Sexual Exploitation of Children, held in Stockholm in 1996; the subsequent passage of the Child Prostitution and Pornography Prohibition Act in 1999;[17] and the hosting of the Second World Congress against Commercial Sexual Exploitation of Children, held in Yokohama in 2001.

In the same year that ECPAT Japan was formed, 300 Japanese delegates went to the Rio Summit on the Environment as part of the Brazil Japan Citizen *Renrakukai*/Liaison Group. The network subsequently became Forum 2001, which monitored the implementation of Agenda 2001 in Japan's National Plan of Action, and lobbied for Japan's ratification of the Convention on Biodiversity in 1993, as well as the passage of the first Environment Basic Law, also in 1993. At around the same time (1992), the NGO Liaison Group for the World Conference on Human Rights was founded by six Japanese human rights NGOs to prepare for the World Conference on Human Rights conference in Vienna. By June 1993, sixteen human rights groups, including Korean residents groups, Burakumin minority groups, women's groups, and AIDS groups had joined, and participated in Vienna. This liaison group, since becoming known as the International Human Rights NGO Network, has lobbied actively for Japan's ratification of the International Convention on the Elimination of All Forms of Racial Discrimination (ICERD) in 1995, and the Convention Against Torture (CAT) in 1996. In addition, it provides periodic shadow reports on Japan's treaty obligations under the Covenant on Civil and Political Rights (CCPR), Covenant on Economic, Social, and Cultural Rights (CESCR), and the ICERD.

In 1994, the Japan's Network for Women and Health, a national network of more than forty NGOs, was initially founded by eleven feminist scholars, activists and politicians as delegates attending the International Conference on Population and Development in Cairo. It introduces the concept of 'reproductive health/rights' to Japan, linking for the first time issues of women's health, sexuality, self-determination, violence against women, women's human rights, population and development. None of the conferences mentioned thus far, however, exerted a bigger impact than the Fourth World Conference on Women in Beijing in 1995. About 6,000 Japanese women attended this conference. Many local, regional and national networks were formed post-Beijing (for example, the Beijing Japan Accountability Caucus). Rallying around the discourse about women's human rights, and focusing in particular on the provisions relating to 'violence against women', the Japanese women's movement in Japan lobbied successfully for a series of unprecedented legal changes, including the revision of the Equal Employment Opportunity Law (1997), the legalization of the contraceptive pill (1999), the first Basic Law on Gender Equality (1999), the Anti-Stalking Law (2000), and the Domestic Violence Prevention Law (2001).[18] In 1999, the Beijing – Plus – Five Alternative Report Group was formed as a coalition of fifty-two NGOs, including several networks across issues of environment, minority, disabilities and migrants to lobby at the Beijing-Plus-Five conference on women.

It was in this historical context of mobilization that a hundred people from Japan went to the World Conference against Racism as part of a first pan-racial non-governmental coalition, Durban 2001 Japan. The coalition, in large part built on the existing International Human Rights NGO Network, consisted of more than twelve NGO networks of Burakumin, Ainu, Okinawans, Koreans, migrant workers and Japanese returnees from China. Although estimating the size of minority populations in Japan remains largely guesswork, there are approximately 3 million Burakumin, 30,000 Ainu, 1 million Okinawans, 650,000 Koreans and 750,000 other registered foreigners, in addition to several hundred thousand illegal overstayers.[19] These estimates put the minority population, as of 1997, at something between 4 per cent and 5 per cent of the total population of 126 million. In Durban, the Japanese coalition networked and lobbied with the Caucuses on the Dalits, Indigenous Peoples, Reparation and Slavery, Migration and Refugees, Trafficking, and Asians and Asian Descendants.

The five official themes of WCAR are: (i) sources, causes, forms and contemporary manifestations of racism, racial discrimination, xenophobia and related intolerance; (ii) victims of racism, racial discrimination, xenophobia and related intolerance; (iii) measures of prevention, education and protection at national, regional and international levels; (iv) provision of effective remedies, recourse, redress, compensatory and other measures; and (v) strategies to achieve full and effective equality, including international cooperation and enhancement of the United Nations and other international mechanisms. One of the contentious issues was to define 'race'. Prior to Durban, Japanese NGOs, notably the Burakumin Liberation League and the Tokyo-based International Movement Against All Forms of Discrimination and Racism (IMADR), were an active part of a global anti-caste discrimination campaign which lobbied successfully for the adoption of a first UN resolution on work- and descent-based discrimination by the Sub-Commission on the Promotion and Protection of Human Rights in 2000. It stated specifically that discrimination of Burakumin in Japan, together with discrimination based on the caste system in South Asia and Africa, are all identified as forms of discrimination that are prohibited by international human rights law. Although Burakumin continue to be omitted in the Japanese government's periodic reports to the CERD Committee,[20] the CERD Committee reiterated, in its final observations to the first and second report by the Japanese government in March 2001, that Burakumin fall under the definition of 'descent' within Article 1 of the Convention.[21] In the final outcome document of WCAR, para. 73, the only provision on descent-based discrimination, was deleted. But WCAR represented the first occasion in which the issue of caste was raised substantively in international law.

On the issue of the Ainu, although the Japanese government now recognizes the Ainu as an ethnic minority within Japan and passed the first Law for the Promotion of the Ainu Culture in 1997, it continues to deny them recognition as the indigenous people of Japan. In 1997, the Sapporo District Court made a landmark judgment on the Nibutani Dam case, in which the Ainu were clearly defined as indigenous people.[22]

The situation for Okinawans proves to be even more tenuous, as military bases are involved. In all of its periodic reports to either the Human Rights Committee or the CERD Committee, Okinawans were categorically omitted. Traditionally framed as an anti-militarism campaign, the movement on and in Okinawa has only just begun to mobilize around an indigenous rights frame.[23] In Durban, both Ainu and Okinawan groups lobbied with the Indigenous Peoples Caucus, albeit unsuccessfully, against paras 23 and 43 concerning the definition of indigenous people and their land usage.[24]

Concerning Korean residents in Japan – an estimated population of 951,000 in 2001, over 61 per cent of whom do not possess Japanese nationality – the movement has long focused on nationality and welfare issues. Stripped of their Japanese nationality at the conclusion of the San Francisco Peace Treaty in 1952, many Japan-born Koreans remain as 'special permanent residents' who require re-entry permits and are subject to deportations 'under certain conditions' according to a special immigration law of 1991. They are denied voting rights and basic welfare benefits. Even those who have acquired Japanese nationality continue to face discrimination in areas such as education. Although only about 10 per cent of all Korean resident children attend North/South Korean schools, these 'miscellaneous schools' are not recognized officially by the Ministry of Education. In Durban, Korean groups from Japan, including the Research Action Institute for the Koreans in Japan (RAIK), worked closely with the Reparation and Slavery, African and African Descendents, and Asia and Asian Descendents Caucuses to press for apologies and reparations from former colonial powers. In the final outcome Declaration and Programme of Action, para. 14 recognizes that 'slavery and the slave trade are a crime against humanity', while para. 99 affirms the 'regret that these practices and structures, political, socio-economic and cultural, have led to racism, racial discrimination, xenophobia and related intolerance'. Despite the fact that reparations were excluded, and that the conference focused heavily on the transatlantic and Indian slave trade, Korean resident NGOs did mobilize around the 'reparations for the past' frame to challenge the Japanese government on a whole range of issues including forced labor, pensions for war veterans, wartime sexual slavery and representation in history textbooks.

Finally, on the issue of migrant workers, despite pressure from an aging society, Japan remains one of the most closed industrialized countries in the world. Since the revision of the immigration law in 1990, Japan technically no longer imports unskilled labor apart from *Nikkeijin*, South Americans of Japanese descent. However, migrant workers continue to arrive, and often overstay their visas. As of 1999, an estimated 1.2 million migrant workers lived in Japan; about 20 per cent of these were overstayers who are denied basic social services. In Durban, the National Network in Solidarity with Migrant Workers, formed in 1997 with more than eighty-nine Japanese and international NGOs, became part of the Migration and Refugees NGO Caucus. Although the 1990 Convention on the Protection of the Rights of All Migrant Workers and Members of Their Families was included in para. 78 in the list of international human rights instruments which states were urged to ratify, 'migrants' did not figure in the list of victims or 'other victims', and the entire outcome document was concerned only with legal, but not undocumented, migrants.[25]

In addition to these group-specific outcomes, feminist groups managed to engender the racism conference. In 2000, CERD issued for the first time a General Recommendation XXV on 'Gender-Related Dimensions of Racial Discrimination' and in 2001, the Commission on the Status of Women issued its first Agreed Conclusions on Gender and All Forms of Discrimination, in particular Racism, Racial Discrimination, Xenophobia and Related Intolerance. By WCAR, feminists had decided to use the concept of intersectionality as a central rallying frame. According to Kimberlé Crenshaw, a feminist legal scholar who was involved in preparatory expert meetings prior to Durban, intersectionality is a conceptualization of the problem that attempts to capture both the structural and dynamic consequences of the interaction between two or more axes of subordination. It addresses specifically the manner in which racism, patriarchy, class oppression and other discriminatory systems create background inequalities that structure the relative positions of women, races, ethnicities, classes and the like.[26]

In the final outcome document, feminists succeeded in inserting the concept of intersectional and multiple discrimination (Declaration: paras. 2, 54a, 69; and Programme of Action: paras. 14, 18, 31, 49, 79, 104c, 172, 212). The preamble urges states to 'apply a gender perspective, recognizing the multiple forms of discrimination which women can face'. Para. 2 affirms that 'victims can suffer multiple or aggravated forms of discrimination based on other related grounds such as sex, language, religion, political or other opinion, social origin, property, birth or other status'. Although 'gender' is not listed as a ground for racism, states recognize that racism and racial discrimination 'reveal themselves in a differentiated manner for women and girls' (para. 69). In particular, in the final Programme of Action, para. 31 addresses the intersectional discrimination faced by migrant women; para. 50 recognizes indigenous, migrant and other women as 'other victims' of racism; and para. 54 links gender-based violence explicitly to racism.[27]

In Durban, Burakumin, Ainu, Okinawan, Korean and migrant women from Japan, in addition to lobbying with the various caucuses mentioned above, also spoke out around the theme of multiple discrimination. At the NGO Forum, Burakumin women, together with Dalit women from India and Nepal, talked about their experiences of intersectional discrimination at the 'Work and Descent-Based Discrimination' and 'Multiple Discrimination Against Minority Women in Japan' workshops. A Korean woman from Japan also gave her testimony in the World Court of Women against Racism, organized by the India-based Asian Women's Human Rights Council and the Tunisia-based El Taller International, with the support of 120 other human rights and women's groups. At the intergovernmental conference, an Ainu woman spoke in 'the Voices of Indigenous Women' panel in the presence of the UN High Commissioner for Human Rights, Mary Robinson. The following section examines the impact of their participation in WCAR on the subsequent Japanese NGO Alternative Report to the 4th and 5th Periodic Report of Japan on CEDAW in 2003.

Multiple discrimination against women of ethnic minorities in Japan

Women of ethnic minorities do exist in Japan, being discriminated against not only on the basis of their gender but also on the grounds of nationality, ethnicity, indigenity, descent, lack of citizenship or documentation, status of migrant worker, asylum-seeker or refugee. Generally speaking, they suffer multiple discrimination with different factors compounded, being socially and economically marginalized, and are faced with more difficulties in almost every aspect of life than both male members of the same group and Japanese women belonging to the majority. Consequently, they are vulnerable to abuse, violence and exploitation.

However, Japan's periodic reports contain hardly any information, either on the actual situation of such women who suffer multiple discrimination, or on measures to protect them from acts contradictory to the treaty provisions, to remedy violations, or to promote their rights and status in society.

In July 2003, the Japan NGO Network for CEDAW (JNNC), made up of forty-three women's and human rights groups, launched a staunch critique of the Japanese government in its consistently missing perspective and policies on minority women in all its periodic reports to CEDAW. After Japan ratified CEDAW in 1985, it filed its first periodic report in 1987 and its second and third reports in 1992 and 1993. The fourth and fifth reports were examined together in 2003. In the two latest reports, in addition to a summary of the general 'situation of Japanese women', which covers aggregated statistics of the participation of *Japanese* women in education, employment, agriculture and non-governmental organization activities, the second part details changes in Japan article by article. In the fourth report, for example, thirteen areas were high-lighted: violence against women (art. 2); national machinery (art. 3); women in decision-making (art. 4); sex role stereotypes (art. 5); prosti-tution (art. 6); public fields (art. 7); women in international decision-making (art. 8); discrimination in foreign service (art. 9); education (art. 10); employment (art. 11); health (art. 12); rural areas (art. 13); and finally, amendments to the Civil Code (art. 16).[28]

In New York, the Director General of the General Equality Bureau, who led a 15-member governmental delegation, summarized the reports in her presentation to CEDAW members in four key areas: (i) strengthened machinery; (ii) legal measures; (iii) targets set; and (iv) international cooperation. Indeed, in the decade since the previous report was filed, quite a few changes had occurred in Japan. The formerly coordinating-only Office for Gender Equality was upgraded to the status of a Bureau within the Cabinet Office in 2001. A Council for Gender Equality, headed by the Chief Cabinet Secretary, who also acts as the Minister of State for Gender Equality, was created at the same time as an expert council.

Second, several significant laws have been passed since 1997. The Equal Employment Opportunity Law was revised in 1997, prohibiting discrimination against women in all stages of employment from recruitment to retirement. It also specifically prohibits sexual harassment in the workplace. The first Basic Law for a Gender-Equal Society was promulgated in 1999, which mandated a national as well as local Basic Plan for Gender Equality, with measures up to the year 2010. The Law for Punishing Acts Related to Child Prostitution and Child Pornography and for Protecting Children, and the Law on Proscribing Stalking

Behavior and Assisting Victims were passed in 1999 and 2000, respectively. In 2001, the Law for the Prevention of Spousal Violence and the Protection of Victims was enacted, which led to the creation of 103 Spousal Violence Counseling and Support Centers around Japan. The law provides for two types of court protective order: Orders to Prohibit Approach and Orders to Vacate. Since the passage of the law, around a hundred of these orders have been issue each month. Finally, also in 2001, the Childcare and Family Care Leave Law was revised to prohibit the disadvantageous treatment of employees related to childcare leave. The Law for Measures to Support the Development of the Next Generation was also scheduled to be passed in July 2003, which would oblige local governments and corporations to create plans of action over a ten-year period. The objective of the government in 2001 was to increase within the next three years the number of men who take childcare leave from less than 1 per cent to 10 per cent, and the figure for women from 58 per cent to 80 per cent. Prime Minister Koizumi had also pledged in 2001 to create 150,000 daycare spots within the next three years.

Third, the Council for Gender Equality has made a recommendation that, by 2020, women will hold at least 30 per cent of leadership positions in all sectors of society. In 2002, in the Human Development Report by the UN Development Program, Japan ranked at 32 out of 66 countries in the Gender Empowerment Measure. In government and the private sector, for example, women hold only 8.9 per cent of all management posts. Three areas that the Council for Gender Equality has targeted specifically include the participation of women in policy decision-making processes; as technicians, engineers, scientists and entrepreneurs; and finally, in their re-entry into the labor market after childbirth and childcare leave.

Finally, in terms of international cooperation, since 1995 the Japanese ODA has earmarked annually around 10 per cent for projects on women's education, health, and social and economic participation under Japan's Initiative on Women in Development. The Japanese government also signed the UN Convention against Transnational Organized Crime in 2000, and its supplementary protocols in 2002. In addition to hosting the Second World Congress against Commercial Sexual Exploitation of Children in 2000 and its follow-up International Symposium on Trafficking of Children in 2001, Japan supports trafficking prevention projects in South East Asian countries through the Trust Fund for Human Security. It included the issue of trafficking, for the first time, in its fourth report.[29]

If these changes indicate progress (especially considering the lack of substantial change between 1985 and 1997), however, the non-governmental community is critical of the contents of some of these laws as well as the unmentioned backlash within Japan. At the NGO Briefing during the 29th Session of CEDAW, JNNC highlighted eight areas of concern: (i) loopholes in the domestic violence law; (ii) wartime sexual slavery; (iii) revision of Family Law; (iv) indirect discrimination in employment; (v) gender stereotypes in the judicial system; (vi) Japan's ratification of the Optional Protocol to CEDAW; (vii) anti-feminism backlash; and (viii) minority women and trafficking in women. First, while the 2001 law on domestic violence prohibition and prevention put an end to one of the greatest taboos in Japanese society, its restricted definitions of 'violence' and 'spouse' means that women suffering from non-physical violence from former spouses or boyfriends fall outside the scope of the law. Second, despite the establishment of the private Asian Women's Fund, the Japanese government has provided neither apology nor compensation to the former 'comfort women'.

Third, despite feminist mobilization against the *koseki* (family register) system where men are the only heads of households by default – family law within the Civil Code remains largely intact. At the time of writing, married women have to adopt their husbands' family name in the *koseki*, and children born out of wedlock are put in a special column within the register, making them immediately recognizable and subject to discrimination. Fourth, while discrimination is legally prohibited in all stages of employment under the Equal Employment Opportunity Law (enacted in 1985 and revised and strengthened in 1997), indirect discrimination is still rampant in Japanese corporate practice. In July 2000, for example, an Osaka District Court ruled that the wage differential of the equivalent of US$2,000 per month between men and women with a similar educational background and who entered the company at the same time was because of a difference in hiring categories and hence did not contravene public order and good morals. Fifth, JNNC also pointed out the gender bias within the Japanese judiciary system whereby, for example, rape cases are examined in accordance with the rape victims' sexual history.

Sixth, the Japanese government does not have plans to ratify the Optional Protocol to CEDAW, which will allow for a personal complaint procedure based on the reason that it may violate the domestic judiciary's independence. Seventh, in contravention of Article 2 of CEDAW, which demands that states adopt measures, 'including sanctions where appropriate, prohibiting all discrimination against women', the Japanese government continues to condone sexist comments by high-ranking politicians. On 26 June 2003, for example, at a public forum of a kindergarten association, Ota Seiichi, a former cabinet minister and member of the ruling Liberal Democratic Party, stated that men who engage in gang rape are virile and normal. Faced with a public outcry, he later defended his comments by saying that 'one cause of Japan's declining birthrate is that men are lacking virility to desire their spouses'. At the same forum, the former prime minister, Yoshiro Mori, also commented that 'women do not bear children because they just want to enjoy their freedom', and that 'real social welfare means issuing pension payments only to women who have given birth', and so on. What was unacceptable to the women's movement was not only the ludicrous comments but also the usual impunity to make such irresponsible remarks. The Asia–Japan Women's Resource Center (AJWRC), for example, vigorously protested 'the comments by Mr Ohta tolerating gang rape, the defensive explanations by his cohort, and also the related comments by Mr Ohta and Mr Mori regarding the declining birthrate that represent a serious infringement of women's human rights' and demanded 'Mr Ohta's resignation and an official apology from the former prime minister Mori'.[30]

However, this is the most comprehensive critique of perhaps not only the Fourth and Fifth Periodic Reports, but also the fundamental conceptualization and methodology used by the Japanese government concerning the situation of women in Japan. It is clear that, in all its five reports, the Japanese government never saw the need to define 'women' in Japan, and that 'gender' had clearly meant the relationship between men and women. As the International Movement Against All Forms of Discrimination and Racism (IMADR), Japan – the lead organization in JNNC – charges in its alternative report, the Japanese government has uniquely focused consistently on 'Japanese women belonging to the majority group, not only in its reporting practice but more importantly in planning actions and taking measures . . . Hardly any statistics or data exists on their situation. Measures, whether legal or administrative, that are specifically targeted at minority women are almost non-existent.' Such an omission, charges IMADR, contravenes the preamble in CEDAW, emphasizing that 'the eradication of apartheid, of all forms of racism, racial discrimination, colonialism, neo-colonialism, aggression, foreign occupation and domination and interference in the internal affairs of states is essential to the full enjoyment of the rights of men and women', as well as Article 24, which obliges states to 'adopt all necessary measures to achieve the full realization of the rights recognized in the Convention'.

The alternative report focuses on six minority groups of women: Burakumin, Koreans, Ainu, Okinawans, migrant workers, women trafficked into the sex industry, and non-Japanese women married to Japanese men. It highlights eight problem areas faced by women from minority groups in Japan, including (i) hate crimes and violence against Korean schoolgirls (incidents having increased dramatically since 2002 as incidents involving the abduction of Japanese nationals by the North Korean government filled the media); (ii) sex crimes by the US military in Okinawa; (iii) lack of support to non-Japanese victims of domestic . violence; (iv) the lack of domestic legislation that prohibits trafficking as well as support measures for trafficked women; (v) discrimination in education, employment and welfare access faced by Korean women, based on their nationality and ethnicity; (vi) the marginalization of Burakumin women in fields of literacy, marriage and employment; (vii) social and economic discrimination faced by Ainu women even after the passage of the 1997 Promotion of Ainu Culture Act; and (viii) access to health care for migrant workers, trafficked women and asylum seekers.[31]

Drawing upon four UN documents – the CERD Concluding Observations on Japan (2001); the CERD General Recommendation xxv on Gender-Related Dimensions of Racial Discrimination (2000); the CEDAW recommendation for WCAR (2001); and the WCAR Plan of Action (2001) – IMADR makes the following specific recommendations. The Japanese government should:

- Recognize its treaty obligations under CEDAW to promote and protect the human rights of all women in its territory regardless of nationality, ethnic origin, citizenship or legal status.
- Disaggregate socio-economic data by gender and national/ethnic groups, and provide information on measures taken to prevent gender-related racial discrimination including sexual exploitation and violence (in accordance with the CERD concluding recommendation No. 22);
- Conduct research on women of minority groups in Japan, and use a perspective of multiple discrimination against such women (in accordance with the WCAR Plan of Action para. 94).
- In collaboration with local governments, take measures to prevent and eliminate multiple discrimination against minority women, provide support for their needs, and encourage their participation.
- Develop legal and administrative measures to criminalize traffickers and protect the rights of trafficked victims.

- Adopt the 1999 Optional Protocol of CEDAW on the individual complaint system, which would make it easier for women of minority groups to obtain remedies from rights violations (in accordance with the WCAR Plan of Action para. 78).[32]

Table 8.1 compares the government report to CEDAW with the NGO alternative reports.

Table 8.1 The missing perspective and policy: women of minority groups in Japan's Fourth Periodic Report to CEDAW *vis-à-vis* Japanese NGO Alternative Report

CEDAW Articles	Japanese Government Fourth Periodic Report 2002	Japanese NGO Alternative Reports
2 Prohibiting *all* forms of discrimination against women	Violence against women – sex crimes, sexual harassment, child pornography, and wartime 'comfort women'	Hate crimes and violence against Korean schoolgirls; lack of apology to, and compensation for, wartime sex slaves; sex crimes by US military in Okinawa; non-Japanese victims of domestic violence; support for trafficked victims
3 Advancement of women in all fields	Reinforcement of the national machinery	Marginalization of Korean, Burakumin and Ainu women
4 Temporary special measures	Target set at 30% of women in national advisory councils by 2005	Absence of minority women representation in targets
5 Elimination of prejudices	National sensitization programs such as the National Conference for the Creation of a Gender-Equal Society	–
6 Traffic in women and exploitation	Prostitution in a 'downward trend'; protection of non-Japanese women through 'strict immigration inspection'	No domestic law; light civil penalties; absence of protection of trafficked victims
7 Women in public life	Women in the Diet (10%); in prefectural and municipal assemblies (4.4% in 1996); one city mayor (1997)	Women of ethnic minorities 'are blocked in politics in the first place before one can say anything about the expansion of their participation'

Table 8.1   (Continued)

CEDAW Articles	Japanese Government Fourth Periodic Report 2002	Japanese NGO Alternative Reports
8 Women in international public service	5,000 women from Japanese NGOs attended 1995 Fourth World Conference on Women	–
9 Nationality	Amendment of Foreign Service Personnel Law	–
10 Equal opportunity in education	Establishment of gender study centers	Discrimination against Korean, Burakumin and Ainu women
11 Equal opportunity in employment	Revision of the Equal Employment Opportunities Law and Childcare Leave Law	Discrimination against Korean, Burakumin and Ainu women
12 Health	'supporting the health of women throughout life'	Lack of access to health care for migrant workers, trafficked women and asylum seekers
13 Women in rural areas	Women in agricultural committees (0.66% in 1996 from 0.06% in 1985)	Poverty of Ainu women living in rural communities
16 Equal rights in marriage and family relations	Amendment to Civil Code (e.g. separate surnames for couples) 'under study'	Discrimination against children born out of wedlock

Conclusion

In this chapter, I have set out to examine the impact of the globalization of human rights norms on women in Japan from an intersectional perspective of gender and race. Whether it is in Japanese feminist theory or movement, minority women within Japan occupy a marginal position. At the level of the UN, women of minority groups in Japan, like their counterparts elsewhere in the world, have been invisible at the intersection between CEDAW and CERD. Accordingly, state reporting to these committees has focused uniquely on 'women' and 'race', respectively, at the expense of a population of women who experience multiple discrimination because of both their gender and their race.

The World Conference against Racism challenged the previously linear/ singular conceptualization of, and methodology on, discrimination. Women of ethnic minorities in Japan used the concept of multiple discrimination to challenge the gender-neutral assumptions of the minority movements, the race-neutral assumptions of the mainstream

Japanese women's movement, and their complete invisibility in the eyes of the Japanese government. While it is too early to show any concrete impact of such an intersectional methodology to discrimination on gender and racial politics in Japan, the newfound political visibility of minority women in Japan raises several important questions. At the grassroots level, does an intersectional approach demand more coherent cross-convention human rights advocacy in Japan? At the state level, will the Japanese government adopt an intersectional methodology in its reporting to CEDAW and CERD, as recommended by the Durban Plan of Action and demanded by the Japanese social movement organizations? What might the impact be of a perspective of multiple discrimination on the anti-discrimination bill when, and if, it is passed? In the current conjuncture of prolonged economic recession and a post-September 11 anti-terrorism climate, it is hard to predict the answers to these questions. One thing is certain, however: the voice of ethnic minority women in Japan is making itself heard, with the women demanding to play their part in constructing a '*tabunkashakai*' (multi-cultural society).

Appendix: List of 43 member organizations in the Japan NGO network for CEDAW (JNNC), as of 1 July 2003

Aboriginal Island People of Ryuku
Ainu Association of Hokkaido, Sapporo Branch
Anti-Eugenic Network for Women and Disabled People Japan
Asia Women's Conference Network
Asia–Japan Women's Resource Center
Association of Employment Development for Senior Citizens
Association of Friendship and Peace
Association of Korean Human Rights in Japan
Buraku Liberation League
Council of Democratic Resident Korean Women in Japan
DPI – Disabled Women's Network
ECPAT/STOP Japan
Equality Action 2003
FEMIN – Women's Democratic Club
HELP Asian Women's Shelter
House for Women 'Saalaa'
International Movement against All Forms of Discrimination and Racism, Japan Committee
International Women's Year Liaison Group
Japan Accountability Caucus, Beijing

Japan Anti-Prostitution Association
Japan Civil Liberties Union
Japan Federation of Bar Associations
Japan Federation of Women's Organizations
Japan Network for Abolishing 'Koseki' and Discrimination Against Children
   Born out of Wedlock
Japanese Association of International Women's Rights
Japanese Organization for International Cooperation in Family Planning
Kanagawa Women's Conference
Kyofukai, Japan Christian Women's Organization
Men Thinking About the Role of Men
National Network on Domestic Violence Law for Victims
New Japan Women's Association
NGO Network of the World Conference on Women, Kansai
NPO Dispatched Labor Network
Okayama Communication Network of the World Conference on Women
PLACE TOKYO: Positive Living and Community Empowerment Tokyo
Saitama 2000 Women's Network
Society for the Study of Working Women
Tokyo Women's Union
Violence against Women in War-Network Japan
Women against Sexist–Ageist Remarks by Governor Ishihara
Women and Health of Japan
Women's Conference
Working Women's International Network

Notes

1 For a detailed analysis of the impact of globalization of human rights norms
   on five issues of sexuality – reproductive rights, sexual harassment, domestic
   violence, wartime sexual slavery, and child prostitution and pornography –
   and five other issues in racial discrimination – Burakumin, Korean, Ainu,
   Okinawans and migrant workers – see Chan-Tiberghien (2004b, forthcoming).
2 Saito (1997), pp. 257, 268.
3 Judith Butler (1999), *Gender Trouble* (New York: Routledge), p. 6.
4 Ueno (1997), pp. 278, 280.
5 Matsui (1997), p. 136.
6 For more details, see Kamitani (1995), p. 5.
7 Quoted in Ehara (1995), p. 290.
8 Asano (1995), p. 78.
9 Quoted in Ehara (1995), p. 314.
10 Yoshimi (1995).
11 See International Women's Year Liaison Group (1989), *Rentai to Kodo: Kokusai
    Fujinnen Renrakukai no Kiroku* (Networking and Action: The Record of the
    International Women's Year Liaison Group) (Tokyo: Ichikawa Fusae Kinenkai).

12 Presentation at the International Symposium, 'Contested Historiography: Feminist Perspectives on World War II', German Institute of Japanese Studies, Tokyo, 13–14 April 2000.

13 See, for example, Cho (1997); the section on 'Minority Feminism' focusing on disability and feminism by Michiko Kishida; lesbian feminism by Minako Tusurga and Miwa Machino; and Korean resident feminism by Isaja Kim in Inoue *et al.*, (1997), vol. 1; Okuda (1997); and IMADR (2002).

14 Since the purpose of this chapter is to highlight the usage of an intersectional method to gender and racial discrimination from WCAR in Japan, this analysis focuses primarily on five groups of minority women in Japan – Burakumin, Ainu, Okinawan, Korean, and migrant. Other minority groups such as lesbian women, women with disability and so on will be the scope of a separate study.

15 See, for example, Apter and Sawa (1984); Margaret Mckean (1981), *Environmental Protest and Citizen Politics in Japan* (Berkeley, Calif.: University of California Press); Broadbent (1998); and LeBlanc (1999).

16 Interview with former Japanese Ambassador to the UN, 2 May 2000.

17 Personal interview with Mayumi Moriyama, a member of LDP and Chair of the Child Prostitution and Pornography Prohibition Law Coalition Team, 27 March 2000.

18 See Chan-Tiberghien (Forthcoming 2004a) for a detailed analysis.

19 See the First and Second Reports by the Japanese government on the International Convention on the Elimination of All Forms of Racial Discrimination (June 1999); 'Collective Report among Japan Based NGOs on the International Convention on the Elimination of All Forms of Racial Discrimination', NGO Committee for the Reporting on the ICERD (January 2001).

20 Tomonaga (1999); the First and Second Reports by the Japanese government on the International Convention on the Elimination of All Forms of Racial Discrimination, June 1999.

21 IMADR (2001).

22 'Comprehensively viewing the above-recognized facts, we can see that for the most part the Ainu people have inhabited Hokkaido from before the extension of our country's rule. They formed their own culture and had an identity. And even after their governance was assumed by our country, even after suffering enormous social and economic devastation wrought by policies adopted by the majority, they remain a social group that has not lost this unique culture and identity. Accordingly, the definition provided above of an "indigenous people" should certainly apply' (NGO Committee for the Reporting on the ICERD, 2001), *Collective Report among Japan Based NGOs on the International Convention on the Elimination of All Forms of Racial Discrimination*. For a full analysis of the case, see Stevens (2001).

23 Personal interview with the Executive Director of the Okinawa Citizen Information Center, 11 December 2001.

24 Paras 23 and 43 in the final Declaration state, respectively: 'We fully recognize the rights of indigenous peoples *consistent with the principles of sovereignty and territorial integrity of States*, and therefore stress the need to adopt the appropriate constitutional, administrative, legislative and judicial measures, including those derived from applicable international instruments'

[emphasis mine]; and 'We also recognize the special relationship that indigenous peoples have with the land as the basis for their spiritual, physical and cultural existence and encourage States, wherever possible, to ensure that indigenous peoples are able to retain ownership of their lands and of those natural resources *to which they are entitled under domestic law'* [emphasis mine].

25   For a more detailed background on these minority groups and their mobilization at the racism conference, see Chan-Tiberghien (Forthcoming 2004a), ch.7: 'Japanese Nongovernmental Mobilization at the World Conference Against Racism'.

26   Crenshaw (2000) p. 7.

27   For a detailed gender analysis of WCAR, see Chan-Tiberghien, (Forthcoming 2004b).

28   For the full report, see http://www.mofa.go.jp/policy/human/women_rep4/index.html.

29   Introduction by Dr Mariko Bando, Director General Equality Bureau, Cabinet Office of Japan, on the occasion of the consideration of Japan's Fourth and Fifth Periodic Reports, Twenty-Ninth Session of the Committee on the Elimination of Discrimination against Women, 8 July 2003, New York.

30   See AJWRC, 3 July 2003: 'We demand the resignation of Mr Seichi Ohta, a former cabinet minister and member of the ruling Liberal Democratic Party as well as an official apology from the former Prime Minister Mori', See www.jca.apc.org/ajwc/.

31   For details on each group, see 'Alternative Reports to the 4th and 5th Periodic Reports of Japan on CEDAW: Voices of Minority Women' submitted collectively by the Burakumin Liberation League, Ainu Association of Hokkaido, Sapporo Branch, Association of Korean Human Rights in Japan, Council of Democratic Resident Korean Women in Japan, and HELP Asian Women's Shelter (see www.imadr.org).

32   For details of the Alternative Report, see www.imadr.org.

References

Allison, Gary (1993) 'Citizenship, Fragmentation, and the Negotiated Polity', in Gary Allison and Sone Yasunori (eds), *Political Dynamics in Contemporary Japan* (Ithaca, NY: Cornell University Press).

Apter, David and Sawa, Nagayo (1984) *Against the State* (Cambridge, Mass.: Harvard University Press).

Asano, Chie (1995) 'Senzaiteki Shohintoshite no Shintai to Sesshoku Shogai' (Anorexia and the Subconsious Commodification of the Body), in Yumiko Ehara (ed.), *Sei no Shohinka* (The Commodification of Sex) (Tokyo: Keiso Shobo).

Broadbent, Jeffrey (1998) *Environmental Politics in Japan: Networks of Power and Protest* (Cambridge University Press).

Chan-Tiberghien, Jennifer (Forthcoming 2004a) 'Gender-Skepticism or Gender-Boom: Poststructural Feminisms, Transnational Feminisms, and the World Conference against Racism', *International Feminist Journal of Politics*.

Chan-Tiberghien, Jennifer. (Forthcoming 2004b) *Gender and Human Rights Politics in Japan: Global Norms and Domestic Networks* (Palo Alto, Calif.: Stanford University Press).

Cho, Yon-Em (1997) 'Feminizumu no naka no Reshizumu' (Racism in Feminism) in Yumiko Ehara and Yoshiko Kanai (eds), *Feminizumu* (Feminism) (Tokyo: Shinyosha).

Crenshaw, Kimberlé (2000) 'Gender-Related Aspects of Race Discrimination' Paper presented at the Expert Group Meeting, 'Gender and Racial Discrimination', 21–24 November 2000, Zagreb, Croatia.

Ehara, Yumiko (1995) 'Shohintoshite no Sei' in Yumiko Ehara (ed.) *Sei no Shohinka* (The Commodification of Sex) (Tokyo: Keiso Shobo).

IMADR (2001) *Kokuren Kara Mita Nihon no Jinshu Sabetsu* (Racial Discrimination in Japan from UN Perspectives) (Tokyo: IMADR).

IMADR (ed.) (2002) *Mainoriti Josei ga Sekai wo Kaeru!* (Minority Women Change the World!) (Tokyo: Kaiho Shuppansha).

Inoue, Teruko, Ueno, Chizuko and Ehara, Yumiko (eds) (1997) *Nihon no Feminizumu*, vols 1–8 (Japanese Feminism) (Tokyo: Iwaba Shoten).

International Human Rights NGO Net (1999) *Wocchi! Kiyaku Jinken Iinkai: Doko ga Zureteru? Jinken no Kokusai Kijun to Nihon no Genjo* (Watch! Human Rights Committee: Where Has It Gone Wrong? International Human Rights Standards and the Status in Japan) (Tokyo: Nihon Hyouronsha).

Kamitani, Masako (1995) ' "Sex Commodification" and Freedom of Expression', in Yumiko Ehara (ed.), *Sei no Shohinka* (The Commodification of Sex) (Tokyo: Keiso Shobo).

LeBlanc, Robin (1999) *Bicycle Citizens: The Political World of the Japanese Housewife* (Berkeley, Calif.: University of California Press).

Matsui, Yayori (1996) 'Interview' in Sandra Buckley (ed.), *Broken Silence: Voices of Japanese Feminism* (Berkeley, Calif.: University of California Press).

Matsui, Yayori and Wakakuwa, Midori *et al.* (1996) (eds) *Feminizumu wa Dare no Mono* (Whose Feminism?) (Shizuoka: Z Kai Peburu).

Okuda, Akiko (ed.) (1997) *Mainoriti toshite no Joseishi* (Women's History from a Minority Perspective) (Tokyo: Sanichi Shobo).

Saito, Chiyo (1997) 'What is Japanese Feminism?' in Sardra Buckley (ed.), *Broken Silence: Voices of Japanese Feminism* (Berkeley, Calif.: University of California Press).

Stevens, Georgina (2001) 'The Ainu and Human Rights: Domestic and International Legal Protections', *Japanese Studies*, vol. 21, no. 2, pp. 181–98.

Suzuki, Yoko (1997) *Senso Sekinin to Jendaa* (War Responsibility and Gender) (Tokyo: Miraisha).

Tomonaga, Kenzo (1999) 'Buraku Mondai' (Buraku Issue), in International Human Rights NGO Net (ed.), *Wocchi! Kiyaku Jinken Iinkai: Doko ga Zureteru? Jinken no Kokusai Kijun to Nihon no Genjou* (Watch! Human Rights Committee: Where is the Gap? International Human Rights Standards and the Situation in Japan) (Tokyo: Nihon Hyouronsha).

Ueno, Chizuko (1996) 'Interview' in Sandra Buckley (ed.), *Broken Silence: Voices of Japanese Feminism* (Berkeley, Calif.: University of California Press).

Yoshimi, Yoshiaki (1995) *Jugun Ianfu* (Military Comfort Women) (Tokyo: Iwanami Shoten).

Part III

Post-Bubble Japanese Business: Adjusting to the New Era

9
Why Does Japan Receive So Little Direct Investment from Abroad?

Shujiro Urata

Globalization of economic activities has been advancing very rapidly in recent years. From the end of the Second World War until the early 1980s, international trade was the single most important means of globalization. Rapid expansion of foreign trade, resulting largely from trade liberalization under the auspices of the GATT, advances in communication and transportation technologies contributed to remarkable growth of the world economy. It is also well known that one of the factors that led to high economic growth in Japan was the expansion of foreign trade.[1]

Entering the 1980s, foreign direct investment (FDI) started to increase rapidly and it became one of the important means of globalization of economic activities. According to the United Nations (2000), world FDI increased at an average annual growth rate of 26.7 per cent between 1982 and 1990[2]. The annual average growth rate declined to 15.7 per cent in the early 1990s (from 1991 to 1995), but rose again to 27 per cent during the period 1996–9. Considering that the average annual growth rates of world GDP and world trade during 1982–99 period were 6.3 per cent and 7.4 per cent, respectively, we understand the rapid expansion of FDI during the period.

A notable characteristic of FDI in recent years is the increasing importance of cross-border mergers and acquisitions (M&As)[3]. The value of cross-border M&As in the world grew at an annual average rate of 23.3 per cent between 1991 and 1995, and to 46.9 per cent between 1996 and 1999. Cross-border M&As are active among the developed countries, particularly among North American and European firms.

As a result of the rapid expansion of FDI, the importance of FDI and multinational enterprises (MNEs), which are major FDI suppliers, increased in the world economy. For example, the share of FDI in global capital formation increased from 2.3 per cent in 1980 to 11.1 per cent in

1998. The increasing importance of FDI/MNEs in the world economy can also be found in international trade, as the share of exports conducted by foreign affiliates of MNEs in world exports rose from 31.2 per cent in 1982 to 46 per cent in 1999.

Although the world economy faced several problems, such as an economic crisis in East Asia in 1997 and 1998, it has expanded steadily since the early 1980s, along with rapid FDI expansion. Japanese firms have undertaken FDI actively since the mid-1980s, and from that time Japan became one of the major suppliers of FDI. By contrast, inward FDI by foreign firms to Japan remained relatively small. The imbalance of inward and outward FDI levels can be seen from the following statistics. The share of Japan in world outward FDI was 6.2 per cent in 1999, while the corresponding value in world inward FDI to Japan was much lower, at 0.8 per cent.

In light of these observations and in recognition of the fact that inward FDI to Japan would bring various benefits to the Japanese economy, which at the time of writing is suffering from low growth, this chapter attempts to discern the factors limiting inward FDI and examines ways to promote inward FDI.

The structure of the chapter is the following. The next section examines recent developments with regard to inward FDI in Japan, while the third section identifies the motives behind undertaking FDI by foreign firms. The fourth section analyzes the impacts of inward FDI on the Japanese economy, and the fifth section investigates the obstacles to FDI in Japan. Finally the sixth section concludes by suggesting some policies to increase inward FDI in Japan.

Inward FDI in Japan: recent developments

Annual FDI inflow to Japan fluctuated around ¥500 billion until the mid-1990s, but increased sharply to ¥770 billion in 1996 (see Figure 9.1). Although Japan's FDI inflow declined to ¥670 billion in 1997, it started to rise again in 1998 to record ¥1.3 trillion. The upward trend continued, as Japan's FDI inflow was recorded at ¥2.4 trillion and ¥2.9 trillion in 1999 and 2000, respectively.

Several notable characteristics can be found for recent FDI inflows to Japan. First, FDI inflows are concentrated in a few sectors. In manufacturing, machinery industries, particularly the automobile industry, attracted large amount of FDI inflows – one notable example, which received wide media attention, was Renault's investment in Nissan in 1999. In non-manufacturing, FDI inflows to finance and insurance, and

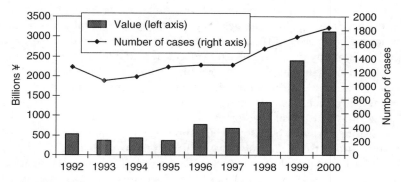

Figure 9.1   Inward foreign direct investment (FDI) in Japan

communications increased sharply. In finance, Ripplewood acquired the Long-term Bank of Japan, while in communications British Telecom and AT&T began to participate in the management of Japan Telecom by purchasing its equity shares. The second notable development, which is related to the first, is the sharp increase in M&As, both in terms of the number of cases and in value. According to the Japan External Trade Organization (JETRO), the number of M&A cases fluctuated at around forty annually until 1997, but increased to fifty-four in 1998, and then further to 104 in 1999. The number increased to 112 in the first nine months alone of 2000 [4]. The third distinguishable development is the increase in the size of FDI. As can be seen from Figure 9.1, FDI in terms of value grew faster than in terms of the number of cases. Indeed, the average value of FDI inflow increased from ¥400 million in 1992 to ¥1.4 billion in 1999.

Several factors can be identified to explain the increasing trend of Japan's inward FDI in recent years. First, declining land and equity prices, resulting from the collapse of the bubble economy and long economic stagnation, increased the attractiveness of FDI in Japan. The Nikkei average stock price index declined sharply after reaching a peak of ¥38,915 in 1989. By the mid-1990s it had declined to ¥20,000 and it continued its decline, to go below ¥10,000 by 2001. Land prices experienced a similar decline. The land price index for the six largest cities peaked in 1992, but then declined sharply in 2000 to a level that was less than half of its peak value. The sharp decline in equity and land prices, which are important determinants of FDI, has enabled foreign investors to undertake FDI at lower costs when compared to the earlier period.

The second factor behind the rapid expansion of inward FDI to Japan is the restructuring of Japanese firms. Many Japanese firms expanded during the bubble economy period, but some of these new operations were later making losses, largely because of the unfavorable economic situation in Japan and their overextended operations. To deal with the problems, many firms tried to get rid of unprofitable operations. Some foreign firms saw this as an opportunity to expand their business into Japan, and they acquired some of the Japanese firms' operations.

The third factor is the change in Japanese policies, not only those concerning FDI but also concerning the domestic economy. The large retail store law, which was enacted to protect small and medium-sized retailers from the large ones, was gradually relaxed in the 1990s and finally abolished in June 2000. Toys R Us opened its Japan operation soon after the abolishment of the large retail store law, as this reduced obstacles to entering retail business. Liberalization of the handling fees for trading stocks in the late 1990s resulted in an increase in FDI by foreign securities companies, as it enabled these companies to compete effectively against Japanese competitors. The introduction of an equity swap system, the removal of a ban on holding companies, the reduction of corporate income tax, and other changes in the policies concerning corporate activities facilitated the undertaking of FDI by foreign firms in Japan. The combined effective corporate tax rate, including corporate income tax, business tax and residential tax, was 49.98 per cent until 1997. The rate was reduced subsequently, being 40.87 per cent in 1999. At 40.87 percent, the effective corporate tax rate is still high compared to corresponding rates in the UK (30 per cent) or France (36.67 per cent), for example, but is lower when compared to Germany (48.44 per cent) or some states in the USA.[5]

The fourth factor is a sharp increase in world FDI, as was noted earlier. World FDI increased substantially in the 1990s because of liberalization in FDI policies, privatization, deregulation in domestic policies and technological progress symbolized by the IT revolution. Indeed, world FDI increased as much as 45.6 per cent in 1997–8. Intensified global competition between MNEs, resulting from deregulation and liberalization, has led MNEs to use FDI as an important means of pursuing their global strategies. One notable example of intensified competition that led to active FDI is the case of the automobile industry. In the late 1990s, the global automobile industry was restructured as a result of several significant business deals, including a mega-merger involving Daimler-Benz and Chrysler, and the acquisition of Volvo by Ford. Such industry restructuring led to active FDI in the Japanese automobile industry by foreign auto producers. Notable cases include Renault's equity participation in Nissan, and an increase in the equity partnership in Fuji Heavy Industries (Subaru) by General Motors.

We found above that FDI inflows to Japan have been increasing remarkably in recent years. It is of interest to compare the level of inward FDI in Japan with other countries. Table 9.1 shows the level of inward FDI stock for five developed countries in 1999. According to the figures in the table, inward FDI stock in Japan is the lowest among these countries. The level of inward FDI stock for Japan in 1999 was US$38.8 billion, a meager one-twenty-eighth of the level in the USA and one-fifth of the level in France, the second lowest country in terms of inward FDI stock after Japan. The level of inward FDI stock in Japan is also found to be low, when a comparison is made against economic size. The share of inward FDI stock to GDP in Japan was 0.7 per cent, the lowest among the countries in the table. The share in Germany was the second lowest, but the value was 9.3 per cent, much larger when compared with the level in Japan.

The low level of inward FDI stock in Japan appears to indicate the low level of internationalization of the Japanese economy. However, this observation may be incorrect, since the level of outward FDI by Japanese firms is comparable to the level for other developed countries. Remarkable is the imbalance of inward and outward FDI. This can be seen from the figures in Table 9.1. For Japan, the level of inward FDI stock was only 13 per cent of the level of outward FDI stock, while the situations are more balanced in other countries. Even for Germany, where the pattern is somewhat similar to the case in Japan, the ratio is 54 per cent.

Table 9.1 showed that the level of inward FDI in Japan was substantially lower when compared with five other developed countries. A simple statistical analysis is carried out in order to conduct a somewhat more rigorous international comparison by expanding the number of sample countries. Table 9.2 presents the results of the analysis of the determinants of inward FDI for twenty-two OECD countries. The dependent variable is the inward FDI stock at the end of 1998, while independent, or

Table 9.1 Inward foreign direct investment (FDI) in selected developed countries, 1999

	FDI stock (US$ bn)	Share of ratio to	
		GDP (%)	Outward FDI
Japan	39	0.7	0.13
USA	1087	9.5	0.96
UK	395	23.3	0.59
Germany	226	9.3	0.54
France	182	11.7	0.61

Source: United Nations (2000).

Table 9.2 The determinants of inward foreign direct investment (FDI) (dependent variable: inward FDI stock in US$ bn)

	c	*GDP*	*Per capita GDP*	*Japan dummy*	*R-squared*
(1)	−2134*	73.4**	30.8		0.443
	(−2.24)	(3.72)	(0.34)		
(2)	−2790**	88.8**	56.8	−342.5*	0.594
	(−3.20)	(4.85)	(0.71)	(−2.59)	

Notes: The figures in parentheses are t-statistics; * and ** indicate statistical significance at 5 per cent and 1 per cent, respectively; GDP is expressed in natural log form; the sample includes 22 OCED countries; data on FDI are taken from United Nations (2000), and the rest of the data from Development Indicators 2000 (CD-ROM), the World Bank; R-squared shows the degree of fit between the statistical model being estimated here and the data (R-squared equals one for a perfect fit and zero for no fit).
Source: Author's estimates.

explanatory variables are GDP per capita and GDP. Use of GDP per capita and GDP is because of the recognition that one of the important motives for undertaking FDI is to expand sales in the host or recipient countries of FDI. As expected sales in the host country are considered to depend on the income level of the population and economic size of the host country, we expect the estimated coefficients of both variables to be positive. We add a Japan dummy variable to test if the level of inward FDI in Japan is statistically different from those in other sample countries.

The estimated coefficients of GDP per capita and GDP are both positive, which is consistent with our expectations. The estimates on GDP are statistically significant, but those on GDP per capita are not. Negative and statistically significant coefficients on the Japan dummy variable indicate that the level of inward FDI in Japan is significantly lower compared with other OECD countries. Predicted levels of inward FDI in Japan are computed by using the estimated coefficients of GDP and GDP per capita. According to the results presented in Table 9.3, the actual level of inward FDI in Japan is only 8 per cent of the predicted level. The results show that the USA is a very attractive host country to MNEs, because the actual level of inward FDI in the USA is 2.2 times as large as the predicted level. Although the UK is not as attractive as the USA, the level of inward FDI in the UK is greater than the predicted value. By contrast to the situations in the USA or UK, the actual levels of inward FDI in Germany and France are lower than the respective predicted levels. These patterns are similar to that in Japan, but the actual levels for these countries are much closer to the predicted levels, compared to Japan.

Table 9.3 Actual and predicted levels of inward FDI for selected developed countries (stock in 1998, US$billion)

	Actual level	Predicted level	Actual/predicted
Japan	26	308	0.08
USA	812	366	2.22
UK	323	225	1.44
Germany	199	262	0.76
France	169	230	0.73

Source: United Nations (2000) and author's estimates.

The motives for inward FDI in Japan

We found earlier that the level of inward FDI in Japan is very low compared to its economic size and the level of income of the population (see the previous section). In this section we investigate the motives of undertaking FDI in Japan by foreign MNEs. Such an investigation would prove useful in formulating the policies for the promotion of inward FDI in Japan. Before conducting the investigation, we review briefly the theories of FDI, to set a framework for the analysis of the motives of undertaking FDI in Japan.

FDI is one way of using firm-specific assets by MNEs (such as technology and management in foreign markets) to maximize profits. MNEs can also use the exporting of their products, licensing technologies and other means as well as FDI. Recognizing these other possible means of exploiting firm-specific assets, in order to identify the motives for FDI we have to explain why MNEs choose this option, and not exporting or technology licensing, for example. One useful theory is the eclectic theory developed by Dunning (1979). As the term indicates, the eclectic theory combines several theories, each of which explains a motive or motives for FDI. One may argue that corporate decision-making on overseas business is very complicated and thus needs more than one theory to explain it.

According to the eclectic theory, FDI is undertaken when the following three 'advantages' exist: firm-specific advantage, locational advantage, and internalization advantage. *Firm-specific advantage* comes in the forms of efficient technology and management know-how, brand names, and so on. Since firm-specific advantage is a source of competitiveness, possession of such an advantage is a necessary condition for the firms to undertake overseas operation such as FDI, exporting and technology licensing.

Locational advantage, which refers to the characteristics of a country or region, which may host FDI, comes in various forms, such as the availability of abundant natural resources and low wage labor, good infrastructure, and stable and transparent policies. Locational advantage provides MNEs with an environment where the costs of transaction and production are low. An MNE with firm-specific assets chooses to undertake FDI in a country with locational advantage over exporting.

Internalization advantage refers to a situation where transactions of firm-specific assets can be better carried out in the form of intra-firm transactions rather than inter-firm, or arm's-length, transactions. To put it differently, internalization advantage arises when arm's-length trans-actions give rise to market failure. The discussion of a concrete example should prove helpful in understanding internalization advantage. Take the case of the transaction of a technology. A seller of a technology knows its content well, and therefore can charge a price reflecting its worth. A potential buyer of the technology generally has a limited knowledge about it, and therefore tends to think that the offered price is higher than the technology's worth. Under such a case of asymmetric information, arm's-length transactions do not take place, because of the differences in the evaluation of the technology by seller and potential buyer. To avoid such a market failure, a firm does not sell the technology but uses it inside the firm through FDI. An MNE interested in using firm-specific assets such as technology in foreign markets undertakes FDI to keep it 'inside' the firm rather than sell it in the form of technology licensing.

Our brief review of the literature on the determinants of FDI points to the importance of locational advantage when we discuss the attractiveness of Japan as a potential FDI host country. In light of this observation, we examine below the motives for FDI in Japan by foreign firms.

Several surveys have been conducted to investigate the motives for inward FDI in Japan by foreign firms. According to a survey conducted by Daiichi Kangyo Bank Research Institute (2001), 82 per cent of foreign firms undertook FDI in Japan to expand sales in the country[6]. This result indicates that Japan, with the second-largest economy in the world, is a very attractive market for foreign firms. As discussed above, foreign firms have several options, such as exporting and FDI, to serve the Japanese market. One can think of several reasons why foreign firms choose FDI rather than exporting to serve the Japanese market. First, it is important for the firms to locate themselves close to potential consumers, to obtain information on consumers' tastes and demand. This is particularly so for the Japanese market, because Japanese consumers are well known for their particular preferences. Second, one may argue that transaction costs associated with exporting to Japan are quite high, as distribution channels are not open and/or transparent because of regulations and closed business practices. Under such circumstances, foreign firms choose FDI as a means of serving the Japanese market.

The survey by Daiichi Kangyo Bank Research Institute identified the establishment of a manufacturing base (19.5 per cent), a base for information collection (18.2 per cent), or a base for R&D activities (11.2 per cent) as motives behind FDI in Japan by foreign firms. These motives are not as important as the sales motive, however. Some foreign firms set up their subsidiaries in Japan to collect market information, not only on Japan but also on Asia as a whole, as a great deal of information on Asia flows into Japan. Some foreign firms undertake FDI in Japan to take advantage of the availability of useful technology and capable R&D personnel. Information on the motives behind FDI in Japan by foreign firms should prove useful in formulating policies for attracting FDI in Japan, which will be discussed later in the chapter.

The impact of inward foreign direct investment (FDI) on the Japanese economy

Inward FDI has various impacts on the host country. Through hosting FDI a host country can obtain financial resources, which are used for fixed investment or capital formation. Stimulation of capital formation leads to the expansion of production capacity, which in turn leads to output and employment expansion. Expansion of output and employment increase incomes of firms and households, which would stimulate fixed investment and consumption, thus promoting economic growth. It should also be noted that inward FDI is likely to increase exports from the host country through efficient and well-developed sales networks of MNEs.

In addition to the quantitative economic expansion that inward FDI would bring to the host countries, it would contribute to the economic growth of the host countries by improving technical and allocative efficiency. One might expect inward FDI to improve the technical efficiency of the host country, as technology is likely to be transferred from MNEs to the host country. Allocative efficiency may also improve, as inward FDI puts competitive pressures on domestic firms to force them to use resources efficiently. Such changes that inward FDI would bring to the host countries may be characterized as qualitative contributions.

One cannot dismiss the possible negative impact of inward FDI on the host countries – for example, the entry of competitive MNEs is likely to force inefficient domestic firms out of business. Although this type of resource reallocation is good for the long-term growth of the host country, it gives rise to the unemployment of resources, at least temporarily. The host government should provide temporary assistance to unemployed workers in the forms of unemployment compensation and provision of education and training, so their hardships can be reduced and they may be reemployed without much difficulty. One may also think of the negative impact of inward FDI when competitive MNEs exploit their market power to reap monopoly profits. To deal with this case, the host government should formulate and implement competition policy, and make sure the policy is enforced. In light of the discussions on the possible impact of inward FDI on the host countries, we shall analyze the impact of inward FDI on the Japanese economy in the rest of this section.

Let us begin with the quantitative impact of inward FDI, and then turn to the qualitative impact. Earlier we found that inward FDI in Japan has been rising remarkably in recent years. However, its impact is rather limited when compared to other countries. In the case of the contribution to capital formation, the share of inward FDI in fixed capital formation for Japan was 0.3 per cent in 1998, significantly lower than the corresponding figures for other developed countries, which were around 10 per cent.[7] Turning to the contribution of foreign firms to output, one finds that the share of output by foreign firms in the total output in manufacturing was 3 per cent in 1998, increased from approximately 2 per cent in the mid-1980s.[8] These shares vary widely among different manufacturing sub-sectors. The share is extremely high at 17.1 per cent in petroleum products, and other sectors with relatively high ratios include transport machinery (4.5%), chemicals (3.5%), general machinery (3.5%), and electric machinery (3.5%). The contribution of foreign firms to employment generation is sizeable in terms of absolute value, but not so significant in comparison with total employment. Specifically, foreign firms in Japan employ 264,000 workers at the time of writing, which amounts to a meager 0.6 per cent of the total number of workers – 43 million. The share of workers employed by foreign firms in total employment is high for manufacturing when compared with the situation in non-manufacturing, but the ratio for manufacturing is still very low, at 1.9 per cent.[9]

Foreign firms have an impact on Japan's foreign trade. For foreign firms in Japan, 36.4 per cent of their procurements come from imports, and 55.7 per cent of their imports come from their parent companies. The information on procurement patterns for Japanese firms is limited. According to the results of the survey, which was conducted among Japanese firms with outward FDI, the share of imports in total procurements was 13.2 per cent, significantly lower compared with the case for foreign firms. It should be noted that 13.2 per cent share is likely to be higher than the figure for any Japanese firm, because Japanese firms with outward FDI are more internationalized than other firms, and therefore Japanese firms with outward FDI are likely to have a higher import-procurement share than other firms.

The situation is very different for exports. The share of exports in total sales for foreign firms in Japan has been lower compared to the case for Japanese firms. Specifically, the exports–sales ratio for the former was 12.7 per cent, while the corresponding ratio for the latter was higher at 18.2 per cent. These observations are consistent with the fact that one of the motives for undertaking FDI in Japan by foreign firms is to expand sales in Japan, not to expand exports. Coupled with the observations on import and procurement patterns, the findings on exports and sales indicate the important contribution that foreign firms are making towards reducing trade surplus, which is one of the important policy issues facing Japan.

Let us turn now to the qualitative impact of foreign firms on the Japanese economy, which is difficult to measure. One useful benchmark against which to measure the quality of management is profitability: the higher the profitability, the better the management. A comparison of profitability by using such measures as profit–sales ratio and profit–equity ratio reveals that the profitability of foreign firms is higher than Japanese firms. For example, in 1998, the average profit–sales ratio for foreign firms in Japan was 3.8 per cent, against 1.5 per cent for Japanese firms. These figures appear to indicate that foreign firms have better management than Japanese firms, thereby implying that inward FDI to Japan contributes to the improvement of management capability within the country. Having made this observation, it is important to realize that management capability is not the only factor that determines profitability. For example, the attitude of the owners of firms, or the shareholders, has an important impact on profitability. If shareholders place importance on short-term gain rather than long-term benefit, managers are forced to make short-term profits, leading to high profitability. Indeed, this is a typical attitude among shareholders in the USA, while shareholders in Japan tend to emphasize long-term gains.

Another qualitative contribution FDI may make in the host country is the transfer of technologies, because MNEs tend to have superior technologies. An examination of the data on R&D by foreign firms in Japan reveals that foreign firms are not as active as Japanese firms in carrying out R&D. Specifically, the ratio of R&D to sales for foreign manufacturing firms in Japan is 3.2 per cent, lower than the corresponding value for

Japanese firms, which is 4.1 per cent. This observation indicates that the impact of FDI on R&D activities in Japan is rather limited. This is consistent with the results of the survey, which show that the share of foreign firms with R&D motives in total foreign firms in Japan is small. So far we have examined the impact of FDI on the Japanese economy by using statistical data. Below we analyze its impact by referring to some specific areas.

Foreign firms in Japan are changing the 'Japanese management style', which was once regarded as being very efficient. A typical case in point is the change in corporate governance structures. Traditionally, Japanese corporate structure has been characterized as non-transparent and irrational. One such example is a long-term, inter-firm relationship – such as a *keiretsu* transaction. Although long-term, inter-firm relationships result in stable business, they deter new entries, thus reducing economic dynamism. To such an inflexible management environment, foreign firms brought accounting and other business practices, which are accepted as the 'global standard'. As a result, foreign firms have contributed to the increased transparency in Japanese-style management, thereby making management style in Japan more consistent with the global standard.

It is also worth noting that foreign firms have contributed to the enhanced mobilization of workers in the Japanese labor market. Life-long employment and a seniority wage structure were special characteristics of the Japanese labor market. These 'systems' worked very effectively and contributed to human resource development in Japan during the period of high economic growth. However, the systems became inefficient when Japan's economic growth declined. Specifically, Japanese firms were faced with very high, and increasing, wage payments and stagnant revenue, resulting in a decline in profitability. The entry of foreign firms not only increased job opportunities but also mobilized the labor market because of their flexible labor practices, which was acutely needed to achieve efficient use of labor.

Let us look at some specific areas where foreign firms have had a significant impact on the Japanese economy. Take the case of the financial sector. Japanese banks were highly protected by excessively interventionist government policies. As a result, they were very slow in introducing new types of services. But foreign banks have entered the Japanese market with many new services, such as investment banking, special transactions for the wealthy, and foreign currency savings, to name just a few, which are benefiting globalized Japanese firms and high-income consumers.

New developments in the distribution sector can be experienced directly by consumers. Toys Я Us entered the Japanese market with a great farfare, because its successful entry was attributable to the strong pressure on the Japanese government by the US government to open up the retail market. Toys Я Us introduced a new business style into the Japanese toy market, as it sells not only toys but also stationary and clothes for children, offering Japanese consumers a wider selection. Furthermore, Toys Я Us introduced a new procurement practice, under which it buys products directly from producers, so bypassing wholesalers. In this way, Toys Я Us was successful in reducing costs and prices. Indeed, the Toys Я Us effect of lowering prices has put a number of less inefficient toy stores out of business. It should be noted, however, that sales and employment in the toy industry *increased* after Toys Я Us entered the market, indicating that its new entry promoted overall sales of toys. In addition to Toys Я Us, new types of business including 'outlets' (which sell mainly overstocked branded products at low prices) and membership discount stores were introduced to Japan by foreign firms.

We examined the impact of FDI on the Japanese economy in this section. So far because of its small scale, the quantitative impact of foreign firms seem to be rather limited. However, qualitative impacts appear to be substantial, as foreign firms have introduced a number of new business methods, which have contributed to improving technical and allocative efficiency and increasing diversity in the Japanese economy.

The obstacles to FDI in Japan

We noted above that inward FDI in Japan has had a favorable impact on the Japanese economy – for example, employment generation, the introduction of new management styles, and so on. However, the level of inward FDI was found to be low when compared to other countries. It is desirable for Japan to increase its level of inward FDI, but to achieve this objective, it is necessary to discover the reasons for the low level of inward FDI in Japan. With this observation in mind, this section identifies the obstacles to inward FDI in Japan, mainly by using the information obtained from various surveys.

Figure 9.2 shows the results of a survey conducted on foreign firms by METI.[10] According to the results, a large number of respondents indicated 'high business costs' and 'high taxes' as serious obstacles. Specifically, the shares of respondents noting these problems were 65 per cent and 60 per cent, respectively. High business costs are largely a result of high office rental fees and land prices. As was noted earlier, land prices and office rental fees fell after the collapse of the bubble economy, but they are still substantially higher when compared to other developed countries, as

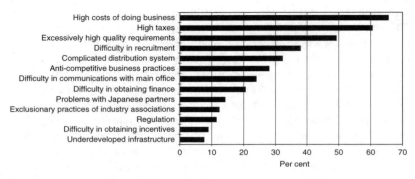

Figure 9.2   obstacles to doing business in Japan

indicated below. Information on office rental fees is not readily available, and we therefore compare housing rental fees, which are closely correlated to those of offices. Housing rental fees in Tokyo are significantly higher than those in other major cities, such as New York (1.56 times), London (1.15 times), and Paris (1.91 times.)[11] In addition to office rental fees and land prices, the high cost of infrastructure-related services, such as energy, transportation and communication services, increased business costs. According to the Economic Plannning Agency (2000), the costs of energy and transportation/communication services in Tokyo are higher than those in New York City by 1.61 and 1.13 times, respectively. It has been argued that wages in Japan are significantly higher than in other developed countries, but in recent years the gaps have been reduced. For example, wage gaps in manufacturing in Japan and the USA narrowed, as the ratio of these rates were 1(Japan):0.71 (USA) in 1991, but this became 1:0.94 in 1995.[12] It is also important to note that wages in Germany and France are, on average, higher than those in Japan.

Many foreign firms point out high tax rates as a serious obstacle in doing business in Japan. In fact, corporate taxes in Japan have been reduced since the mid-1990s, and, at the time of writing, levels are comparable to those in other developed countries. Many foreign firms also indicate a high expectation of Japanese consumers being an obstacle. Although this may be a serious problem for foreign firms, which are accustomed to different types of consumers, foreign firms have to do business with the presence of inquisitive consumers as a given. The recruitment of capable personnel and the establishment of distribution channels are also problems faced by foreign firms. Static labor and the underdevelopment of a well-functioning labor market make it difficult for foreign firms to find capable staff. Long-term, interfirm relationships such as *keiretsu* transactions are obstacles to foreign firms attempting to develop their distribution systems. It should be noted that these obstacles have been disappearing for several reasons, including globalization, technological progress and long-term recession in Japan. For example, the development of e-commerce resulting from technological progress has enabled firms to bypass whole-salers or complicated distribution systems, while long-term recession has resulted in an increase in the number of unemployed workers, creating a pool of potential employees from which foreign firms are able to find staff.

So far we have analyzed the problems facing foreign firms by using the information obtained from the survey discussed above. However, we did not analyze the characteristics of foreign firms, which tend to face such problems frequently. Urata (1996) examined this question and found that joint ventures with Japanese firms and foreign firms with a high proportion of Japanese employees overall tend to be relatively free from these problems. These findings may indicate that localized foreign firms are able to avoid the problems.

Government regulations were indicated as problems by 11.3 per cent of the respondents. Although this average figure is lower when compared to other problems, one finds that the shares differ widely among foreign firms in different sectors. The sectors with the highest proportion include the medical and pharmaceutical industry (54.2%), textiles (28.6%), and transportation and communication services (26.1%). The medical and pharmaceutical industry is regulated for health and safety reasons, while transportation and communication services are regulated for purposes of national security and social order.

Japanese policy toward inward FDI was liberalized gradually in the post-Second World War period. Immediately after the war, the Law on Foreign Investment, enacted in 1950, restricted inward FDI in order to develop domestic industries, but the restrictions were liberalized gradually with economic growth. Liberalization took place in the industries that were considered to have become competitive. The 1980s saw substantial liberalization, as the inward FDI approval system was replaced by a reporting system. As of 2001, only a few sectors, such as agriculture, forestry and fishery, air and marine transportation are restricted. It is worth noting that Nakamura *et al.* (1997) found, by conducting a cross-industry study, that regulations on inward FDI did not have any significant impact on the level of FDI in Japan.

Regulations on inward FDI still remain, but at the same time various promotion measures, including low-interest loans, and the provision of information and consultation are implemented by central and local governments to attract FDI because of the recognition that inward FDI would contribute to the reactivation of the Japanese economy. One of the problems of these measures is that they are formulated and/or implemented without consistency or coordination, so their impact so far has appeared quite limited.

Promoting FDI in Japan

Inward FDI contributes to the recovery and sustainable economic growth of the Japanese economy not only in terms of quantitative expansion but also in terms of qualitative improvement. Despite the favorable contributions that inward FDI would make to the Japanese economy, however, the level of inward FDI in Japan has been quite low, and therefore Japan has not been able to utilize efficiently resources owned by foreign firms. To mobilize these resources by expanding inward FDI in Japan, the obstacles to its acceptance have to be removed. The analysis of the obstacles to inward FDI in Japan in this chapter revealed the 'high costs' of operating business as the most serious obstacle: specifically, the high costs of labor, land, transportation and communications services, which are essential elements in doing business. It is important to recognize that these same elements are major obstacles to the recovery from the long recession in Japan. The high cost structure of the Japanese economy is attributable to various factors such as regulations and the anti-competitive behavior of Japanese firms, such as *keiretsu* transactions. The recognition of these problems points to the need for deregulation and the effective application of competition policies in order not only to promote inward FDI but also to revitalize the Japanese economy.[13]

The expectation of high profits induces the entry of firms. As such, the optimistic future economic outlook for Japan would encourage new entries into the Japanese market by Japanese as well as foreign firms. It is therefore essential for Japan to construct an economic system under which optimistic economic developments can be expected, by implementing rigorously structural reforms and other necessary policy changes. If the inhibiting economic structure is replaced successfully by a vibrant and flexible structure, entry by Japanese firms as well as foreign firms via inward FDI will be activated, leading to sustainable economic growth.

The importance of restructuring the economic system was emphasized to promote inward FDI in Japan. It is also important to emphasize the need to carry out further liberalization in FDI policies. As the discussions on the policies toward FDI indicated, there are several areas that are excluded from inward FDI for national security, people's safety, and other reasons. Although some of the restrictions may be justified, it is important to reexamine their validity. It is also important to assess the effectiveness of FDI promotion policies based on their costs and benefits.

Finally, it should be emphasized that the internationalization of Japanese society is necessary to promote the internationalization of the Japanese economy via various means, including inward FDI. Specifically, the Japanese have to deepen the level of understanding of foreign countries and foreign people, and to learn to communicate with them. Without the internationalization of Japanese society, increase in inward FDI will not have a significant impact on Japanese economy and society.

Notes

1 Many studies including Minami (1994) have pointed to the important contribution that export expansion made in Japan's economic growth. Lawrence and Weinstein (2001) argued that imports had a positive impact on Japan's economic growth, as they contributed to the improvement of productivity.
2 The figures used in this section are in nominal values, and are taken from United Nations (2000).
3 FDI typically takes two forms – M&A and green-field investment, or setting up new establishment.
4 Japan External Trade Organization (2001). The information on M&As is difficult to obtain, as no official statistics are compiled. Therefore, the main sources of information are surveys and newspaper articles.
5 Web page of the Ministry of Home Affairs, the government of Japan.
6 The survey questionnaire was sent to 2,408 foreign firms operating in Japan, and a response was obtained from 272 of them.
7 United Nations (2000). For reference, the share of outward FDI in fixed capital formation was 2.4 per cent in 1998.
8 The figures are taken from Ministry of Economy, Trade and Industry (2001). It is well known that these figures underestimate the true value, because the figures are obtained via a voluntary survey, and the survey does not cover some industries such as finance and insurance.
9 As noted in note 8, the figures reported in Ministry of Economy, Trade and Industry (2001) underestimate the true figures. Using different information, Fukao (2001) reports that the number of workers employed by foreign firms in Japan was 490,000 in 1997.
10 The questionnaire was sent to 3,150 foreign firms, and 1,613 (51.2%) responded.
11 The numbers, which are taken from Economic Planning Agency (2000), indicate the level of housing rental fees in Tokyo by setting those in the cities in comparison as unity.
12 Daiichi Kangin Sogo Kenkyusho (2001).
13 The results of the METI survey show one of requests to the Japanese government that are most frequently noted by foreign firms is an improvement in 'transparency in government administration'. It is therefore important for the

Japanese government to disseminate information on regulations and other administrative services to foreign firms, which are in a disadvantageous position with regard to Japanese firms in obtaining such information.

References

Daiichi Kangyo Bank Research Institute (2001) *Tainichi Chokusetsutoshi Sokushin Seisaku no Hyoka to Kongo no Shisaku no Arikatanikansuru Chosa* (Report on the Evaluation of Inward Foreign Direct Investment Promotion Policies) (Tokyo) (in Japanese).

Dunning, John H. (1979) 'Explaining Changing Patterns of International Production: In Defense of the Eclectic Theory', *Oxford Bulletin of Economics and Statistics*, November.

Economic Planning Agency (2000) *Bukka Report* (Report on Prices) (Tokyo).

Fukao, Kyoji (2001) 'The Facts about Foreign Direct Investment in Japan', *Nippon Keizai Shimbun* (Japan Economic Daily), 3 and 4 April.

Japan External Trade Organization (JETRO) (2001) *White Paper on Foreign Direct Investment in Japan and the World* (Tokyo) (in Japanese).

Lawrence, Robert Z. and Weinstein, David E. (2001) 'Trade and Growth: Import-Led or Export-Led? Evidence from Japan and Korea', in Joseph E. Stiglitz and Shahid Yusuf (eds), *Rethinking the East Asian Miracle* (New York: Oxford University Press).

Minami, Ryoshin (1994) *The Economic Development of Japan: A Quantitative Study*, (London: Macmillan).

Ministry of Economy, Trade and Industry (METI) (2001) *Gaishikei Kigyo no Doko* (Survey on the Activities of Foreign Firms in Japan), Report on the Survey on the Activities of Foreign Firms in Japan, No. 33 (Tokyo).

Nakamura, Yoshiaki, Fukao, Kyoji and Shibuya, Minoru (1997) *Why is Inward Foreign Direct Investment in Japan Low?*, Policy Series No. 31 (Tokyo: Research Institute of Ministry of International Trade and Industry).

United Nations (UN) (2000) *World Investment Report 2000* (New York and Geneva: United Nations).

Urata, Shujiro (1996) 'Obstacles to Inward Foreign Direct Investment', *Nihon Keizai Kenkyu* (Research on the Japanese Economy), no. 31, Japan Center for Economic Research (in Japanese).

10
Japanese Society under Marketization and Globalization

Takanobu Nakajima

Who could have imagined the miserable performance the Japanese economy has displayed since the 1990s? The average real GDP growth rate during the 1990s was 1.4 per cent, and the unemployment rate reached 5 per cent in July 2001. The recession period after the bursting of the bubble in 1991 has been called *the lost ten years*. What was wrong during that time? Many hypotheses have been presented: demand shortage, policy failure, bad loans, and a pessimistic view of the future. The truth may not be known for another ten years.

'No growth is attained without a structural reform.' Prime Minister Junichiro Koizumi, the eighth prime minister in the previous ten years, announced structural reform as the main political issue of his administration in his keynote address in April 2001. When the economic downturn occurred in 1991, the government at first considered it to be a temporary business shock that would disappear quickly, and tried to stand by its monetary policy. While the Bank of Japan made a 180-degree turn from a tight-money policy, designed to calm down the bubble, to an easy-money policy to accelerate the economy, the government stuck to the reduced budget principle to maintain the soundness of national finance.[1] But just when the recovery process looked encouraging, another downturn appeared on the horizon in 1997. The Hashimoto administration, criticized for passivity in its economic policy, was replaced by the Obuchi administration after the national election in 1998. Mr Obuchi and his successor, Mr Mori, converted drastically to a positive fiscal policy. Government bond issues increased by 46 per cent in 1998, 32 per cent in 1999 and 21 per cent in 2000, finally reaching ¥90 trillion (US $0.75 trillion) in 2001. Both regional and central government loans soared to ¥666 trillion (US $5.5 trillion): this equates to ¥5.55 million per capita. As we saw earlier, these policies did not produce good GDP growth or unemployment numbers.

To discuss the meaning and effectiveness of a structural reform, it is necessary to understand the structure itself: it is a mechanism or a system upon which a society is constructed. It is a set of laws and rules that determines the direction of peoples' activities. From an economic point of view, the structure provides a basic incentive mechanism to companies and individuals that take action for the maximization of their own net benefit. If the economy does not work well for a long time, even though individuals are doing their best, there is probably something wrong with the mechanism.

There are numerous discussions about when the Japanese traditional social system was constructed. Urushiyama (2001) explains that the rational and productive rice farming system, established more than a thousand years ago, is the key to understanding the origins of the system. According to his discussion, the best way to raise productivity in rice farming is to organize regional communities and promote cooperative activities. Ihara (2001) emphasizes that the structure was originally built when the Tokugawa administration, established in 1603, restricted the transfer of human resources between industries and regions, and designed a stable, closed social scheme viable for 260 years. Noguchi (1995) called the basic framework of the current Japanese economy the *System of the year 1940* because the essential system components such as bureaucracy, centralized finance, the Japanese style of management, and administrative guidance, were all established in 1940 in order to manage the economy in wartime.

Regardless of when the present system was constructed, it is a good question as to whether this old-fashioned structure is finally out of date for the beginning of the new century. Orthodox empirical studies could show the answer to the question about what really changed in the 1990s, if ample time series of data were available. At the present time it is possible to discuss the structure issue only based on anecdotal episodes and to present the evidence that shows discrepancies between the old-fashioned structure and the present reality.

In this chapter I investigate the recent structural change in the Japanese society from three viewpoints. The first is to analyze progress in individualization. We show that individualization is inevitable in the process of economic growth, which makes it possible for an individual to enjoy his/her private space. This can be a driving force for structural change.

Next is the failure of prior cost intensive rules, which has been one of the characteristics of the traditional Japanese social system. According to the Coase Theorem, if a transaction cost is negligible, resources are automatically allocated so that the most efficient party bears the cost of accomplishing the goal. In fact, however, a high transaction cost destroys the validity of the market mechanism, which requires a new rule to encourage smooth transactions in the market. In this chapter I define two kinds of rule – (i) the prior cost intensive rule; and (ii) the *ex-post-facto* cost intensive rule – and consider which rule is applicable to the present situation.

The final point is an outsider's effect on the traditional system. Applying the 'marginal interested party' hypothesis in Ramseyer (1990) to the Japanese social system, it can be shown that increasing numbers of new incomers, such as younger generations, female workers, immigrants and foreign ventures, could put pressure on traditional rules to change and converge to the transparent law system.

The rest of the chapter is organized as follows. The second, third and forth sections discuss in turn the three viewpoints introduced above. Their relationships to Koizumi's Structural Reform are discussed in the fifth section. The chapter ends with conclusions in the sixth Section.

Progress in individualization

One of the most amazing facts in recent years is the explosive spread of cellular telephones, especially among the younger generation.[2] At the same time, traditional fixed phones are disappearing in homes because of the high installation cost.[3] Is this phenomenon interpreted as a simple substitution of a new product for an old one in the phone equipment market? Seemingly, yes – however, we can account for a different meaning of this product substitution in the trend of the times since the high economic growth period.

Modern conveniences are influential not only because they raise peoples' standard of living, but also because they make qualitative changes in human life. In Japan's case, the introduction of new products generated by technological innovations has made a great contribution towards a shift of peoples' behavior from group behavior to an individual focus. Before the period of high growth, most ordinary apartment buildings did not have bathrooms. The inhabitants went to the public baths and were in close communication with their neighbors. Economic growth raised the average income level and enabled middle-class workers to afford to install private bathrooms in their houses. The introduction of private bathrooms has certainly improved personal privacy, but it has also lowered community interaction and consequently also the power that can be enforced through information exchange among neighbors.

Individualization has continued to flourish, even at home. Owning refrigerators and microwave ovens allow people to preserve meals and reheat them whenever they wish: the economics of eating together to save money is no longer valid. With all the amenities available in housing now, children are comfortable and entertain themselves more. As a result, parents obviously spend less time with their children.[4]

This trend was encouraged by Sony's handy cassette-tape player, the Walkman. Before the Walkman's appearance, music had not been a perfect private good in Japan. Family members commonly listened to the same music from the TV or a radio, and a compromise had to be reached as to which programme to listen to. This had an effect on the children, who had no chance to experience new styles of music that their parents were not familiar with or did not like. The Walkman's tremendous impact was in allowing individuals their own private space where they could enjoy listening to whatever music they wished, whenever they wished. This has radically changed the music of Japan, where once everyone knew the popular 'folk' music. Now there are as many varieties of music as there are generations and special interests. Did this bring on a decline in the music industry? Quite the contrary; the market share of music has greatly expanded since the 1980s.

But, let us return to the cellular phone issue mentioned at the beginning of this section. According to the context so far, we can easily see that a cellular phone is not just a simple substitute for a traditional fixed one; it helps us to experience a completely private space for human communication. We are now able to contact our acquaintances at any time and anywhere. In other words, people carrying cellular phones are potentially connected to each other at every moment. Before its appearance we relied on organization to make sure when, where and whom to meet. We had to stay at a certain place to be able to be contacted with someone by telephone. Cellular phones give people freedom in their communications. Parents have no idea to whom and about what their children talk on cellular phones.

We now turn our attention to the effects that these new trends could have on the Japanese economy. Progress in individualization has the effect of encouraging variety in individual taste. Products that help people to enjoy their private space will grow in market size. Some decades ago, when family organization was closer than at present, typical ways of spending leisure time were to go to department stores or amusement parks, and have dinner together at restaurants. What department stores did at that time was merely to open their doors and wait for customers to come in – they provided easily available entertainment for families and no effort was needed to attract customers with specific needs. Facing the serious decline in sales after the bursting of the bubble, department stores have finally found that traditional sales methods do not match the diversified tastes of individuals. But companies that have provided products and services to support comfortable individual life-styles and needs have experienced great success. Personal goods such as information devices and their related services will continue to gain a greater market share in Japan.

Individualization, on the other hand, can impose additional costs on society.[5] When regional community and family organizations were robust, anticipating what people were going to do required no additional cost. People's communication was open and a known entity. There were no additional costs of checking up on one other. Now parents have more difficulty in knowing what their children are doing in private. With the availability and ease of personal and private communications, and children's exposure to so much more information, teachers in elementary schools have difficulty in knowing what children are planning and doing in class. Under the old structure, this was not a problem, but current society has changed and presents new challenges. Traditional service sectors that have been protected by government regulation in the past, and rarely experienced severe competition, are having difficulty coping with this new individualism. Service providers have to spend more time and money on discovering what customers really want, and increase their efforts to develop new service products.

We have discussed the costs and benefits of the recent trends in Japanese society. Weakening traditional organization and increasing individualization will impose more transaction costs and monitoring costs on society. On the other hand, they will enlarge business opportunities in two ways: (i) by expanding market size to meet the diversified needs of individuals; and (ii) by creating new services that save transaction costs for individuals.

Prior cost and *ex-post-facto* cost

Definitions

It goes without saying that accomplishing specific new goals generates costs. The same rule can be applied in establishing a social system. According to the economic theory of comparative institutional schools, the social system adjusts to environmental change to minimize the total cost people have to pay. In this section we consider the issue of the timing of cost payment in the creation of the social system to accomplish a social goal.

The principle of 'law and economics' teaches that social cost should be charged to those who can pay for it most efficiently. If the transaction cost for negotiation is negligible, efficient resource allocation is automatically accomplished, and a system of law is not relevant. When the 'Coase Theorem' is perfectly applicable to society, what we do is to put ourselves into the invisible hands of the market mechanism with no consideration of how the social system should be constructed.

If people are close to each other through everyday association as in organizations, the 'Coase Theorem' might be true. However, in many cases the transaction cost for negotiation is significantly large. Even if the resource allocation is inefficient, the high transaction cost prevents interested parties from negotiating for the Pareto-optimal situations. In this case, law is used to realize efficiency in society: the system of law can be constructed to induce interested parties to allocate resources most efficiently.

Concerning the role of the law system, it is important to account for two kinds of costs imposed on society to accomplish the optimal resource allocation: prior cost and *ex-post-facto* cost. We consider realities as sets of events that occur continuously in society. The optimal situation – that is, a satisfactory equilibrium in the system – exists corresponding to reality. When an event occurs, the exogenous environment has its equilibrium changed through resource reallocation. In this process, prior cost is defined as the cost that is paid *before* the event to make the adjustment process easy. In contrast, *ex-post-facto* cost is paid after the event to move the equilibrium from before to after the event.

One extreme case is when society pays all in prior costs and nothing in *ex-post-facto* costs. Prior resource allocation is apt to continue whatever happens, because nothing is paid to lower transaction costs for resource reallocation after the event. In another extreme case, no prior cost is paid and resource allocation is promoted by spending *ex-post-facto* costs. A typical example of the prior cost rule is the license system. Suppose there is a high school student who wants to be a medical doctor in Japan. That student has to spend a great deal of time and money and study hard to pass the entrance exam for medical school. S/he may fail initially, and try again by going to a cramming school or getting private tutoring. Even after the exam is passed, the student will incur significant expenses over the six years of medical school training. Finally, the national exam has to be passed to acquire a formal doctor's license before graduation. All these costs are defined as prior costs to become a doctor. Then other events may occur: the student may find that his/her choice of medicine as a career is wrong, and may have the desire to follow another career. However, paid significant prior costs have already been paid to get the license, and these are all sunk costs. For economic reasons, the person may continue working as a doctor, which may lead to problems caused by resource misallocation. If *ex-post-facto* cost were paid for monitoring the doctor's performance or reconfirmation of his/her aptitude and desire, s/he might be motivated to get another job that would be more appealing.

Japanese society as a prior cost intensive system

The rationality of paying prior costs can be explained from an economic point of view. One of the purposes of prior costs is to limit the variety of results that would occur after the event by reducing the number of choices before the event. Suppose that three events occur consecutively, and there are five options for each event among which one person makes a choice. Theoretically, if s/he makes a choice of whatever s/he wants at the three events, 125 combinations of choices would occur in total, and it is costly to examine the efficiency of choices made from among 125 combinations after the three events occur. Consider the case that we reduce the five options to four for each event in the prior examination. The number of combinations is then reduced by half.

Let me apply the theory mentioned above to some practical examples. While a license system generates a barrier to a new entrant and a monopoly rent for an incumbent, it saves a monitoring (*ex-post-facto*) cost that would be paid for resource reallocation. An entrance exam for a college imposes high prior cost on students and their parents, but saves *ex-post-facto* costs for labor resource allocation because an academic degree primarily determines the choice of career. Disabled people in Japan are classified into several classes based on doctors' diagnosis, which determines the level of support that the government provides for them.[6] It can save *ex-post-facto* costs, because resources for the government welfare services are allocated to them mechanically according to given classes.

The Japanese social system, spending more for prior examination before the occurrence of an event, certainly played a significant role during the economic growth period following the post-Second World War recovery. The fundamental factor behind the success is the behavior of individuals harmonized to others as a member of an organization.

It was easy and cost-free for the government to pick up and select options that could continue to be satisfactory to citizens for a long time.

The Japanese legal system has been consistent with a prior-cost-intensive society.[7] Basically, the law of tort in Japan is based on the negligence rule. In this rule, the law determines the necessary precaution level. If an agent clears this level, it does not have to take responsibility for the results. The negligence rule realizes efficient resource allocation automatically if the level is settled at the appropriate position, and saves *ex-post-facto* monitoring costs. The discussion above, however, ignores one important point – that is, the investigation cost for the government to determine the appropriate precaution level. If the government fails to accomplish the precise investigation and necessary reexamination of the precaution level, the negligence rule leads to the distortion of the resource allocation.[8]

The education system in Japan typically takes the prior cost intensive rule. The obstacles to be overcome before entering a college are much higher than the requirements for graduation. Children heading for privileged universities spend a great deal of time studying so as to excel among the severe competition for admission; but once admitted they go on a spree for four years as a reward for their long-term effort to gain admittance to the university. The system of research funds provision from the government to colleges is also based on the prior investigation rule. Past performance is the most important factor for the prior investigation to decide where the money goes, while the *ex-post-facto* examination is comparatively poor.

The shift to the *ex-post-facto* cost intensive rule

The prior cost intensive system is certainly effective if it saves *ex-post-facto* costs and brings about efficient resource allocation. However, we can see many cases where this system does not work well because of changes in circumstances.

The rationality of a prior cost intensive system assumes that the government has the advantage in collecting precise information for the determination of appropriate rules through prior investigation. It would be easy to extrapolate a precise prediction for future occurrences if people had homogeneous tastes. As mentioned earlier in the chapter, however, thanks to changes in technology, various individual tastes that had been hidden for economic reasons are now being exhibited. The collapse of the tight family organization, for example, has deprived parents of the ability to control the tastes of their children. The mass-education style, formerly based on the homogeneous family structure and interests of children, has fallen into disarray in many classrooms.[9] The previous determination of fault level in tort law is old-fashioned and out of date. This changing environment has removed the advantageous position that government once had in being able to collect precise information and define a predicable set of possible outcomes.

Another problem of the prior cost intensive system is the lack of an incentive to encourage more effort. Let me give examples. Examinations to enter schools and get licenses are prior cost for candidates. The prior examination system presents an incentive for candidates to study only what will be asked in the examinations. They will spend no additional cost to prepare for the issues that do not appear in questions, although that would be very useful information. The negligence rule also undermines concerned parties' stimulus to apply more effort to pursue efficiency. Under this rule they do not have to bear the cost of damages, provided they have equaled the required precaution level. This rule does not encourage them to develop more efficient ways of avoiding damages. It is often said that the Building Standards Act of Japan makes construction companies focus, not on developing ways to reduce total costs (construction cost and damage cost), but on searching for inexpensive ways to just meet the law's requirements.

Considering that the conditions supporting the prior cost intensive system are disappearing, it is time to switch more toward the *ex-post-facto* cost intensive system. Instead of paying a prior cost for investigation before an event, more resources should be allocated for examination after the event. More options should be prepared to widen the range of choices for people. Although the *ex-post-facto* cost of examining appropriateness of the choices is necessary, new combinations of choices may lead to a breakthrough in societal behaviors.

One important issue to be considered is who will pay the *ex-post-facto* cost. If the transaction cost is negligible, the market mechanism automatically realizes the efficiency. If not, a law system should be established to make the party bear the cost who can save it most efficiently. Applying this principle to the tort law system, for example, we can adopt the strict liability rule: if injurers have full knowledge of how to prevent damages, then they are responsible.

'Marginal interested parties' hypothesis

J. M. Ramseyer stated in his book, *Law and Economics* (Ramseyer, 1990), that when a significant discrepancy exists between the legal system and reality, a 'marginal interested party (MIP)' appears and takes on the role to fill the gap via an arbitrary transaction. An MIP is an outsider who temporarily enters a societal interaction and profits through opportunistic behavior.

It is economically rational for interested parties to cooperate with each other if they are involved in a long-term transaction relationship. With cooperative activities they can avoid the situation of a 'prisoner's dilemma' that would occur through a member's selfish behavior aimed at temporary profit. The cooperation is supported by a relationship of mutual trust between interested parties. Once a solid relationship is constructed, they can save the additional cost of monitoring one other.

In the traditional Japanese organized society (*'mura'*, community), the formation of trust was promoted automatically through cooperation among farmers. This formation and reliance on trust was an indispensable factor in increasing the total rice harvest.[10] When someone benefited by betraying the *'mura'*, they incurred a 'village ostracism penalty'[11] which was executed against that person, excluding him or her from the village's cooperative effort. Being in an isolated position in a *'mura'* community penalized the betrayer greatly and made living there difficult. Urushiyama (2001) pointed out that even after the beginning of modern economic growth this traditional social system is still active in many areas. Especially in the manufacturing process of Japanese firms, this cooperative system has been essential in raising productivity. Urushiyama has stressed that this is why Japanese manufacturing firms have been so successful in reaching a very competitive position in the world market.

This discussion of trust formation can also be interpreted in the context of the prior cost intensive system discussed in the previous section. Such trust formation is easily fulfilled in a society with homogeneous desires among its community members. If the prior cost for standardizing peoples' desires is less than the *ex-post-facto* monitoring cost for preventing divergence, the trust formation intensive society is preferred from an economic point of view. In this sense, a prior intensive society is consistent with a trust formation intensive society.

The recent trend of economic marketization and globalization has gradually been demolishing the stability of a trust intensive system in Japan. Progress in information technology has enlarged the market size and lowered transaction costs in the market, particularly in matching the costs of demand and supply. Buyers and sellers are able to find transaction partners all over the world easily through the Internet.[12] Anyone can access the market from anywhere and profit without prior examination. In fact, Japanese companies that have traditionally relied on transactions with group (*keiretsu*) members are now beginning to form fundamentally different business relationships. They try to anticipate buyers' needs from the market and make products and services as inexpensively as possible by shifting factories to countries with lower costs of production, and obtaining high-quality materials at the lowest prices.

There are large numbers of potential MIPs in Japan. The younger generation is considered to be the key to new opportunities. Young workers, who job-hop from company to company for higher salaries, are initiating change in the traditional lifetime employment system in Japan. Female workers, in many cases, have not received the same benefits and salaries as their male counterparts, even if they have similar talents and achieve similar results to male workers. Immigrants and other foreign residents in Japan have been discriminated against, not only in the labor market but also in daily life. Before the revision of the Alien Registration Law in 1999, all foreigners apart from diplomats who stayed in Japan for more than one year had an obligation to register their fingerprints. Even now the registration (except fingerprinting) is compulsory for them. After the registration process is completed, they are given certificates of 'registered immigrants' and are obliged to produce them upon request. Joint ventures and foreign companies, who are new entrants to the market, have to overcome such difficulties before making inroads into the traditional transaction system in Japan.

Increasing MIPs will put pressure on Japanese society to reform the traditional rule that limits the number of participants by prior examination and encourages cooperation among insiders. For example, long-term employment in the Japanese labor market, although it obviously violates the basic human right of equality, has hardly been revised. MIPs have been silent because of the high judicial cost and lack of public understanding. As these obstacles are removed, revolt against the traditional method is being seen, companies and governments are being sued for the violation of basic (human) rights, and people are regaining their lost benefits.

According to Ramseyer (1990), social standards that conflict with laws are repeatedly exposed to attack by MIPs and gradually change the approach to laws. However, MIPs do not always play a part in enforcing the law. Ota (2001) stressed that a certain number of people with a strong sense of justice and a few simple and honest people are necessary for the legal system to function properly. Some dishonest MIPs may enter the market where a contract law system is functioning and try to gain temporary profits through devious behavior. In such markets, we have to reinforce the *ex-post-facto* monitoring and reexamination process.

What 'Koizumi's structural reform' means

On 26 June 2003 the Koizumi administration announced the 'Basic Principles for Economic and Financial Management and Structural Reforms' which is often called the Large-boned Principle, or the Principle for short. This report aims at rebuilding the Japanese economy via the utilization of market mechanisms, and outlines the following seven reformation programs.

(1) Privatization and deregulation programs
  (1-1) Privatization of the postal service and reconsideration of public financial institutions
  (1-2) Introduction of the principle of competition into medical, nursing, welfare and education service sectors
  (1-3) Abolition of regulations that impede the free activities of private sectors
(2) Challenge supporting programs
  (2-1) Reinvestigation of institutional systems to support investors and entrepreneurs
  (2-2) Promotion of information technology (IT) innovation
(3) Insurance facilities reinforcing programs
  (3-1) Making the social security system understandable and reliable
  (3-2) Construction of a reliable pension system
  (3-3) Reduction of medical service costs, retaining the nationwide insurance system and free access to medical services
  (3-4) Control of increasing medical service costs for elderly people within a range of economic growth
(4) Intellectual property doubling programs
  (4-1) In order to utilize human capital more effectively in this science- and technology-intensive nation, double intellectual property in the fields of life sciences, IT, environment, nanotechnology and materials
  (4-2) Support ambitious individuals with substantial scholarships; encourage grants for education and research from the private sector
(5) Life restoration programs
  (5-1) Promotion of city life with multi-functional high-rise buildings
  (5-2) Construction of a female-worker-friendly society
  (5-3) Promotion of a barrier-free society
  (5-4) Planning toward an environmentally advanced country
  (5-5) Guarantee human security and public peace

(6) Self-reliance and invigoration programs for regional economies
   (6-1) Economic development by making use of region-specific strengths
   (6-2) Suspension of financial reliance on central government
   (6-3) Creation and maintenance of a 'beautiful Japan' policy
   (6-4) Structural reform of primary industries
(7) Financial reformation program
   (7-1) Improve excessively rigid allocation methods of budget.

The Large-boned Principle (the Principle) classifies these seven programs into three categories. Programs (1) and (2) aim at the construction of a society where individual personal efforts are rewarded. Programs (3) to (5) are concerned with quality of life and social safety nets. Programs (6) and (7) look toward strengthening government facilities and fundamental reform of the role-sharing between various governmental and private sectors.

In this section we evaluate the programs listed above, based on the discussions in the previous sections. As a whole, the Principle intends to reactivate the private sector and diminish the presence of the government in the economy. The basic method of reactivation is to give individuals more involvement and freedom in economic activities. Instead of distributing a little social support widely to everyone, more intensive support will be provided to those who are eager to achieve high levels of education, do more research, and start new businesses. At the same time, the government will refrain from participating in businesses such as the postal service, insurance, banking and toll road management, providing more business opportunities for the private sector.

In order to promote and realize individual initiatives appropriately, however, we need special facilities to ease high transaction costs and other market failure issues. Furthermore, since free competition inevitably accompanies risk, a system to ameliorate risk should be properly established. As is discussed earlier in the chapter, there are fundamentally two ways to solve these problems: (i) paying a prior cost to avoid failures and risks; or (ii) paying *ex-post-facto* costs after they occur. The Principle obviously attaches more importance to the latter. Instead of limiting participants in the market in advance, it encourages free entrants and checks their accomplishments by *ex-post-facto* examination. Advancing transparency in the social security system and the construction of a safety net system for some level of reemployment are necessary procedures to allow individuals willingly to take risks. Although this may induce possibilities of moral hazard, the Principle assumes that the overall benefits these new entrants will generate are much greater than the costs incurred through negligence.

Program (6) means a transfer of the governing authority from central to regional governments. The economic complexity of Japan is too great to be managed perfectly only by central government. Regions have their own specific characteristics, but laws and rules that are largely uniform over all regions manage them. Under the same conditions, an area that has an efficiently designed infrastructure and is blessed with good demographic and geographical conditions is in a very advantageous position. Because of political pressure from locally elected officials, central government has had to utilize part of the national budget to supplement the poorer prefectures that did not benefit as much from the high growth period as did other prefectures, but as a result of this dependence on central government funds, local areas have lost regional originality and autonomy. Now a governor's job is not so much to create new business opportunities but to acquire part of the central budget for local public works such as the construction of roads, bridges and airports. While the local financial structure cannot exist without support from central government, the national budget has also been placed in a deficit position because of long-term recession and active fiscal policy. This requires the government to reconsider the traditional budget reallocation system.

It should be noted that the budget distribution system in Japan has also adopted the prior cost intensive rule. Once a distribution rule is enacted in Parliament, it is never reconsidered again, even if *ex-post-facto* accomplishment appears to be very poor. It is pointed out frequently that the utilization rate of local infrastructure is quite low. *Ex post facto* reexamination of the plan has not been done at all in the case of public utility construction. If local governments are made more responsible for collecting taxes for public expenditure, the flexibility of budget utilization will be greatly improved.

Conclusions

In this chapter I have examined the features of the Japanese traditional social system and evaluated their compatibility with current circumstances. The core of the traditional system is standardization. The role of central government is to determine criteria in advance that provide basic information to evaluate and pre-judge the characteristics of resources and products. The private sector, placing its faith in government-produced rating information, can save transaction costs for monitoring other firms in the market. Although society pays the cost for prior investigation to determine criteria, *ex-post-facto* costs for reallocation and reexamination are not necessary.

In view of recent technological progress and its accompanying diversification and individualization, however, it is time to reconsider the traditional system. Weakened centripetal force of family organization, community and company has increased the prior cost for standardization. Even if a certain criterion is optimally determined for one situation, progress in technology and a shift in peoples' needs can easily make this criterion obsolescent. This chapter has presented typical examples where the prior cost intensive rule is collapsing and stresses a necessity to migrate toward more *ex-post-facto* cost intensive rules.

Another pressing function is the appearance of the 'marginal interested party (MIP)' defined in Ramseyer (1990). An MIP is someone from outside the traditional system and not bound to an existing relationship with an insider. In this sense, an MIP is expected to play a role in making Japan's traditional social system transparent and global.

Prime Minister Koizumi's structural reformation program, as detailed above, can be interpreted as supporting a shift from the prior cost intensive society to an *ex-post-facto* cost intensive society. In the process of this reformation, laws and rules will need to be modified to fit the target goals.

What is unfortunate for Japan is that the financial bubble appeared just when the Japanese economy was about to convert its direction from a government initiated economy to a market driven one. In the 1980s, public finance was greatly improved by reducing bond issues, and two large government enterprises – the Nippon Telegraph and Telephone Public Corporation and the Japanese National Railways – were privatized. However, the bubble economy lessened the mood of reform. Rising land and stock prices kept the Japanese economy enjoying the successes of high economic growth. Banks that should have raised the profitability of their business through qualitative improvement in loans, pursued traditional managerial strategies – that is, quantitative expansion of loans guaranteed only by land as collateral. As was discussed in detail in Nakajima *et al.* (2000), however, it was an illusion of apparent growth. Because of the bubble economy, Japan missed the perfect opportunity to institute reform.

One thing that should be mentioned in conclusion is about people's trust in the market mechanism. When business is on a healthy track, structural reform is never considered, although it is easy and costless to carry out reforms when business is good. The necessity of such a reform is only realized when serious economic turmoil occurs. However, reform under a recession causes much pain to people, because resource reallocation may temporarily raise unemployment. It is trust in the market, and not in the government, that is required if a reformation program is to be put in place. The problem is that Japan is still a socialist nation in the sense that people do not yet fully understand the real meaning of the market mechanism. We frequently see on TV people who are unemployed or who have lost money on the stock market asking the government to do something to help them. Some commentators on TV news shows criticize privatization or the abolition of the Housing Loan Corporation (HLC), allowing huge amounts of debt for housing loans, saying that the abolition means shutting the door to poor people wishing to buy their own homes. It is not widely known that the HLC's excessive lending and very low interest rates over incredibly long terms, which should only be implemented at a time of stability and high growth, caused these debts. What seems more predictable is that another destructive fall in the economy will happen in Japan while it is still in a state of confusion, and the Japanese people will suffer.

Notes

1   The official bank rate was lowered continuously from 4.5% in 1991 to 0.5% in 1995.
2   According to the report of the Ministry of General Affairs of Japan, at the end of 1999, the number of subscribers in Japan to the cellular phone network was 57 million. At that time 45% of the total population owned a cellular phone. Specifically, 62% of people in their twenties were subscribers to cellular phone networks.
3   It costs ¥72,000 (US $600) to subscribe to the NTT fixed telephone network. In addition to the subscription fee, there is a regular monthly charge, plus call fees.
4   NHK (2000) reports that, on average, Japanese children only spend six minutes per day at home talking with their parents.
5   Conflicts between individual wishes and public needs are occurring in public spaces, caused primarily by an attempt by individuals to make private space in public places. Talking on cellular phones on trains is now widely prohibited as a general rule.
6   There are seven classes (Classes 1 to 7) for those who are physically disabled and three (A, B1, B2) for learning disabled people.
7   Cooter and Ulen (1997) provide a basic theoretical framework of 'law and economics', a part of which is applicable to the discussion here. According to their explanation (ch. 5), while contract laws are suitable for the situation where prior negotiation cost is low enough to make a contract, a tort law is utilized for the people who are unable to make contracts because of a high negotiation cost. Although in the traditional Japanese 'village (*mura*)' society, contract law was more popular, collapsing regional communities caused by the economic growth gave more weight to tort law.

8   There is one reason why the Japanese government prefers the negligence rule. When accidents happen, victims often sue not only those who caused the injury, but also related government agencies on a charge of mismanagement. This custom gives an incentive for the government to set the range of negligence to avoid its own implication.

9   Disorder at home is brought into classrooms, but teachers have no idea how to control it. One traditional Japanese custom, on the second Monday in January, has regional communities holding ceremonies to celebrate the coming-of-age of 20-year-old men and women. Recently these ceremonies have often fallen into disarray because of the unconth manners of participants. According to news reports, they continue talking and drinking while the governor is making his congratulatory speech, even throwing trash at him. This phenomenon is a typical example showing the failure of the old Japanese social system. Parents and teachers have stopped paying the prior cost of upbringing. If prior cost is denied from the viewpoint of efficiency, we have to pay *ex-post-facto* cost to control them. If economic efficiency still supports prior cost, we need to establish a law that internalizes the social cost of turmoil to parents and teachers caused by their abandonment of a proper upbringing of their children.

10 See Urushiyama (2001) for more details about the relationship between the trust formation process and rice production in traditional agricultural villages of Japan.

11 The village ostracism at that time was called '*mura hachibu* (80%)', which means that a betrayer was not allowed to receive cooperation from other community members for eight out of ten activities; the only activities exempted are a funeral and a fire.

12 Yahoo's Internet auction provides a convenient way of selling used goods. Instead of having a garage sale, for example, people who are moving can easily find buyers for items they wish to dispose of before moving.

References

Cooter, R. D. and Ulen, T. S. (1997) *Law and Economics*, 2nd ed (Boston: Addison-Wesley).

Ihara, T. (2001) *400 nen burini nihono kaeru kigyo kaikaku* (Company's Revolution after 400-year Interval) (Tokyo: Toyo-keizai).

Nakajima, T., Nakamura, M. and Yoshioka, K. (2000) 'Japan's Economic Growth: Past and Present', in M. Nakamura (ed) *The Japanese Business and Economic System* (Basing stoke/New York: Palgrave/St. Martin's Press).

NHK Nihon Hoso Kyokai (2000) *Nihonjin no Seikatsujikan 2000* (Survey of Nation's Living Time) (Tokyo: NHK Institute of Broadcast and Culture).

Noguchi, Y. (1995) *1940 nen taisei* (System of the Year 1940) (Tokyo: Toyo-Keizai).

Ota, S. (2001) 'Consumer Contract Law: Honest and Dishonest Parties,' in M. Hosoe and S. Ota (eds), *Economic Analysis of Law* (Tokyo: Keiso Shobo), pp. 119–55.

Ramseyer, J. M. (1990) *Law and Economics* (Tokyo: Kobundo).

Urushiyama, O. (2001) *Kome tsukuri shakai to bijinesu shakai* (Rice farming society and business society) (Tokyo: Nikkei Business Press).

11
The Post-Bubble Japanese Business System and Globalization: Implications for Japanese Society

Masao Nakamura and Kozo Horiuchi

In its modern history since the mid-nineteenth century Japan has experienced a number of major events that caused fundamental changes to Japanese society. The Meiji Restoration in 1868 and the end of the Second World War in 1945 are undoubtedly two such events. For example, who was in control of political and economic power in Japan changed a great deal after these two events. At the same time, these events reshaped the feelings of ordinary Japanese people about their life – present and future. The supremacy of the controlling samurai ranks, together with the Japanese caste system,[1] were formally abolished in the Meiji Restoration, which encouraged the development of free thought and modern entrepreneurship. The Meiji Restoration opened up new possibilities for many Japanese to be connected, in terms of business and otherwise, directly to world affairs. After the Second World War, the major land reforms implemented by the Allied Forces, unprecedented in scale in world history, forced the massive transfer of ownership of agricultural land from landlords to contract farmers. The *zaibatsu* families,[2] who controlled their pyramids of enterprises and possessed much of the political and economic power in prewar Japan, were also disbanded by the Allied Forces.

While the wealth of the former *zaibatsu* families was literally driven down to a negligible level, corporations and banks under their control survived and formed powerful *keiretsu* groups, a unique Japanese institution of business organization that has shaped many of Japan's postwar industries. Undoubtedly the postwar developments in the Japanese economy, and Japanese society at large, were affected significantly by these reforms undertaken by the occupying Allied Forces.[3] However, despite significant efforts by the Allied Powers to change Japan's postwar institutions and social practices to conform with those prevailing in the West, certain things in Japan did not change in any fundamental way. The reliance of Japanese businesses on groupings such as *keiretsu* is one such example. There are no Western counterparts to *keiretsu*, which are likely to violate anti-trust laws in the both USA and the European Union (EU).[4]

The purpose of this chapter is to discuss certain changes that have taken place in Japan from the 1990s to the early 2000s, and discuss the implications of these for the globalization of Japanese society. One question of interest is, which of many of Japanese business practices will change to become more compatible with the US and Western European models. How Japanese society will cope with the present challenge to reform itself is also of interest. Our tentative conclusion is that, despite the globalization pressure to change many aspects of Japanese society, the Japanese business system will preserve certain key features of current postwar practices.[5] Any adoption of Western practices by Japan will be selective and evolutionary.

At the time of writing, many agree that Japan needs a significant restructuring of its practices in business, economy and society to return the Japanese economy to a normal state with minimum yet steady growth prospects. Japan has already paid a significant price for delaying the implementation of required changes to its business and social practices during the 1990s.[6] However, any significant change will be also very costly, since such a change would require readjustments of the existing equilibrium involving interrelationships and the associated distribution of power among people, firms, government and other actors in Japanese society.

The general globalization trends since the 1960s have put pressure on many countries, including Japan, to conform to global standards in many aspects of society, and these are often Western standards. We believe that the bursting of the financial bubble in 1990, which had started in the late 1980s in Japan, and the subsequent developments in Japanese business and social policies, will have a long-lasting impact on Japanese society. We do not yet know whether the impact of the bubble burst on Japanese society will be as widespread and deep-rooted as the impacts of the Meiji Restoration or the end of the Second World War. Nevertheless, by the early 2000s, the decade-long recession since the bursting of the bubble has forced many Japanese economic and business practices to change. Such changes have in turn forced Japanese people to lower their expectations significantly about what they can expect from their employers or the government over their lifetime.

While the financial bubble itself was to a large extent formed endogenously in Japan,[7] the environment for a bubble to form was created by the Bank of Japan's prolonged low interest and expanded money supply policies which were initiated in 1986 to prop up the Japanese economy, which was suffering at the time from a severe recession caused by the massive appreciation of the yen in 1986. (Following the Plaza Accord of January 1986, the yen appreciated rapidly against the US dollar, from ¥251 per US dollar at the beginning of 1985 to ¥122 per US dollar by the end of 1987.)[8] As the Bank of Japan failed to bring its interest and money supply gradually to normal levels, a financial bubble was able to form. The Bank of Japan's sudden and massive increase in interest rates resulted in the bursting of the bubble in late 1990. Unfortunately, the Bank of Japan did not respond adequately and promptly to the economic recession following the bursting of the bubble. The post-bubble period coincided with the increasingly intense global competition facing the Japanese economy. Yet Japanese banks and corporations, suffering from the aftermath of the massive amounts of bad investments made in the 1980s, could not channel enough new capital into preparing themselves to combat the global competition. And this global competition made it clear that the Japanese economy had to reform itself to regain competitiveness. Unfortunately, this reform, which involved both economic and political reform, had to be done in the midst of the post-bubble recession.

In our discussion below we shall pay attention to Japan's responses to the bursting of the bubble as the country tried to cope with the international pressure to globalize.[9] We are particularly interested in the impact of the bubble on the stability of Japanese society, and how changing Japanese practices compare with their Western counterparts.

The rest of this chapter is organized as follows. We first summarize the kinds of policy changes that have been taking place in Japanese business and more generally in the Japanese economy, in response to the post-bubble recession. These policy responses are often addressed not only at the post-bubble recession but also at Japan's aging population and globalization in general. We then discuss what types of impact these policy changes have had on firms, workers, households and Japanese society as a whole. We are also interested in the impact of business and economic policy changes on the Japanese people's expectations, and how they reacted to those changes.[10]

Changing business and economic conditions and globalization in Japan: the post-bubble period in the 1990s and 2000s

It is generally agreed that the failed Bank of Japan (BOJ), and Japanese government macro-economic policies, have forced the post-bubble recession to be prolonged unnecessarily.[11] The economic conditions were worsened by a serious deflation, the first of its kind to appear in world history in an economy as large as Japan's. Also during this period some of the Japanese industries that used to be globally competitive lost this competitiveness.[12] Japanese firms face the difficult task of reforming themselves to regain global competitiveness while little growth in the Japanese economy is expected and little capital is available from the Japanese banks, which are suffering from massive non-performing loans. The suggested reform consists of new business practices in industrial relations and labor management, supplier management and corporate governance. Such reform is needed to enable Japanese corporations to acquire skills and prepare themselves to deal with global competition when they can no longer expect an expanding domestic market. In addition, significant global pressure is being placed on Japan to introduce new environmental management practices that contribute to the creation of an environmentally friendly and sustainable society. Finally, aging, a demographic condition observed in many developed countries, is taking place at a particularly rapid pace in Japan.[13] Aging of the Japanese population, though predicted decades ago, is taxing Japanese households in terms of increasing government expenditure on health care and social security. The burden for these expenditures is expected to continue to increase over decades to come. One public policy issue is concerned with how to convince Japanese workers of the younger generations to bear the cost of the aging society when the young Japanese themselves face historically high unemployment levels.[14]

Changing Japanese business practices

Japanese business practices, often collectively termed 'Japanese management' attracted much attention in the 1980s. These practices evolved gradually after the Second World War based on conscious efforts by various stakeholders of Japan's firm sector. These practices, together with other aspects of the Japanese economy and society (for example, the education system), have co-existed in harmony in Japan since the late 1950s.[15] The severe post-bubble recession has forced many Japanese firms, workers and government officials to reevaluate the social equilibrium that had existed in Japanese life for more than four decades after the Second World War.[16] It is possible that various massive, and often fundamental, changes that are taking place in many aspects of Japanese business practices will change how Japanese people feel about their life and society in a significant way. From a societal point of view it is of interest how such changes in people's feelings are changing Japan's long-valued social stability.

Industrial relations[17]

In postwar Japan, firm managers have been constrained by the so-called 'three sacred treasures' of industrial relations: lifetime (or long-term) employment; the *nenko* (length-of-service reward) wage system; and enterprise unionism. These contemporary industrial relations practices developed over time as a result of the conscious efforts by both firms management and their workers to avoid the types of serious labour disputes that took place between the early 1900s and the 1950s (Fruin, 1983).[18] The severe decade-long recession from the 1990s and into the early 2000s prompted many Japanese firms either to modify or to give up some aspects of these practices. This will be discussed below.

Success stories

The benefits of the Japanese industrial relations system is most easily conveyed by examining some of these success stories (see, for example, Krafcik, 1988). In the automobile industry, for example, Toyota perfected its production system (sometimes called the just-in-time (JIT), or *kanban*, production system) by the early 1970s and then disseminated it to other Japanese competitors by the late 1970s. By the early 1980s, many Japanese manufacturers had adopted JIT. JIT inventory management requires that (i) all needed parts and/or semi-complete products are delivered to where they are needed, as they are needed and in the quantities needed; and (ii) a production flow is set up so that automobiles with various specifications are produced in sequence according to demand fluctuations. It is often the case that two successive vehicles produced on a production line are of different types. (See, for example, Lieberman and Asako, 1997 and Nakamura and Nakamura, 1989).

JIT inventory management, as implemented by Toyota and its parts suppliers requires close-to-zero defect rates in all stages of the production process in order for the system to run smoothly. To this end, production-line workers participate actively, often in teams, in solving local production problems. Thus separate repair and maintenance positions are eliminated. This cooperation is possible because the workers are familiar with many aspects of the production process and view cooperation in production management as being essential for their own long-term goals.[19]

Job rotation and on-the-job training combined with long-term employment security allow firms and workers to make long-run investments in workers' human capital; it can take as long as ten years to master some skills. Fewer job classifications are conducive to the multi-skill development of workers. It is generally the case that the number of job classifications for Japanese auto plants are fewer compared to the number in traditional Big Three plants. For example, in the mid-1980s, a Honda USA plant had three different job types – team leader, production and maintenance – while a typical GM plant had 95 job types (US General Accounting Office, 1988). A substantial amount of R & D takes place in Japanese auto plants to design production facilities that utilize fully multi-task production workers.

Japanese firms do not lay off workers except under extreme circumstances.[20] US employment indexes, for example, follow production indexes much more closely than is the case in Japan. Job security, which prevailed in Japan until the late 1990s, helped workers to accept new production technologies.[21]

Problems associated with Japanese industrial relations practices

Because of their industrial relations policies, personnel development in Japanese firms is carried out primarily through internal labour market policies. Managers and workers cooperate to develop employee skills through job rotation, on-the-job training and formal employer-supplied training. This is the case not only for production (blue-collar) workers but also for office (white-collar) workers. This system is believed to have helped Japan achieve its national goal of macro-economic growth, with the rewards of this growth being shared by workers, shareholders and other stakeholders of firms. This macro goal, however, is thought to have been largely achieved by the 1980s. Japanese industrial relations practices that were designed and implemented successfully in Japan's high-growth era are no longer suitable for the start of the twenty-first century, when Japanese society demands more variety: for example, more job opportunities for women, for disabled workers, older workers, ethnic minorities and other types of workers who are not young and middle-aged men (Japan's traditional regular workers);[22] labor markets for the growing number of workers who want to change jobs; and the accommodation of issues engendered by the internationalization of Japanese firms as well as Japanese society as a whole (for example, foreign workers, immigrants).

Secondary labour markets

It is customary for most Japanese firms to hire workers at the time they graduate from school. While Japanese firms do hire workers at various stages of their careers, the fraction of workers hired in mid-career is quite small compared, for example, with the practice in North America. Furthermore, the probability of a male worker changing his job voluntarily is considerably smaller in Japan than in Canada or the USA. This also implies that secondary labour markets in Japan are relatively weak compared to the primary labour market for new graduates. These patterns are consistent with the longer lengths of service with single employers observed for Japanese workers compared to US and Canadian workers.

An obvious implication of the weak secondary labour market in Japan is that it is difficult, if not impossible, for workers to adjust their employment to changes in their own tastes, preferences, qualifications and personal life-cycle planning without substantial wage loss. Also, training that is not provided or encouraged by the employer may not be rewarded within a firm's internal labour market. Yet workers who have obtained additional education or training on their own may not be able to find other positions where their efforts would be rewarded.

The lack of an adequate secondary labour market is a particularly serious problem for Japanese women, who often have to drop out of regular work to have children. These women have great difficulty in locating new jobs with pay commensurate with their qualifications when they wish to return to work.

Corporate groups (*keiretsu*)

There are two main types of corporate group in Japan: production-based corporate groups (sometimes called capital or vertical *keiretsu*) and bank-based corporate groups (sometimes called financial or horizontal *keiretsu*). The membership of these corporate groups often includes a number of foreign-affiliated firms. A production-based corporate group often consists of a major manufacturer and its much smaller supplier sub-contractors. Relationships between the manufacturer and its suppliers are based on economic transactions (for example, supplying parts) and are often quasi-permanent; the terms of transacting conditions (including prices) are often influenced by the relative bargaining power that the selling and buying firms have in bilateral negotiations (Aoki, 1988).[23]

For example, it was estimated that, in the late 1970s, Toyota had a direct relationship with 122 first-tier suppliers and an indirect one with

5,437 second-tier suppliers and 41,703 third-tier suppliers. The quasi-permanent nature of the Toyota group is illustrated by the fact that, between 1973 and 1984, only three firms ceased to be members of the association of Toyota's first-tier suppliers, while twenty-one firms joined the association (Aoki, 1988). In 1999, Toyota had 343 firms under its control, and additional sixty firms over which it had partial control. The largest company in the Toyota group is Denso, which began as Toyota's electrical equipment division. At the time of writing, Toyota owns 24 per cent of Denso.[24] Comparing the auto industry in Japan and the USA, it is often said that Toyota buys 80 per cent of its parts from outside, while GM makes 80 per cent inside.

Capital keiretsu (production-based vertical corporate groups)

The production-based corporate group is often characterized by the following factors: (i) ownership by the prime manufacturer (or the dominant company at the centre of a group) of small fractions of its subsidiaries or suppliers (typically 10–20 per cent of the total outstanding shares of first-tier suppliers); (ii) little or no ownership by the suppliers of their prime manufacturer's shares; (iii) long-run business associations based on vertical technological relations; and (iv) sub-contractors who often do business with other production-based corporate group companies (in fact, the prime manufacturer sometimes encourages its group suppliers to retain orders from firms outside the group for the purpose of attaining scale economies of production).

The prime manufacturer has a significant (and often overwhelming) influence on its group firms' corporate governance (for example, retaining the due shares of board directorship). The prime manufacturer, as the owner of large blocks of its group firms' shares and also as the primary customer of its group firms, can often dictate the group firms' plans for new investment, new product development and other business decisions. Provided that common long-term business goals and risk-sharing arrangements are agreed upon between a prime manufacturer and its supplier firms, a production-based corporate group can be an efficient producer of complex, assembly-based products such as cars and electrical/ electronic goods.

The advantages of a production-based corporate group over a vertically-integrated company include: (i) the size of each firm in the group, including supplier firms and the prime manufacturer firm, remains small and is therefore easier to manage; (ii) incentives for corporate performance are less likely to be lost in small, separate firms; and (iii) small firms pay lower wages. Long-term business relationships also allow the suppliers and the prime manufacturer to cooperate in activities such as developing parts for new products. On the other hand, it is not difficult to imagine that if the long-run goals of a prime manufacturer and its supplier firms are not well aligned in terms of incentive and risk-sharing schemes, then the corporate group may not function as well as would a vertically integrated firm.[25] Japanese firms have accumulated substantial knowhow in dealing with interfirm business relationships (see Fruin, 1992). Aoki (1988) discusses some types of interfirm contracts used in production-based groups. To date, these production-based corporate groups in Japan have been quite successful in the global market in the auto and electronics industries and other manufacturing industries.

Financial keiretsu *(bank-based or horizontal corporate groups)*

Until the recent major restructuring of the banking industry, which began in 1998 as a result of the massive non-performing loans carried by Japanese banks, there were six major city-bank-based corporate groups in Japan. These were Mitsubishi, Mitsui, Sumitomo, Fuji, Dai-Ichi Kangyo and Sanwa. Each of these banks created a financial *keiretsu* which still exists at the time of writing. Each group typically consists of (at least) one city bank, one trust bank, one general trading firm (Sogo Syosha) and firms in non-competing lines of business. There are, however, exceptions to this rule of general group membership, as a number of companies belong to several groups – for example, Hitachi Ltd belongs to three groups. Both the Mitsubishi and Mitsui groups have several group firms competing in the chemical and petrochemical industries. In 2002, Mitsui Bank and Sumitomo Bank merged to form the Mitsui Sumitomo Financial Group, and in 2003 the Fuji Bank, DKB and the Industrial Bank of Japan merged to form the Mizuho Financial Group. As a result, some reorganization took place of firms belonging to the former Mitsui and Sumitomo groupings discussed above (for example, formation of Mitsui Sumitomo Life Insurance and Mitsui Sumitomo Fire and Casualty Insurance) but to date no industrial firms in the former Mitsui, Sumitomo, Fuji and DKB bank groups have merged. Merger talk between Sumitomo Chemicals and Mitsui Chemicals (two of Japan's largest chemical companies) from the Mitsui and Sumitomo groups collapsed in March 2003. It appears that, for the moment, most of the member companies of the Mitsui and Sumitomo horizontal groups will continue their groupings with their respective general trading firms (Mitsui & Co. and Sumitomo Corp.) as the cores of their groups. So far little change has taken place in the Fuji and DKB groups either.

Main banks

Most listed Japanese firms, both independent (non-group) and group firms, have a main bank. ('Main bank' is not a legal term.) The main bank of a (client) firm is usually the largest bank shareholder of the client firm as well as its largest bank lender. It is profitable for a bank to be the main bank of an industrial firm, since it can charge interest on loans to firms in its group at interest rates that are above the market rate, and it also retains the business accounts of these firms which often carry no interest (Caves and Uekusa, 1976; Aoki, 1988).

When a client firm is faced with financial problems, however, its main bank is expected to take part in the management of the troubled firm on behalf of the syndicate of financial institutions involved with the firm, including other banks, and it is expected to absorb more than its proportional share of any loss. For example, the Sumitomo Bank wrote off ¥113.2 billion in 1977 when Ataka Industries failed because of, among other things, a major investment loss in a Newfoundland oil refinery. Nippon Light Metal, Alcan's listed subsidiary in Japan, also received substantial subsidies from its main and sub-main banks (the Daiichi Kangyo Bank and the Industrial Bank of Japan) during the 1970s and 1980s, when the Japanese aluminum industry went through restructuring (Sheard, 1991).

Generally, the main bank for bank-based corporate group firms is the bank at the centre of the group. The group bank and other financial institutions act as major, but not exclusive, financial intermediaries for group firms. Banks are allowed to hold up to 5 per cent of the equity in industrial firms and they often hold this upper limit in each group firm, while group firms hold equity in the bank as well. (It should be noted, however, that non-group firms and other banks also act as stable shareholders of group banks and firms.)

Because of their horizontal nature, covering many industries, bank-based corporate groups are often suspected of having (and exercising) considerable market power. However, others feel that the presence of independent competitors, as well as competitors in other bank-based groups, provides sufficient competition to keep bank-based group firms' profitability low relative to independent firms (Caves and Uekusa, 1976; Nakatani, 1984). Caves and Uekusa (1976) failed to find any monopsonic or monopoly power exercised by firms in bank-based corporate groups. While some preferential intragroup transactions seem to take place, for example, between general trading firms and steel producers, it is also the case that some of the strong producers in the automotive, electronics and other industries have chosen not to rely on general trading firms to distribute their products in domestic or overseas markets. Group firms' continuous profit maximization processes may not always lead to the preferential use of existing group firms. This seems consistent with the findings of Caves and Uekusa.

Although bank-based group firms' profitability may be somewhat lower, risk-sharing activities and a secure demand for their products from other group firms probably make profits more stable over time than is the case with independent companies. We should note that this risk-sharing or insurance aspect of a corporate group does not necessarily, of itself, make group firms more competitive.

Another function that both production-based and bank-based groups perform is to facilitate the movement of excess labour when, for example, some group firms in declining industries must scale down their operations. (Government policies encourage such intra-group transfers of redundant personnel, but this type of placement does not help to develop a transparent secondary labor market for such workers.)

Other inter-firm relationships

We have discussed two main types of corporate group found in Japan. It is important to note, however, that there are many other types of interfirm relationships in Japan, and Japanese firms, regardless of their more formal *keiretsu* affiliations, participate in these interfirm activities. Morgan and Morgan (1991, p. 171) note: 'The Japanese are the masters of partnering, and any large company has many investors and partners, relationships and contracts, consortium activities and joint projects. Never discount Japanese flexibility and interest in new opportunities.'

We have argued that the corporate groups and partnerships prevalent in Japan implement risk-sharing and incentive mechanisms which have a positive impact on long-run economic growth. Another, perhaps more important, contribution of the presence of corporate groups and possibilities for corporate alliances of different kinds in Japan is that this brings competition to markets where high monopoly rents are being earned. This type of competition among corporate groups was relied on in Japanese industrial policies in the 1960s (see Nakamura and Vertinsky, 1994, chs 4 and 5).

Keiretsu *and market access for foreign firms*

It is not difficult to imagine that many foreign firms trying to enter the Japanese market feel the potential difficulty in access to the Japanese market posed by Japanese corporate groupings and alliance practices. The US government has been arguing this point, particularly with respect to auto supplies, in its trade negotiations with Japan. No clear-cut strategy to deal with this type of non-visible trade barrier has yet been found for foreign firms affected in this way.[26]

Corporate governance

One aspect of Japanese firm behavior that is quite controversial is who really controls a Japanese firm. In the North American literature, the standard model of control is that a firm's shareholders delegate the responsibility to run a firm to hired managers and executives, who in turn work as the agents of the shareholders. The shareholders have the ultimate power for corporate control. When a company's management is not performing adequately, share prices become too low and that management may be replaced, possibly after a hostile takeover, with a resulting increase in share prices. Corporate control mechanisms in Japan are much more complex than this. The influences on the control mechanisms of a Japanese firm include workers on (implicit) long-term employment contracts, enterprise unions, other companies, banks and other financial institutions as stable (long-term) shareholders, the main bank, the core manufacturer in case of a vertical *keiretsu* group firm, as well as the management itself.

Workers on long-term employment contracts accumulate substantial firm-specific skills over time which are indispensable to the firm. They also have a serious stake in the firm's long-run performance. These concerns are often represented effectively by their enterprise unions. This implies, for example, that, under some circumstances, long-term employees can prevent a proposed merger of their firm with another firm.

Since large fractions (often up to 70 per cent) of most listed Japanese firms' outstanding shares are held by stable shareholders such as other companies, banks and other financial institutions that are expected not to behave in an opportunistic manner, individual and other investors who are hostile to the existing management can largely be ignored. A typical situation where a coalition of shareholders can effectively replace the existing management is when the firm's main bank and other banks and institutional shareholders decide that the present management is not acting in the interests of the large shareholders'. This may occur, for example, when a firm is in financial difficulty. The role of the main bank is particularly important in replacing the (incompetent) management, since, as it is a large shareholder of the firm and also the largest bank lender, it is expected to take a leading role in the management of its troubled client firm on behalf of the consortium of banks and other financial institutions that have loans outstanding to the firm. Morck and Nakamura (1999) present an empirical analysis of main banks' involvement in their troubled client firms, and conclude that in Japan the market for corporate control has been replaced by banks' involvement in the management of troubled firms.[27]

Because Japanese main banks are usually the largest bank shareholders and creditors, they have considerable power over their client firms' decisions regarding not only corporate governance but also corporate investment. This dual role played by Japanese banks as their client firms' creditors and shareholders is a potentially problematic practice when seen from the perspective of the client firms' individual shareholders, since the banks may always use their power as the largest shareholder (or one of the largest shareholders) of their client firms to promote their position as their (largest) creditors. It is quite possible that this type of behavior by Japanese banks has contributed significantly to the formation of Japan's ongoing bad-loan problem (see Morck and Nakamura, 2001).[28]

Legal environment in corporate governance: anti-trust and other issues in Japan

Japan's antitrust environment is characterized by its anti-monopoly laws which were introduced originally by the Allied Forces during their occupation of Japan after the Second World War. In addition, the commercial code and other laws stipulate the legal environment relevant for corporate governance in Japan. Holding companies were also prohibited at that time, and became legal as recently as 1997.[29]

Vertical keiretsu

Japanese manufacturers in particular have taken full advantage of their vertical corporate groups to achieve high levels of production efficiency. In this system of production, suppliers need to accept many of the demands (for example, scheduling and new product development) made by their core manufacturers, who are typically much bigger than the suppliers and hence have a much greater bargaining power. This may become in some cases almost like a master–slave relationship, which is viewed as being largely acceptable under the Japanese anti-monopoly law. Yet suppliers need to be part of such a vertical *keiretsu* group, since most core manufacturers require their suppliers to be part of their *keiretsu* group. Such a vertical *keiretsu* system is prohibited on anti-trust grounds in the USA and most other Western countries. In addition, the owners of smaller suppliers in the West typically demand freedom to make their own production and other business decisions, even though they may have large assemblers as their customers. For these reasons, in

Western countries, Japanese-type vertical *keiretsu* are not likely to be formed and hence manufacturers need to rely on independent suppliers or integrate themselves vertically.

Ownership of their client firms' equity by banks

The anti-monopoly law enacted by the Allied Forces also allowed banks to hold up to 5 per cent of the equity in other firms, but made no provision with regard to their behavior. Thus Japanese banks act as aggressive investors in their client firms from time to time. The 5 per cent limit was subsequently raised to 10 per cent, but then brought back to 5 per cent in 1987. However, this limit on bank ownership of other industrial firms was never effective because banks, if they so desired, could include shares held by other firms in their corporate groups for control purposes. As a result, main banks typically control the largest blocks of their client firms' outstanding shares. The exceptions to this include cases where the banks' client firms are members of vertical *keiretsu* groups. In such cases the core manufacturers of these firms usually own the largest blocks of their outstanding shares. The Japanese anti-monopoly law legally allows bank ownership of equity in other firms, including the banks' client firms; has allowed Japanese banks to form their own horizontal financial *keiretsu*; and to play the most important role as main banks in corporate governance in Japan. See Morck and Nakamura (1995, 2001) for further discussions of the historical developments of Japanese and other banks as universal banks.

In the USA, bank holding firms are also allowed to hold up to a 5 per cent of the equity in any industrial firm, but by law, bank holding firms in the USA are not permitted to be active shareholders involved in board decision-making in the firms of which they are part owners. Because of this legal constraint, very few US banks have an interest in holding equities in industrial firms. Canada has more relaxed rules about banks' holding of equities in other firms, but historically Canadian banks do not own equities in other industrial firms, and if they do, they are not involved in the active corporate control of these industrial firms. The stated reason for this is that Canadian banks find it unprofitable to become an aggressive equity investor in other industrial firms (Morck and Nakamura, 1995, 2001).

Globalization, Japanese businesses and Japanese society

Globalization has changed in several significant ways the way that Japanese businesses operate. The global relaxation of investment rules throughout the 1970s and 1980s enabled many Japanese companies to expand their overseas production facilities. Its foreign direct investment (FDI) made Japan the world's largest creditor nation. At the same time the developments in North America and Western Europe of such societal movements as deregulation, global environmentalism and individual rights became well known in Japan. But the new concepts involved in these overseas developments were not necessarily accepted or implemented in their original forms among the Japanese themselves. The new concepts, however, did begin to affect the behavior of the Japanese government, businesses, people and NGOs. In this section we shall discuss how some of these global developments in business and societal activities had an impact on Japanese firms, its economy and society. In particular, we focus our discussion on the impact on Japanese society of FDI, deregulation and environmentalism.

Foreign direct investment

US multinationals have developed standardized methods of localizing the management of their FDI operations over many decades, and they can therefore delegate significant portions of the management tasks of their FDI operations to local personnel.[30] On the other hand, Japanese multinationals still lack expertise in controlling local management and rely heavily on their own home office personnel to run their foreign operations. (Most Japanese firms' FDI operations became significant parts of their businesses in the 1980s.)[31] However, another major reason for this difference in the style of global management between Japanese and US multinationals is that, while US firms depend on market-based management practices, Japanese firms rely on firm-specific Japanese management practices.

For example, IBM Japan operates under IBM's global strategy, but its primary management functions are delegated to Japanese locals. Its CEO and president are typically Japanese. This style of management of US multinationals' subsidiaries is standardized to a large extent and is found not only in Japan but also in other countries. Few Japanese multinationals have adopted this model of management for their overseas subsidiaries.

Japanese multinationals' methods of management of their overseas operations are quite consistent with how they run their home operations. Japanese firms rely significantly on the in-house training of their workers over a long period of time in various aspects of the company's operations. Overseas management assignments are clearly part of such career developments for most of their employees at home and cannot be ignored.

Another reason is that Japanese firm operations are based on long-term *keiretsu* and other inter-firm relationships. Most Japanese firms believe that only employees with a long-term commitment to the firm are able to become familiar with the intricate fundamentals of interfirm relationships that are vital in managing their operations. Foreign locals are often thought to lack this kind of commitment to the company.

Knowledge transfer between multinationals' home operations and subsidiaries

It is well known that many multinationals transfer their knowledge on many aspects of company operations between their home operation and their overseas subsidiaries, or between the subsidiaries. It is not difficult to imagine that it is more difficult to transfer know-how, production methods or management skills than strictly scientific knowledge such as chemical or mathematical formulae. This is particularly so when significant differences exist in the economic environment (for example, how markets operate) and culture between the home and host countries. For example, workers and suppliers in the US markets operate very differently from their Japanese counterparts. This has been a significant barrier, for example, to many Japanese auto makers attempting to transfer their own just-in-time (JIT) production methods from their home operation to overseas bases, though such transfer is essential since their production methods are the source of their global competitiveness.[32] It is also of interest to ascertain to what extent Japanese multinationals did or did not transfer back their knowledge they learned from their US operations to their home operation.[33] For example, the types of equal employment laws and associated company employment practices that apply to female workers in the USA were never introduced in Japan, even though Japanese multinationals operating in the USA face these issues every day. Similarly, the types of flexible labor markets that could accommodate female and other mid-career job-seekers that are found in the USA are not (at least at the time of writing) developing in Japan.[34]

We have seen that, despite the globalization of Japanese multinationals' production activities, by design some knowledge from abroad is not transferred back to Japan. It is likely that the traditional culture and existing home-grown business practices, which fit better with the tastes and preferences of the Japanese, impede the rapid adoption and implementation of certain areas of knowledge into Japanese society. This seems to imply that the impact of globalization on Japanese society has limitations, and convergence in certain societal areas may not take place.

Hollowing out

One implication of Japanese companies' liberal foreign expansion, which became possible with globalization (and the relaxation of investment rules) has been that a significant part of domestic employment opportunity has been lost overseas. While there is a debate regarding the long-run net impact of Japanese firms' FDI on domestic employment, the short-run effects have been negative and have contributed to the persistently high unemployment rate in the 1990s and 2000s.[35]

Environment

One global issue that has generated much interest in Japan is the environment. Japan has had to cope with many environmental problems since the 1960s,[36] but has been successful to a large extent in raising its level of environmental awareness. Perhaps because of their own experiences, the Japanese are also very conscious of global environmentalism. As in Europe, Japanese consumers have become more concerned about the food they eat. One recent example is their preference for avoiding food made from genetically modified (GM) ingredients, such as tofu made from Monsanto's GM soybeans. In fact, virtually all soybean products sold in Japanese supermarkets are now made from non-GM soybeans.[37] An important current global environmental problem is global warming. Japan ratified the Kyoto protocol to manage emissions of global-warming gases in 2002 and is in the process of implementing its specific policy measures. Many, but not all, Japanese firms have shown an interest in becoming more environmentally friendly in their operations, as well as in the products they sell. Japanese and foreign customers of Japanese auto makers are given the choice of buying environmentally friendly cars, such as Toyota's Prius, at a price which is somewhat higher than ordinary cars. It is possible that Japanese firms may be able to make significant contributions to the development of new technologies that provide fuel efficiency for many areas of industry.[38] It is not yet the case, however, that Japanese firms have found environmentally friendly business practices profitable; however, they are hoping to make them pay in the long run. Their strategic success depends in particular on a strong leadership that believes in environmental management, and on their customers' preferences – especially Japanese customers' preferences for environmentally friendly products.

Environment and the Japanese auto industry

The top executives of leading Japanese firms understand that the survival of their firms is closely tied to their firms' global environmental strategies.

In these companies the top management is at the forefront of the firms' responses to these global issues. Typically, they lead middle managers and other employees in dealing with these issues. For this reason it is very important for firms to orientate their middle managers and other employees to the new environmental paradigm they face. The recent rapid introduction of ISO 14001 in Japanese firms, for example, has helped firms to achieve the goal of raising the awareness of their employees in understanding the new realities of the global environmental movement, even though the stated objective of ISO 14001 to continue to monitor and improve the firms' environmental management processes has been equally important.[39]

The Japanese auto industry is one of the industries in Japan that is proactive in dealing with environmental issues. Auto manufacturers in Japan, Europe and the USA face common fundamental problems: improvements in fuel consumption, reduction in nitrogen oxides emissions; and the promotion of the recycling of used car parts, all of which are important strategic issues in auto firm management. Companies' survival in the global market may well depend on how they perform among the keen competition to achieve these environmental goals.

For example, Toyota claims the preservation of the natural environment as one of the most important objectives of its management (Toyota, 1998). The company adopted a formal policy on the environment in 1992 which states that it is Toyota's mission to provide clean and safe products and to contribute, through its corporate activities, to the creation of a prosperous society and a pleasant earth to live in. Based on this policy, Toyota formalized its earth environmental constitution in 1992, which set out the following three basic principles: (i) overall treatment of the environment; (ii) the prevention of unexpected accidents; and (iii) contributions to society. In order to achieve these three basic principles, seven goals to guide Toyota's corporate behavior were implemented, and these goals in turn led to Toyota's environmental plan in 1993, consisting of twenty-two specific action plans. These action plans include, for example, the reduction in gas emissions, an improvement in mileage, and the development of clean-energy cars (Horiuchi and Nakamura, 2001).

In 1998, Toyota also established the Department of Environment consisting of environmental experts promoting environment improvement activities. The Environment Department reports to and advises the office of the CEO. Its functions include providing guidance on the company's overall environment policy, coordinating cross-functional conflicts in environmental policies, and serving as the secretariat to the various Committees on the environment. This is how Toyota implemented its framework in which the top management's strategies can be disseminated throughout the entire organization.

According to estimates calculated by the Japan Automobile Association for emissions of carbon dioxide throughout the lifecycle of an automobile with a 2000cc engine, about 88 per cent of the emission occurs while it is being driven, with the remaining 12 per cent occuring in the production and scrapping stages. For this reason Toyota prioritized the development of environmentally friendly engines, and in 1997 produced the Prius which is powered by a hybrid gasoline-electric engine. Prius attracted considerable interest in the Japanese auto market and received many prizes for its environmental friendliness and innovative design.

In December 2002, Honda and Toyota began selling their fuel-cell-motor-driven passenger cars, the first cars of this type in the world. This may be the beginning of a global race for auto makers to become the first company selling environmentally sustainable vehicles. Such companies must lead the world with their environmental management policies for coping with the problem of global warming, arguably the most important environmental problem of the early twenty-first century.

Shareholders and corporate governance

In the 1980s, Japanese methods of corporate governance relying on the role of the main bank as the firm's largest bank lender as well as a shareholder were thought to reduce significantly the agency cost caused by the deviation of the firm management's interests from those of the firm's shareholders. The main bank, as a large, informed shareholder of the firm, potentially could monitor the firm's management to make sure that the firm's shareholders' interests are protected. This notion that Japanese bank-based corporate governance leads to more efficient firm management was questioned significantly in the 1990s, when many Japanese corporations and banks became poor performers and lost competitiveness in the post-bubble recession.

Virtually all aspects of Japanese business practice were held responsible, and Japanese corporate governance in particular was criticized. The primary point at issue here is the rights of shareholders. Firms' shareholders by definition demand the maximizing of the market value of the firm in which they have shares. In the 1990s, the Japanese government instituted certain changes in the laws governing the accounting rules and management structures of firms, so that Japanese corporate governance would be more consistent with that of the USA. To protect shareholders, consolidated reporting is now required, and mandated quarterly reporting is being introduced.[40] In addition, firms are encouraged to have outside directors on their boards. The legal structure of company boards is also being revised, to be more consistent with the US model. Despite these reform movements in corporate governance, however, many Japanese firms, including ones that are performing well, are still opting to use the old governance methods.[41]

One of the main reasons for many Japanese industrial firms' reluctance to change their governance methods is that they are not yet fully convinced that the traditional style of governance was primarily responsible for the demise of the Japanese economy. Given that Japanese banks will continue to provide significant portions of capital the firms need, they cannot be ignored by firms' management or shareholders. Furthermore the banks are also large shareholders of many firms. No change is being contemplated in the parts of the Japanese anti-monopoly law that allow Japanese banks to be aggressive investors so long as their share of holdings in a firm is limited to 5 per cent. Many other aspects of interfirm relationships, particularly *keiretsu* relationships, seem still to be operational, though some firms have realigned their suppliers. As discussed earlier, the firm's workers have a significant voice on corporate management, particularly through their enterprise unions. Though the size of Japanese firms' regular (permanent) worker ranks has clearly shrunk, the firms' management still relies heavily on these workers to conduct their business.[42]

It is clearly premature to conclude that Japanese firms, or more broadly, Japanese society, have accepted the US style (Anglo-American) corporate governance method. It is, at the same time, safe to say that whatever emerges as a new corporate governance system in Japan will be some combination of the existing Japanese system and the imported US one. It is not likely that Japanese firms choose fully to operate on a US-type system, since such arrangements will not be compatible with many other aspects of Japanese business practices.[43] This again suggests the limitations of globalization.

We have discussed how globalization interacts with Japanese business practices. In the next section we discuss where Japanese business practices performed poorly during the recession in the 1990s and early 2000s, and where they have resulted in serious social problems.

Changing Japanese business practices: implications for economic performance and social stability, 1990s and 2000s

Japan is known for valuing stable relationships in society. There is also some empirical evidence that the Japanese as a people tend to be group-orientated and risk-averse.[44] The long-term employment practice and the industrial organization of the postwar Japanese economy, for example, reflect the behavioral preferences of Japanese people. Naturally, the erosion in recent years of some of these practices, which had existed in equilibrium for many years since the Second World War, has adverse implications for Japanese society. At the same time, despite strong global pressure to reform Japanese practices along the lines of those that are more consistent with Western-style practices, we argue that certain aspects of Japanese practices do not show many signs of changing. For example, the lack of a substantial labour market for skilled, mid-career workers, the closed nature of the markets for suppliers, and the lack of a market for corporate control all reflect special features of the Japanese business system.

In the following section we discuss the social implications of Japan's post-bubble economic reform in the 1990s and 2000s, and the limitations of globalizing certain Japanese business practices.

Labor markets

We have argued that many of the postwar Japanese management practices are based on long-term relationships, and these practices have helped to create a highly efficient production system in Japan. Another consequence is that the markets associated with such practices are often difficult for newcomers – foreign or Japanese – to crack.

Long-term employment practices make it difficult for mid-career job changers to locate new jobs, since secondary labour markets are very narrow, particularly for highly-skilled workers from large firms. Older workers made redundant face similar labor market conditions. Most large Japanese firms are not yet in a position to take advantage of available skill from outside the firms.

The massive layoffs of workers, unthinkable to the Japanese in the 1970s and 1980s, when workers were in short supply, took place in the 1990s as a result of restructuring and the failure of many of the Japanese businesses. As was pointed out above, the globalization of the world economy caused brutal competition across all areas of the Japanese economy[45] and accelerated both domestic layoffs and the loss of many manufacturing and R&D jobs to FDI operations in Asia. This process was accelerated by the massive non-performing loans that immobilized most of the Japanese banks throughout the 1990s and early 2000s. It is not clear at yet when many of these Japanese firms and financial institutions will return to a normal profitable position.

Because of the uncertainty facing Japanese employers, secure employment will continue to be scarce well into the 2000s. Yet there is no clear-cut sign that Japanese firms have given up their traditional long-term employment policy for their regular workers, though their seniority-based methods of promotion policy and compensation are being replaced to some extent by merit-based methods. Traditional bonus payments continue to be used for most Japanese employees, and these provide significant amounts of flexibility to firm management.

The massive layoffs happened typically to middle-aged as well as older workers. Given Japan's very narrow labor markets for older workers, it has been difficult for these laid-off workers to locate any jobs, let alone the types of jobs that pay salaries similar to those they used to get. This has created serious social problems in Japan. For example, suicides in Japan for economic reasons increased significantly in the late 1990s and early 2000s.[46]

In addition to the increased suicide rate, there are other social indicators which suggest the increasing presence of social unease in Japanese society. These include: (i) increasing distrust by the young in the future of Japan's public pension system; and (ii) an increasing number of Japanese people who feel worried and uneasy about their daily life. The Japanese public pension system requires all adults, including students and the unemployed, to pay into the system. Despite continuing increases in its premiums, the expected payout from the system for the retired has been decreasing. As a result, many young people have refused to pay their premiums in recent years. This problem is most serious for the national public pension fund that covers all individuals who are not covered by an employer-based pension system. For example, 37.2 per cent of those required to pay into the national public pension fund did not contribute to the plan in 2002, and unpaid premiums have reached ¥1,000 billion. The potential lack of, or an inadequate level of, future security is a primary source of unease among the Japanese. According to the government household survey undertaken in 2003, the fraction of Japanese who feel worried or uneasy about their daily life increased from 50 per cent in 1990 to 67 per cent in 2003. This clearly reflects Japanese households' deteriorating levels of confidence, for example, in their future social security and public health care, as well as an increasing level of mistrust in government policies.

One consequence of the restructuring process of the Japanese economy in the 1990s and 2000s is that the number of regular employees who enjoy long-term secure employment has declined considerably. Many workers who cannot obtain regular positions end up with temporary jobs, many of which do not add much to their skill profile. Public or private training programs are still not well established in Japan, where employers typically train their workers in-house over a long period of time. The lack of enough regular jobs has caused many young workers and new graduates to become unemployed, or very much under-employed. As discussed above, new graduates traditionally have the best chance of gaining employment, and the probability of finding regular employment diminishes as workers get older. The presence of a large number of young workers who are unemployed, or under-employed in temporary jobs, is of serious social concern. They may eventually be in the ranks of permanently unemployed and underemployed people, a situation Japan did not see in its postwar economy. This will cause a serious social problem, particularly if Japan cannot support these people by using public funds in the long run. Such a scenario could occur if the present severe budgetary deficits at all levels of government continue.

As was pointed out above, Japanese policy-makers believe that Japan's rapidly aging population and the associated decline in the size of the country's working population will also result in a serious social problem. They worry that it would be difficult for fewer workers to support the increasing number of aged people who will incur pension and health costs.[47] Interestingly enough, this policy concern ignores the presence of the potentially large number of unemployed or under-employed female workers, as well as older workers. As at the time of writing, no effective labor market policies have been put forward nor implemented by the Japanese government or companies to deal with this dilemma. We discussed earlier that some of the characteristics of postwar industrial relations practices discriminate against female and other workers who are forced to become mid-career job-seekers.

We believe that these employment problems are potentially a source of future social instability in Japan. The country's past policies that maintained a reasonably level income across its population by guaranteeing employment through government policy[48] do not seem to work any longer, given the massive number of unemployed workers and the inability of the Japanese economy to generate new employment in emerging industries.

We also point out that these unemployed or under-employed workers do not contribute to their own pension, or Japan's national pension or other income-maintenance programs, which will weaken Japan's future financial base for public programs.

The market for suppliers

Keiretsu relationships provided long-term interfirm relationships which shared business risks among companies and guaranteed prosperity for all the companies involved. The economic benefits of such interfirm relationships (particularly vertical *keiretsu*) appear to be significant, as was discussed above. Many Japanese suppliers enjoyed some form of affiliation with large assembler firms' vertical *keiretsu*, which in turn provided them with some level of guarantee for their output purchases, technology transfer and sharing of unforeseen business risks. In turn, the suppliers had less autonomy in their unequal relationships with their assembler firms. At this time most assembler firms continue to use their *keiretsu*-based suppliers, though the size of the supplier population has reduced. (Exceptions to this include the Nissan Motor Company.)[49] Clearly, most assembler firms still see some advantages of using such a *keiretsu* system of suppliers, though many of them complain that such *keiretsu*-based procurement imposes constraints on their business plans and hence reduces their global competitiveness.[50]

Some manufacturers, such as Toyota Motor, are tightening their grip on their *keiretsu* suppliers. As of 2003, we do not yet see any clear signs that Japanese-style *keiretsu*-based supplier networks are disappearing. This may be in part be because the alternative, an open US-type market for suppliers, has not yet developed in Japan. Unless many firms choose to abandon their *keiretsu* systems, development of such open markets may not occur.

Corporate governance and economic performance

Since the bursting of the bubble, the profitability of Japanese firms has been persistently low. This is in contrast to US firms, which recovered their profitability fairly quickly in the early 1990s after restructuring to achieve cost reductions. The long-term employment practices and corporate group mechanisms have been blamed as part of the reason why Japanese firms could not cut costs quickly enough, and why Japanese firms could not change their product lines fast enough to capture market shares for new products. We have already discussed the fact that Japanese firms have much less flexibility to lay off their workers. Vertical *keiretsu* relationships, which served Japanese manufacturing industries well in the high growth periods until the end of the 1980s, are also often viewed as a significant burden in the 1990s and the 2000s, because the core manufacturers are often obliged to use vertical *keiretsu* suppliers even if their production costs are much higher than those of independent suppliers in the global market. The recent dissolution by Nissan Motor of its *keiretsu* suppliers may illustrate this point.

Nissan's experience

Renault took over control of the Nissan Motor Company in March 1999, when Nissan was facing bankruptcy. After the take-over, the

Renault-appointed Nissan president, Carlos Ghosn, reduced Nissan's *keiretsu* significantly, and Ghosn's managerial competence is thought to be the chief reason for Nissan's speedy revival from its near-bankrupt state to the profitable performance current at the time of writing.[51] According to Ghosn, Japanese management is characterized by seniority-based wages, long-term employment practice and the concentration of management decision power in the hands of middle management (Ghosn, 2003). He argues that successful Japanese firms with global operations incorporate result-orientated global management practices[52] into their Japanese-style management, and that Nissan failed to do this before the Renault take-over. Ghosn clearly thinks the traditional *keiretsu*-based interfirm relationships are of questionable value. He sold all the shares Nissan held in financial institutions and other industrial firms, and has reduced the number of Nissan suppliers from 1,200 to 700. Ghosn thinks the relationship between a core assembler such as Nissan and its suppliers should be results-orientated and rely on trust. In this regard, he views Nissan's current relationship with Hitachi Ltd as its supplier as being ideal. Though they do not own any equity in each other's companies, Nissan can demand from Hitachi long-term reductions in the costs of parts, and improvements in the quality of parts. At the same time, Nissan co-operates with Hitachi's parts production.[53]

Ghosn's view of interfirm relationships in Japan is clearly not necessarily shared by all globally successful firms, including Toyota.[54] As a subsidiary of Renault, Nissan no longer has as large shareholders Japanese banks or firms which might demand certain supplier connections be maintained.[55] It is also possible that Renault wants Nissan to use certain suppliers. These may also be reasons why Ghosn was able to disband Nissan's *keiretsu*. It is of interest to see how Nissan continues to maintain its supplier firms. It is also of interest to see if any other major Japanese-owned assembler firms adopt the Ghosn-style management of their supplier firms.

Misalignment in vertical keiretsu group firms' objectives

Despite the advantages of vertical *keiretsu* over vertically integrated production operations, a manufacturer and its suppliers do not always share equally in the profit opportunities available to a production-based corporate group. It is known[56] that the windfall profits the Japanese auto industry enjoyed as a result of the 1981 US–Japan voluntary export restraint agreements benefited car manufacturers, large-scale manufactures of parts, and suppliers of specialized parts and services, but did not benefit many other suppliers. If the long-run goals of a prime manufacturer and its supplier firms were to diverge seriously for some reason, the production-based corporate group might no longer function as well as a vertically integrated firm. This misalignment in the goals of capital *keiretsu* firms is likely to be one of the most serious reasons for the prolonging of the current recession in Japan. Despite the implicit contracts of bonded assembler–supplier relationships, assembler firms have been trying globally to locate the lowest-cost non-*keiretsu* supplier where possible. At the same time, the assembler firms also have to expend much energy in developing *keiretsu* suppliers' technical skills required for new technologies.

Current realignments in process

Many Japanese firms, particularly those in the construction and real estate industries, have been in financial distress since the bursting of the bubble, causing a serious non-performing loan problem for their Japanese bank creditors. Yet there is empirical evidence that Japanese banks use their power as equity holders to enforce their rights as creditors of their client firms (Morck and Nakamura, 1995; Weinstein and Yafeh, 1998). For example, these banks encouraged their client firms to borrow funds from them in the 1980s. But once these loans turned sour in the 1990s, however, the banks have been reluctant to allow the prompt reorganization of the failing firms because of their vested interests in securing their loans. This aspect of the Japanese corporate governance system, which assigns relatively little weight to the rights of individual shareholders, served domestic-market-orientated Japan well until the 1980s but has not been functioning satisfactorily in contemporary Japan, which is exposed to the competitive pressure arising from globalization. The conflict between firms' shareholders and creditors is more significant in Japan now than before, and the lack of a realistic process to resolve this conflict promptly under the present Japanese corporate governance system is another reason for the slowness to complete the current effort to restructure the Japanese economy (Nakamura, 2002).

Their poor performance because of the post-bubble bad debt problem forced the established Japanese banks, both national and regional, to consider merging with each other in the 2000–01 period. While some proposed mergers are more group-specific (for example, the merger of the Bank of Tokyo-Mitsubishi with the Mitsubishi Trust Bank, and the merger of the Sanwa and Tokai Banks and the Toyo Trust Bank), some others are across the traditional *keiretsu* groupings (for example, the merger of the Sumitomo and Sakura Banks, and the merger of the Fuji and Daiichi Kangyo Banks with the Industrial Bank of Japan). The effort to complete new groupings by Japanese banks and other financial institutions will undoubtedly continue further into the twenty-first century. It remains to be seen, however, whether the newly emerging financial *keiretsu* will behave differently than their predecessors in the twentieth century in resolving the conflict of interest between creditors and shareholders.

Can the Japanese corporate governance system cope with the diverse interests of its constituents?

One policy problem the Japanese public and private sectors must now solve is the formulation of a logical basis (a conceptual framework) for developing practical methods of dealing with diverse needs and interests of their respective constituents, such as taxpayers, workers, shareholders, debt holders and customers. Japanese society demands more diverse varieties than ever before in educational and employment opportunities, investment opportunities and the like, but the existing institutions, both government and corporations, continue to behave according to their norms developed between the 1960s and the 1980s. Revised Japanese corporate governance practices must be compatible with these diverse interests of the public. Unfortunately this has not yet been achieved.

The market for corporate control: factors discouraging both friendly and hostile large-scale mergers to improve efficiency

Large Japanese firms have long-term employees who have accumulated substantial firm-specific skills. This deters both friendly and hostile mergers between large firms because of the extreme difficulty in combining two firms with different firm-specific practices.[57] These factors explain why there is no market for corporate control, at least for large firms, in Japan.

The high level of firm-specificity in management methods and personnel management cultured by long-term employment at Japanese firms makes it very difficult for two separate firms (even in the same financial *keiretsu* group) to have a friendly merger, let alone a hostile merger. That is, long-term employment practices and associated management practices represent a barrier to mergers between Japanese firms, and the height of this barrier increases with the size of a potential merger.

For example, in 1971, when the Daiichi Bank and Kangyo Bank joined in a friendly merger to form the Daiichi-Kangyo Bank (DKB), no employee of either the Daiichi or the Kangyo Bank was laid off. DKB maintained intact the two personnel management systems inherited from the former Daiichi and Kangyo Banks for ten years, during which period the former employees of the Daiichi Bank and the Kangyo Bank were assessed and promoted according to their former respective banks' personnel management criteria. Many financial analysts cite the merger as a source of DKB's inefficiency (for example, lower profits per worker) relative to its competitors. Other examples of this sort include the mergers involving Yawata Steel and Fuji Steel in 1970 (to form Nippon Steel), and the Mitsui Bank and the Taiyo Kobe Bank (to form the Sakura Bank). In the 1990s, failed friendly merger attempts include those between the Mitsui Chemicals and Sumitomo Chemicals (both in the chemical products industry) and Sega and Sammy (in the entertaiment/computer game industry).

Firm-specificity in management is not the only barrier to large-scale mergers in Japan, however. Large fractions of listed Japanese firms' outstanding shares are held by stable shareholders. Because of this, individual and other investors who are hostile to the existing management can usually be, and are, ignored. Long-term investments in workers' human capital by both firms and workers might be worthless if a sudden change in firm management policy occurred as a result, for example, of a hostile take-over. Stable shareholding practices help to provide long-run protection for human capital investments.

Stable shareholding practices and the high level of firm specificity in personnel and other management methods are two important reasons why there is virtually no market for corporate control in Japan, particularly for large firms. Foreign firms generally cannot count on being able to purchase large Japanese firms outright in order to gain entry to the Japanese market.[58] This is in contrast to some purchases by Japanese firms of large US corporations that took place in the 1980s.

Because of the relatively slight weight that Japanese firms give external shareholders who are not part of stable shareholding arrangements, Japanese firms' boards of directors are mainly company executives, with the company CEO being the chairman of the board.[59] In the USA, the board often exercises its power to restructure a firm's management when the firm is under-performing compared to its industry peers. Board oversight does not function well, however, when all firms in an industry are performing poorly (that is, under-performing against the economy). It is in this latter case that a hostile takeover, or the threat of it, disciplines the firm's management.

In Japan, board oversight of a firm's management is not effective because most directors of the board are executives in the company management team. Unlike the case in the USA, there is no market for corporate control that could discipline a firm's management when the entire industry is doing poorly.[60]

Faced with poor management performance, it is the larger shareholders, such as the main bank and other related firms, that play a disciplining, or propping-up, role in Japan. (Large, informed shareholders can enhance firms' value (Morck *et al.*, 2000; Shleifer and Vishny, 1986).) The role of a firm's main bank is particularly crucial. As discussed above, Japanese banks' dual role as many firms' shareholders and creditors is not necessarily desirable from the point of view of shareholder value maximization, the standard criterion for firms' managers in the West. It is suspected that this dual role of Japanese banks is used by the banks to promote their positions as creditors, and hence undermines the performance of their client firms (Morck and Nakamura, 2001).

Concluding remarks

The Japanese business system in the 1980s before the bursting of the financial bubble was in equilibrium. This means that, in order to bring about restructuring to achieve a better equilibrium, it is not sufficient simply to undertake marginal or unidimensional adjustments to specific practices. Comprehensive changes would be needed, and these would become possible only when the Japanese business system as a whole finds them to be in its own interest. It may require simultaneous radical change in many market elements of the system.

For example, to promote more large-scale friendly mergers would require a significant relaxation of the current long-term-based employment system and the development of secondary labor markets. At the time of writing, many Japanese firms, which have been suffering from serious global competition, have removed or modified downward automatic wage increases related to workers' seniority, but little systematic change seems to have taken place in terms of long-term employment practices.[61] This implies that continuing importance is being placed on firm-specific worker skills. In these circumstances, labor mobility still seems to be constrained, and well-functioning secondary labor markets do not appear to be developing. Also, workers may continue to have a strong input into firms' corporate governance decisions such as mergers with other firms.

A new corporate governance system and an emerging market for corporate control?

Some large and competitive firms have switched their financing method from the traditional indirect bank financing to direct financing from domestic and foreign capital markets. (Direct financing by ordinary corporations has recently largely been deregulated.) Nevertheless, Japanese banks still provide significant parts of Japanese firms' capital needs (Nakamura, 2002). Main banks still play an important role in dealing with their client firms' financial difficulties. If many of what the Japanese banks regard as desirable client firms were to desert them in favor of direct financing, the main bank system would become less profitable to the banks: then they might decide to abandon it. Even with such a scenario, however, Japanese banks would probably try to retain their dual role as creditors and shareholders in some form, since doing so is legal, and to be an active investor in their client firms would allow banks to reap extra profits as creditors from these firms.

The prolonged recession has seriously eroded the power enjoyed by Japanese workers and labor unions. Major firms employ considerably fewer regular employees, and the continuing pressures to downsize have also reduced the extent of the workforce among Japanese firms. The administrators of the proposed large-scale mergers say that they would not be able to tolerate the 'two-companies under one roof' approach that was used consistently in earlier large-scale mergers. Where immediate economic efficiency becomes an important criterion for successful mergers, the Japanese market for corporate control allows the entry of foreign firms into the market – for example, to act as acquirers of Japanese firms. Historically, foreign firms could come in during a recession period and purchase failing Japanese firms that no Japanese firm would rescue. This has happened in both the finance and the manufacturing sectors. For example, many Japanese automobile manufacturers, anticipating serious cash flow problems in meeting required massive investments in the environment in the near future, have given up their control to foreign competitors. Now Nissan is controlled by Renault, Mazda by Ford, Mitsubishi Motor Company by Daimler-Chrysler, and Fuji and Isuzu by GM. Only Toyota and Honda are entirely Japanese-controlled (see Horiuchi and Nakamura, 2001). The question still remains regarding whether or not the current flow of foreign capital to buy into failing Japanese firms represents a permanent change in the Japanese system (in both private practice and public policy) for corporate control in the Japanese market.

What will change?

We have argued that some of these Japanese management practices and policies are not about to change, despite the current severe and prolonged recession. For example, Kato (2001) finds that participatory management – one of the key industrial relations practices in Japan – is still widely used in Japanese firms. At the same time, many Japanese management practices have begun to incorporate Western (particularly US) practices. So which aspects of the Japanese system are likely to change first?

Historically, the Japanese system has been based on some forms of risk-sharing, with such arrangements often taking a private form. One could view Japanese practices, such as bonus payments, *keiretsu*, and even business–government relations, as part of the contemporary risk-sharing system that functioned successfully in the postwar period. Successful risk-sharing mechanisms increase economic efficiency. (See Korkie and Nakamura (1997) for an estimate of *keiretsus'* portfolio diversification effects in the stock market.) The Japanese risk-sharing system was successful because the private incentives and, more broadly, incentives at the corporate and national levels of risk-sharing practices were well aligned.

This type of private alignment of risk-sharing seems to have been eroded during the 1990s, and clearly some forms of risk-sharing arrangements, involving perhaps the public sector, are required. What kinds of public arrangements, for example, will replace the failing parts of the existing private risk-sharing system which is at the root of the current policy debate in Japan?[62] It seems likely that, with an introduction of some type of public mechanism to support redundant workers, Japanese society will begin to accept short-term employment and more frequent layoffs. In fact, the current spread of short-term employment contracts may be consistent with this. On the other hand, the *keiretsu* practice, whether capital or bank based, does not appear to be vanishing; it appears only to be being reshaped and refocused toward group goals.

In conclusion, the Japanese system will continue to explore various configurations until it finds one that is satisfactory to all the participants of the system. Until then, Japan may continue to appear less confident and experimental, and experience low economic growth, which reflects the cost of adjustment to a new equilibrium.

Notes

1   For a few hundred years up to the Meiji Restoration, the Tokugawa Shogunate maintained the rigid feudal rankings of social classes, with the samurai ranks at the top, followed by farmers, craftsmen and merchants.

2   Well-known pre-Second World War *zaibatsu* families include Mitsui, Iwasaki (Mitsubishi *zaibatsu*), Sumitomo and Yasuda.

3   Broadly speaking, the following two factors contributed to Japan's rapid postwar economic growth: (i) the three major domestic reforms (*zaibatsu* dissolution, land reform and liberalization of labor movements – for example, the legalization

of labor unions) undertaken by the Allied Forces democratized Japanese society, and hence social mobility, unprecedented in Japan's prewar I history became a reality; (ii) the postwar adoption by the world economic powers of the IMF–GATT system as a global framework for international trade promoted world economic growth and allowed the Japanese economy to grow rapidly in the 1960s without generating any serious trade friction with its trading partners (Horiuchi, 1993).

4 One important factor that allowed the *keiretsu* groupings to form in the late 1940s and early 1950s was that the Allied Forces did not include Japanese banks in their dissolution list. In addition, the Allied Powers also allowed Japanese banks to own limited amounts of equity in their client and other industrial firms for control purposes, a practice that is prohibited in the USA. See, for example, Morck and Nakamura (2003).

5 These include risk-sharing and group-based business organizations.

6 This is not to say that Japan necessarily knows what to do. In fact, one of the primary reasons for the delay is that Japan is still searching for a new set of practices to form a new social balance to replace the postwar equilibrium that served the country well up to the end of the 1980s.

7 The primary cause of the bubble was greed. Both Japanese investors (including many households) and corporations thought they could obtain high returns from many of their investments in land and stocks, among other assets, and continued investment in these assets. Much of their investment capital was debt from Japanese banks, which were more than willing to lend money, using the inflated value of land and stocks as collateral. However, the Bank of Japan's sudden increase in interest rates put an end to the bubble. This process of the growth of a financial bubble has been repeated many times in world history (see, for example, MacKay, 1841) and unfortunately may well be repeated in the future.

8 We should note, however, that the US high dollar policy adopted within the 'Reaganomics' environment in the early 1980s also contributed to the rapid appreciation of the Japanese yen after the Plaza Accord.

9 Such globalization pressure is not limited to business and economic activities. For example, throughout the 1990s and the 2000s, both during and after the Gulf and Iraqi Wars, Japan has been subjected to continuing pressure internationally to contribute military forces for global peace-keeping purposes. However, the current Japanese constitution is not fully compatible with Japan's liberal participation in such global peace-keeping activities.

10 Most of Japan's major policy changes in the post-bubble recession era have been tied to the country's responses to economic and social problems caused by the recession.

11 For example, the BOJ's low interest and lenient money supply policy following the Plaza Accord in 1986 lasted too long and resulted in the formation of a bubble. The BOJ's policy change to increase interest rates burst the bubble, but then its lack of policy to combat the rapid deterioration of economic activities following the policy change simply worsened the recession. The recession was further deepened by the Japanese government's decision to increase its consumption tax rate from 3 per cent to 5 per cent on 1 April 1997. The deflationary trend that followed continued into the 2000s. No other country with an economy as large as Japan's ever experienced the kind

of massive deflation in price levels as Japan did from the late 1990s. Unfortunately, the BOJ has been resisting taking effective measures, arguing that such measures would invite uncontrollable inflation.

12   The most notable one is Japan's semiconductor industry, which at one point in the 1980s was the most competitive in the world. But other industries and companies, including Japanese banks, and machinery, electrical appliance, computer and communication equipment industries lost their global standing dramatically in the 1990s after the bursting of the bubble.

13   The Japanese birthrate began to decline steadily in the 1970s and has never recovered. At the same time, the Japanese death rate has continued to decline for many decades. The net change for Japan, however, is negative population growth. Japan's National Institute of Population and Social Security (2002) predicts that the Japanese population will start to decline at the earliest by 2009.

14   Japan's unemployment rate increased from 2.2% in 1992 to 5.4% in 2002. In 2002, the unemployment rate for the age group 15–24 was 9.9%, the highest among all the age groups. Older workers (age group 55–64) also have an unemployment rate of 5.9% – above the national average. In particular, the unemployment rate for men in this age group is quite high (7.1%). The high unemployment rates for both young and older workers are a serious source of social concern.

15   Such harmony does not imply fair distributions, for example, of *ex ante* work opportunities or *ex post* work benefits among all the participants in the Japanese system.

16   See, for example, Nakamura (2000, ch.1).

17   For a more detailed analysis of this topic, see Nakamura *et al.* (2003) and Nakamura (1993).

18   It should be pointed out that these three pertinent features of industrial relations practices were observed primarily for the sorts of jobs that have traditionally been filled by men in their prime. Many women, older workers and foreign workers are in jobs where this is not the case.

19   The multi-task capabilities of workers are also relied on in combining the production of cars of different types. Producing a passenger car of type A followed by, say, a station wagon of type B on the same production line requires the retooling of press machines in a very short time. Workers skilled in a variety of tasks make it possible to design a production line where cars of different types are produced in accord with the time-varying demand distributions for these types of cars. Flexible manufacturing of this sort contributes to high capacity utilization rates which, in turn, lead to high productivity gains compared to North American companies (see, for example, Fuss and Waverman, 1990). On the other hand, some US firms implemented JIT on a selective basis in their own ways and improved their productivity performance successfully (Nakamura *et al.* (1998)).

20   This still seems true for the core workforce (regular employees) of many Japanese firms, but the number of those covered by this no-layoff practice has been declining. Contemporary Japanese labor laws require considerable efforts by employers to justify layoffs among their workers. This has been one factor preventing more extensive layoffs in Japan. However, the recession in the 1990s and early 2000s has faced Japan with such extreme adverse

circumstances that many firms, some more successfully than others, have implemented redundancies.

21 This may partially explain why Japanese factories are now equipped with large numbers of industrial robots compared to their Western counterparts. In 1989, the estimated numbers of operating industrial robots (excluding fixed sequence robots) were: 219,700 for Japan; 37,000 for the USA; 22,395 for (West) Germany; 7,063 for France; 7,463 for Sweden; and 5,908 for the UK.

22 High-paying jobs are generally available only to those workers with long seniority who have been given increasingly challenging assignments. It is expected that women will have intermittent career patterns, to allow for child-bearing and rearing. As a consequence, female workers interested in pursuing demanding careers are likely to be (and often are) subjected to statistical discrimination by employers. Unfortunately, Japan's Equal Employment Opportunity Law of 1986 (revised in 1999) has no enforcement provisions.

23 Firm groups of this type exist in the US auto industry, but on a much smaller scale than in the Japanese auto industry.

24 Other Japanese firms with large vertical *keiretsu* groups include Hitachi, Matsushita, Sony, Honda, Toshiba, Fujitsu, Bridgestone and NEC. After Renault took over control of Nissan Motor, Nissan is said to have dissolved its production *keiretsu*.

25 It is well known that Toyota has been trying, unsuccessfully, to take away some of Denso's highly profitable auto electrical components business (for example, GPS navigators). Electrical components have become the most important part (in terms of value added) of automobile output in recent years. In response, Toyota has been trying to strengthen its control over Denso and set up a joint venture with Toshiba to produce automotive electrical components (Toshiba and Toyota both belong to the Mitsui group – a horizontal *keiretsu* group).

26 Many foreign firms of different sizes that have established successful operations in Japan have succeeded in developing long-term relationships with Japanese firms, distributors and/or customers. Some of these relationships take the form of corporate groups. The lesson of these successful operations may be 'if we can't beat them, let's join them'. It should also be pointed out that the successful operations of foreign firms in Japan may have different forms of ownership structure: fully owned, or jointly owned subsidiaries. There are several corporate groups (vertical *keiretsu*) involving foreign firms' subsidiaries which are either fully owned by foreign parent firms or jointly owned by both foreign and Japanese parent firms (See Nakamura and Vertinsky, 1994, ch. 6; and Lawrence, 1993).

27 It is important to note that Japanese banks have been reducing their holdings in many client firms since the 1990s, so their financial performance becomes less dependent on stock market fluctuations. The massive non-performing loan problem and the recent change in accounting rules require firms and banks to include unrealized gains (losses) from their financial assets, including stocks at market value, in their financial statements. For example, during the 1990s, large Japanese banks sold off part or all of the equity they held in 1,600 out of the 3,500 client firms with which they had cross-holding arrangements. Interestingly, these client firms rarely sold off their banks'

shares. We should also note, however, that, despite this steady decline in the equity holding of Japanese banks, Japanese firms' dependence on bank loans as a source of capital have been increasing during the 1990s and early 2000s.

28   Since transparent financial disclosure is not required of Japanese banks, the total amounts of non-performing loans held by Japanese banks are still unclear, but they are estimated to be equivalent to hundreds of billions of dollars and are still increasing under the present deflation. A number of large Japanese banks failed in the 1990s and more are likely to fail in the future. Although they have been reluctant to do so, it is most likely that Japanese taxpayers will, in the end, have to absorb most of these non-performing loans. The large Japanese banks have always had a powerful political base in the Japanese government and Parliament, and a political victory by which they could transfer most of their non-performing loans to the taxpayers without much sacrifice on their part is quite possible.

29   Subject to certain conditions. For example, financial institutions as holding companies are not allowed to own companies from other industries, as was done by pre-Second World War *zaibatsu* groups. Another recently implemented provision is that Japanese firms are now allowed to buy back their own shares.

30   This also applies to most multinationals from Western European countries.

31   Exceptions include Japanese trading firms such as Mitsui & Co., which has, for example, kept its own importing and exporting operations since the early 1900s. Nevertheless, their overseas operations are still organized and controlled by their head office in Tokyo, and most of the key management personnel in their foreign operations are Japanese nationals.

32   See, for example, Nakamura *et al.* (1998, 1999).

33   Japan has always been selective in the types of knowledge that are allowed into the domestic system from abroad.

34   As mentioned above, such flexible labor markets could help Japan to get out of the current decade-long recession.

35   Some FDI projects are designed specifically to serve currently unserved customers abroad and may increase domestic employment because of the gains, for example, in parts exports. If the foreign market is already served by exports from Japan, FDI investments in that country will replace such exports and hence eliminate the demand for the domestic labor that used to be engaged in producing the exported items. Another argument for outward FDI is that, by allowing certain operations to go abroad, the resources committed to the old industry could become available for use by newer emerging industries.

36   These include air pollution in major cities and industrialized areas, water pollution caused by pulp mills, and mercury poisoning in Minamata.

37   This has created a new market for the farmers who grow non-genetically modified soybeans in the USA and China. Such soybeans are exported to Japan in significant quantities.

38   Japan did improve its energy efficiency considerably during the 1970s and early 1980s, when Japan faced two oil shocks that had a serious negative impact on the Japanese economy.

39   See Nakamura *et al.* (2002).

40   Interestingly enough, Japan, noting the problems of short-sighted management increasing short-run share prices, abandoned the quarterly reporting requirement in the 1970s to enable firms to focus on long-term business planning.

41 Japanese firms have significant legal flexibility in choosing the forms of their governance. According to the July 2003 survey of 876 Japanese firms by the Japanese Ministry of Finance, about 36% of these firms have appointed outside directors, an increase of 5% over the previous survey in 1999. About 40% of these outside directors appointed, however, come from the firms' parent firms, *keiretsu* group firms and main banks. These figures show that many Japanese firms are still using inside directors exclusively, and many of the outside directors appointed at other firms come from traditional *keiretsu* connections. Such outside appointments may be interpreted as reflecting the firms' intentions to strengthen their *keiretsu* ties.

42 Little is understood about the implications of the long-term employment practice with associated internal promotion system for firms' long-run perform-ance. Anecdotal evidence seems to suggest, however, that such a practice works better for industries with competitive product markets (for example, auto-mobiles, electronics) than for industries with highly protected product markets (for example, communications, utilities).

43 As discussed above, these include banks, suppliers and workers, among other actors in the Japanese corporate governance system, all of whom have significant power over the firm's management.

44 See, for example, Hofstede (1983) and Reischauer (1988, ch. 13).

45 The global competition forced Japanese firms in the industries where they were traditionally highly competitive, such as electronics and machinery, to downsize and restructure. These firms (for example Hitachi, Toshiba, Sony, NEC, Fujitsu) are, at the time of writing, still struggling to return to profitability.

46 The number of suicides in Japan ranged between 20,000 and 24,000 for the period 1978–97, but increased significantly in the late 1990s to 32,863 (in 1998), 30,3048 (in 1999) and 32,143 (in 2002). About 45% of those who commit suicide do so for economic reasons. Also, about 53% of those who commit suicide are in the prime-working-age group (30–50 years old) (Japanese Police Agency, 2003).

47 A similar policy issue involving the intergenerational conflict of interest exists, to a less degree, in Germany (Ewing, 2003).

48 This is seen, for example, in Japanese policies towards agriculture.

49 We shall discuss the Nissan experience below.

50 Production-based corporate group firms tend to buy and sell goods among themselves more than through external markets. This characteristic would not be viewed as a market problem if the group supplier firms were owned by the prime manufacturer, since group transactions would simply become the prime manufacturer's intra-firm transactions. Since most group supplier firms are independent firms which transact with the group's prime manu-facturer as well as other manufacturers on a long-term basis, there is the potential for an outsider to become one of the suppliers. Full vertical inte-gration eliminates such potential, of course. It is apparent that considerable effort is required on the part of a newcomer to be included in group transactions that are long-term-based.

51 Nissan's recent consolidated sales revenues (profits) were as follows: ¥6,039 billion (¥–88 billion); ¥6,580 billion (¥–27 billion); ¥5,977 billion (¥–684 billion); ¥6,089 billion (¥33,075 billion); ¥6,196 billion (¥372 billion); and ¥6,828 billion (¥495 billion), respectively, for fiscal years ending in March

1996, 1999, 2000, 2001, 2002 and 2003. Nissan's debt in 1999 exceeded ¥2,000 billion.

52   This includes top-down management.

53   Both Nissan and Hitachi were in the same prewar Nissan *zaibatsu* group and tied closely to the Industrial Bank of Japan (currently a part of the Mizuho Financial Group) since the war. In this sense, Nissan and Hitachi may still feel reasonably close to each other.

54   As noted above, Toyota has been strengthening its supplier *keiretsu* relationships.

55   Nissan's ten largest shareholders in March 1997 and March 2002 are as follows: (1) Daiichi Life Insurance (5.6% equity in Nissan); (2) Fuji Bank (4.6%); (3) Industrial Bank of Japan (4.4%); (4) Nippon Life Insurance (4.2%); (5) Asahi Bank (3.0%); (6) Sumitomo Bank (3.0%); (7) Nissan Fire & Casualties (2.0%); (8) Tokyo Mitsubishi Bank (2.0%); (9) Sumitomo Trust Bank (2.0%); and (10) Yasuda Fire & Causalties (1.9%) for March 1997; and (1) Renault (44.4%); (2) State Street Bank & Trust Co. (3.3%); (3) Mitsubishi Trust Bank trust accounts (2.8%); (4) Japan Trusty Service Trust Bank trust accounts (2.3%); (5) Daiichi Life Insurance (2.1%); (6) Chase Manhattan Bank N.A. London (1.9%); (7) Chase Manhattan Bank N.A. London S.L. omnibus accounts (1.9%); (8) Nippon Life Insurance (1.8%); (9) Boston Safety Deposit B.S.D.T. Treaty clients omnibus (1.5%); and (10) UFJ Trust Bank trust accounts (1.4%) for March 2002.

56   Ries (1993).

57   The ongoing problem of integrating Mizuho financial group's information systems, which were inherited from the former DKB, Fuji and Industrial Bank of Japan (IBJ), caused a massive failure in early 2003 in Mizuho's on-line banking operations. This failure is attributed to the refusal by the personnel of the former DKB and IBJ to adopt Fuji Bank's technically superior banking system as Mizuho's system.

58   The only exceptions occur when failing Japanese firms cannot find domestic rescuers. Then foreign firms can come in.

59   Sony and some other Japanese companies chose to adopt new forms of corporate governance in the 1990s involving various executive committees and outside directors. New Japanese laws on corporate governance allow such a choice. At the same time, another excellent company, Canon, chose to strengthen its internal board director system. Japanese firms' responses to the new laws appear quite variable.

60   The recent revisions of corporate governance laws have introduced the notion of outside board directors and more transparency in the governance mechanisms for Japanese corporations. Yet these new governance structures have not yet been widely implemented. It is unclear how much power will be given, for example, to the firms' individual shareholders.

61   For example, Fujitsu has recently introduced a new wage system, which does not have seniority component in the employees' wage determination.

62   This covers virtually all areas of Japanese life: for example, employment, health, education and social security.

References

Abe, M., Higuchi, Y., Kuhn, P., Nakamura, M. and Sweetman, A. (2002) 'Worker Displacement in Japan and Canada', in P. Kuhn (ed.), *Losing Work, Moving On:*

International Perspectives on Worker Displacement (Kalamazoo, Mich.: W. E. Upjohn Institute for Employment Research), pp. 195–300.

Aoki, M. (1988) *Information, Incentives and Bargaining in the Japanese Economy* (Cambridge and New York: Cambridge University Press).

Caves, R. E. and Uekusa, M. (1976) 'Industrial Organization in Japan', in H. Patrick and H. Rozovsky (eds), *Asia's New Giant: How the Japanese Economy Works* (Washington, DC: The Brookings Institution), pp. 459–523.

Ewing, J. (2003) 'Revolt of the Young', *Business Week*, 22 September, p. 48.

Fruin, W. M. (1983) *Kikkoman: Company, Clan, and Community* (Cambridge, Mass.: Harvard University Press).

Fruin, W. M. (1992) *Japanese Enterprise System: Competitive Strategies and Cooperative Structures* (Cambridge and New York: Cambridge University Press).

Fuss, M. and Waverman, L. (1990) 'Productivity Growth in the Motor Vehicle Industry, 1970–1984: A Comparison of Canada, Japan, and the United States', Working Paper No. 1735 (Cambridge, Mass.: National Bureau of Economic Research).

Ghosn, Carlos (2003) *'Waga nihongata keieino shinzuio kataro'* (My Japanese-style Management) (in Japanese), *Bungei Shunju*, August, pp. 138–46.

Hofstede, C. (1983) 'The Cultural Relativity of Organizational Practices and Theories', *Journal of International Business Studies*, Fall pp. 75–89.

Horiuchi, K. (1993) 'Factors Contributing to Corporate Growth in Japan', *Keiei Shirin*, vol. 30, no. 3, Hosei University, Tokyo, pp. 113–21.

Horiuchi, K. (1998) *Nihon keizaino vision to seisaku* (The Japanese Economy: Vision and Policy) (in Japanese) (Tokyo: Toyo Keizai).

Horiuchi, K. and Nakamura, M. (2001) 'Environmental Issues and Japanese Firms', in M. Nakamura (ed.), *The Japanese Business and Economic System: History and Prospects for the 21st Century* (Basingstoke/New York: Palgrave/Macmillan/St. Martin's Press), pp. 364–84.

Kato, T. (2001) 'Participatory Employment Practices in Japan', in M. Nakamura (ed.), *The Japanese Business and Economic System: History and Prospects for the 21st Century* (Basingstoke/New York: Palgrave/Macmillan/St. Martin's Press) pp. 46–80.

Korkie, R. and Nakamura, M. (1997) 'Block Holding and Keiretsu in Japan: The Effects of Capital Markets Liberalization Measures on the Stock Market', *Journal of International Money and Finance*, vol. 16, pp. 113–40.

Krafcik, J. F. (1988) 'Triumph of the Lean Production System', *Sloan Management Review*, vol. 30, pp. 41–51.

Lawrence, R. A. (1993) 'Japan's Different Trade Regime: An Analysis with Particular Reference to Keiretsu', *Journal of Economic Perspectives*, vol. 7, pp. 3–19.

Lieberman, L. B. and Asaba, S. (1997) 'Inventory Reduction and Productivity Growth: A Comparison of Japanese and US Automotive Sectors', *Managerial and Decision Economics*, vol. 18.

MacKay, C. (1841) *Extraordinary Popular Delusions and the Madness of Crowds.* Reproduced at: http://www.litrix.com/madraven/madne001.htm.

Morck, R. and Nakamura, M. (1995) 'Banks and Corporate Governance in Canada', in *Corporate Decision-Making in Canada*, Industry Canada Research Series, University of Calgary Press, pp. 787–805.

Morck, R. and Nakamura, M. (1999) 'Banks and Corporate Control in Japan', *Journal of Finance*, vol. 54, pp. 319–39.

Morck, R. and Nakamura, M. (2001) 'Japanese Corporate Governance and Macroeconomic Problems', in M. Nakamura (ed.), *The Japanese Business and Economic System: History and Prospects for the 21st Century* (Basingstoke/New York: Palgrave/Macmillan/ St. Martin's Press), pp. 325–49.

Morck, R. and Nakamura, M. (2003) 'Been There, Done That: The History of Corporate Ownership in Japan', Working Paper, (Cambridge, MA: National Bureau of Economic Research).

Morck, R., Nakamura, M. and Shivdasani, A. (2000) 'Banks, Ownership Structure, and Firm Value in Japan', *Journal of Business*, vol. 73, pp. 539–67.

Morgan, J. C. and Morgan, J. J. (1991) *Cracking the Japanese Market: Strategies for Success in the New Global Economy* (New York: Free Press).

Nakamura, A. and Nakamura, M. (1989) 'Inventory Management Behavior of American and Japanese Firms', *Journal of the Japanese and International Economies*, vol. 3, pp. 270–91.

Nakamura, A., Nakamura, M. and Seike, A. (2004) 'Aging, Female and Foreign Workers, and Japanese Labor Markets: An International Perspective, ch. 6 in this volume.

Nakamura, M. (1991a) 'Japanese Direct Investment in Asia-Pacific and Other Regions: Empirical Analysis Using MITI Survey Data', *International Journal of Production Economics*, vol. 25, pp. 219–29.

Nakamura, M. (1991b) 'Modeling the Performance of U.S. Direct Investment in Japan: Some Empirical Estimates', *Managerial and Decision Economics*, vol. 12, pp. 103–21.

Nakmura, M. (1993) 'Japanese Industrial Relations in an International Business Environment', *North American Journal of Economics and Finance*, vol. 4, pp. 225–51.

Nakamura, M. (2001) 'Introduction', in M. Nakamura (ed.), *The Japanese Business and Economic System: History and Prospects for the 21st Century* (Basingstoke/ New York: Palgrave/Macmillan/St. Martin's Press), pp. 1–9.

Nakamura, M. (2002) 'Mixed Ownership of Industrial Firms in Japan: Debt Financing, Banks and Vertical Keiretsu Groups', *Economic Systems*, vol. 26, pp. 231–47.

Nakamura, M. and Hubler, O. (1998) 'The Bonus Shares of Flexible Pay in Germany, Japan and the U.S.: Some Empirical Regularities', *Japan and the World Economy*, vol. 10, pp. 221–32.

Nakamura, M. and Nakamura, A. (1991) 'Risk Behavior and the Determinants of Bonus versus Regular Pay in Japan', *Journal of the Japanese and International Economies*, vol. 5, pp. 140–59.

Nakamura, M. and Vertinsky, I. (1994) *Japanese Economic Policies and Growth: Implications for Businesses in Canada and North America* (Edmonton, alberta: University of Alberta Press).

Nakamura, M., Sakakibara, S. and Schroeder, R. (1998) 'Adoption of Just-in-Time Manufacturing Methods at U.S. and Japanese Owned Plants: Some Empirical Evidence', *IEEE Transactions on Engineering Management*, vol. 45, pp. 230–40.

Nakamura, M., Sakakibara, S. and Schroeder, R. (1999) 'Just-in-Time and Other Manufacturing Practices, and Market Environment: Implications for Manufacturing Performance', in P. Adler, M. Fruin and J. Liker (eds), *Remade in America: Transplanting and Transforming Japanese Production Systems* (Oxford University Press), pp. 361–81.

Nakamura, M., Takahashi, T. and Vertinsky, I. (2001) 'Why Japanese Firms Choose to Certify: A Study of Managerial Responses to Environmental Issues', *Journal of Environmental Economics and Management*, vol. 42, pp. 23–52.

Nakamura, M., Vertinsky, I. and Zietsma, C. (1997) 'Does Culture Matter in Inter-firm Cooperation: Research Consortia in Japan and the U.S.', *Managerial and Decision Economics*, vol. 18, pp. 153–75.

Nakatani, I. (1984) 'The Economic Role of Financial Corporate Grouping', in M. Aoki (ed.), *The Economic Analysis of the Japanese Firm* (Amsterdam: North-Holland), pp. 227–58.

National Institute of Population and Social Security (2002) 'Estimates for Japan's Future Population', National Institute of Population and Social Security, Tokyo, January.

Reischauer, E. O. (1988) *The Japanese Today* (Cambridge, Mass.: Harvard University Press).

Sheard, P. (1991) 'The Role of Firm Organization in the Adjustment of a Declining Industry in Japan', *Journal of the Japanese and International Economies*, vol. 5, pp. 14–50.

Shleifer, A., and Vishny, R. W. (1986) 'Large Shareholders and Corporate Control', *Journal of Political Economy*, vol. 94, pp. 461–88.

Weinstein, D. and Yafeh, Y. (1998) 'On the Costs of a Bank-centered Financial System: Evidence from the Changing Main Bank Relations in Japan', *Journal of Finance*, vol. 53, pp. 635–72.

Index

Action Program for the Return of
    US Bases   90, 91
administrative institutions   21
Africa   125
aging   107
    population in Japan   6, 108, 128,
        130, 223
Ainu   158, 163, 166, 167, 169,
    174, 175
    Association of Hokkaido   158, 177
AIDS   43
Akebono   150, 152
Alliance   21
Allied Forces   80, 221, 232, 233, 251
American
    military bases   77, 78, 79,
        80–93, 97–101
    society   24
annual wage round (*shunto*)   136
anti-alliance   26
anti-discrimination measures   8
anti-monopoly laws   232, 233
Anti-Stalking Law (2000)   165
anti-trust   232
anti-trust laws   3
Asashoryu, Ozeki   144, 146, 150, 151
Asia   vii
Asia-Pacific Economic
    Cooperation   49
Asian Center for Women's Human
    Rights   163
Asian sex workers   161
Asian Women's Fund   163, 172
Australia   62
autonomy   viii

Bank of Japan   203, 222, 223,
    251, 256
Bank of Tokyo-Mitsubishi   245
bank-based or horizontal corporate
    groups (*keiretsu*)   108, 109, 113,
        115, 196, 200, 212, 220, 221, 226,
        231, 232, 233, 239, 242, 243, 244,
        245, 246, 250, 253, 255, 256
    see also keiretsu
Banzuke (the ranking order of all sumo
    wrestlers)   149

Basic Law on Gender Equality
    (1999)   165
Baumeister, Roy   56, 63
bribery   3
bonus payments   111, 112, 241, 249
BSE (bovine spongiform
    encephalopathy)   41, 47–8, 49
bubble economy   36
Bunka korosha   *see* Person of Cultural
    Merits
Bunka Kunsho   *see* Order of Culture
Buraku   158
Burakumin   163, 166, 169, 174, 175
    Liberation League   166
bushido   25, 31
business practices   11

Canada   12, 13, 62, 122, 226
Canada–US Free Trade
    Agreement   114
Canadian   57
    government   57, 69
    policies   109
    population   125
capital *keiretsu* (production-based
    vertical corporate groups)   227
capitalism   viii
Career Owl system   141
CEDAW   *see* Committee on the
    Elimination of Discrimination
    Against Women
Center for Japanese Research
    (CJR)   75
centre–local relations   93, 96,
    99, 100, 101
CERD   *see* Committee on the
    Elimination of All Forms
    of Racial Discrimination
Cheney, Dick   82
Child Prositution and Pornography
    Prohibition Act in Japan   162
Childcare and Family Care Leave
    Law   171
China   vii, 51, 254
Chinese
    civilization   21–2
    Ming dynasty   80

choices   10
Choshu domain   36
CISG (Convention on Contracts
   for the International Sale
   of Goods)   viii
   see also United Nations
civilization   21
Class-A war criminals   51
Coase Theorem   205, 208
Cold War   vii, 77, 80, 81, 82, 99
colonialism   xi
comfort women   162, 163
Committee on the Elimination of
   All Forms of Racial Discrimination
   (CERD)   159, 166, 167, 168,
   174, 175
Committee on the Elimination
   of Discrimination Against
   Women (CEDAW)   159, 163,
   164, 169, 172, 173, 174, 175,
   176, 177
competitive markets   1
conformity   ix–x
Confucianism   70
Consulate General of Japan in
   Vancouver   73
Consultative Body on the Problems
   of US Military Bases   87
contraceptive pill   165
corporate control mechanisms   231
corporate governance   231–3, 238–9,
   246, 248–9
Council for Gender Equality   170, 171
culture   21
corporate governance   11

Daiichi Kangyo   228, 245
   Bank (DKB)   246, 247; Research
      Institute   193
Daimler-Chrylser   249
Defense Agency   103
democratic society   3
democracy   1
Denso   227, 253
deregulation   188, 214
discrimination   117
dispute resolution ('Dispute Resolution
   Understanding')   viii
diversity   ix
Domestic Violence Prevention Law
   (2001)   165

economic crisis in East Asia   186
Edo era   12

electronic job matching information
   systems   141
Emperor Meiji   20
employment   107, 115, 133, 136, 242
   authorization   59
End Child Prostitution in Asian
   Tourism (ECPAT)   164
enforcement mechanisms   7, 117, 119
English as Second Language (ESL)
   57, 72, 73
environment   236–38
   Basic Law   165
environmentalism   236
Eto, Shimpei   22
equal employment opportunities   7
Equal Employment Opportunity Law
   (1997)   165, 253
ethnic minority   225
   women   169
Europe   12
European Union (EU)   3, 13, 221
   policies   109
Ex-post-facto   215, 216
   cost   207, 208–13, 217
   rule   205
   system   10
Ex-post responsibilities   10

family register (koseki)   172
female
   workers   115, 213
   labour   119
financial bubble   36, 107, 129,
   221, 222
firm-specific
   advantage   191
   management methods   246, 247
Ford   249
foreign direct investment (FDI)
   9, 115, 185–201, 234–6, 240
   inward   186–201
   outward   186, 194, 195
   promotion of   200–1
foreign firms   192–200, 230
foreign workers   6
   in Canada   123
   in Japan   123–4
fraud   10
Fuji   228, 249
   Bank   228, 245
   Heavy Industries   188
Fujitsu   256
Fukuda, Taiichi   12, 18
Fukuyama, Francis   13, 139

Fukuzawa, Yukichi   33, 38
  Gakumon no susume   34
full-time workers   121
Futenma Air Station   98

gaijin (foreigner, foreign)   144
GATS (General Agreement on Trade
    in Services)   viii
GDP (Gross Domestic Product)
    growth   203, 204
gender   169, 174
  as intersectionality   158
General Maresuke Nogi   19
General Motors   188, 225, 227, 249
genetically modified (GM)   236
geopolitics   80
Germany   140
Ghosn, Carlos   244
Ginowan City   81
global competitiveness   113, 114, 223
global-local linkages   77, 79
globalization   vii, xi, 17–18, 37,
    47, 50, 55, 212, 221, 233, 235,
    239, 240
  Asian experience with   xii
  and Canadian immigration   128
  economic   77
  impacts of   99, 139
  Japan's   1
  of Japanese economy   123
  of Japanese society   11, 203, 221
  social cohesion and   xi
  the bubble and   114
  values and   31
  world economy   107
government   2
  of Kumamoto Prefecture   42
  regulations   9
Grand Sumo (*Ozumo*)   154
G8 Summit   40, 80, 87, 97, 101

Hashimoto, Ryutaro   92, 96
Harvard University   37
Hawaii   73, 146, 148, 150, 152, 153
Heiankyo   31
Heijokyo   30
hemophiliac   43
Hewlett-Packard   122
Hirohito (Emperor Hirohito)   163
Hokkaido   13, 46, 158
hollowing out   115, 236
Honda   238, 249
  USA   225
honesty   32

hostile takeover   247
Housing Loan Corporation
    (HLC)   218
human capital   110, 214
human rights   70
  violation   161, 162
hyperinflation   137

'identity deficit'   56, 63–4, 66, 74
illegal foreign workers   6, 124, 140
IBM Japan   140, 234
IMF–GATT system   251
immigration   123, 124, 125
  in Canada   124–8
  laws   139
immigrants   6, 56–7, 124
  equal employment opportunities
    for   7–8
Inamine, Keiichi   96, 99
individual
  rights   7
  tastes and preferences   10
individualism   viii
individualization   205, 206, 207
Indonesia   vii
Industrial Bank of Japan   228, 245
industrial relations   109–11, 224, 249
industrial structure   129
information technology (IT)   214
intellectual property   214
inter-firm relationships   230,
    239, 242
international migration   65
International Movement Against
    All Forms of Discrimination and
    Racism (IMADR)   166, 173
internationalization   1, 17, 20, 25
  advantage   192
Internet   65
ISO (International Organization for
    Standardization) 14001   237
Isuzu   249
Italy   140

Japan   vii, xi
  birth rate   140
  education system   4
  environmental problems   40, 47
  foreign trade   194
  Grand Sumo Association
    (Kyokai)   144, 146, 147, 152, 154
  health problems   41, 47
  industrialization   26
  internationalization   20

Japan (*Continued*)
　immigration policies　24
　land　28–31
　NGO Network for CEDAW
　　(JNNC)　170, 172, 173, 177
　social problems　40, 47
　Inc.　12
Japan Sumo Association (Nihon
　　Sumo Kyokai)　6
Japan–USA Security Treaty　5, 81
Japanese
　Army　163
　auto industry　236–8
　business　183
　business practices　223, 238,
　　239, 240
　business and economic system
　　8, 11, 248
　Canadian Citizens' Association
　　Human Rights Committee　60
　capitalism　29
　Community Volunteers'
　　Association　75
　corporations　11, 114, 117, 122,
　　131, 134, 186, 187, 195, 212,
　　230, 231, 243
　culture　6
　economy　11, 107, 197
　Equal Employment Law　117, 119
　External Trade Organization
　　(JETRO)　187
　feminism　160, 161, 163, 164
　immigrants to Canada　56–7, 69
　industrial relations　109–11, 224
　internationalization of　9
　isolation　22–3
　government　10
　labour markets　107, 130–1, 139
　local government　86, 88
　management methods　6
　media　65
　National Railways　217
　Overseas Development Assistance
　　(ODA)　171
　'self'　56, 69, 74
　Social Services Network　60–1
　society　2 , 203, 220
　women　5, 226
　workforce　134
Japanese–Canadian　69, 70, 73
job rotation　225
just-in-time (*kanban*) production
　　system　224, 235
　see also kanban

Kadena
　Air Base　98
　town　81
Kamakura period　33
kanban (just-in-time production
　　system)　224, 235
Keio University　38
keiretsu　108, 109, 113, 115,
　　196, 200, 212, 220, 221,
　　226, 231, 232, 233, 239, 242,
　　243, 244, 245, 246, 250, 253,
　　255, 256
　financial　228
　vertical groups　108, 232, 233, 242,
　　243, 244, 245
Kikkoman dispute　139
Koizumi, Junichiro　10, 36, 40, 203,
　　214, 217
Konishiki, Yasokichi　146, 150, 152
knowledge　vii
　transfer　235
Korea　vii, 51, 62, 83, 146
Korean residents　163, 166, 167, 169,
　　174, 175
Korean Council for the Women
　　Drafted for Military Sexual
　　Slavery in Japan, the　163
koseki (family register)　172
Kumamoto University　41
Kyokutenhou　150
Kyokushuzan　150
Kyoto　31
　Protocol　236

locational advantage　192
labor
　contracts　112
　disputes　109
　management　11
　market　6, 129, 240–2;
　　demand　129; supply　129
　unions　109, 136, 249
land speculation　28
landowners　84, 85
large-scale mergers　249
Large-Boned Principle　214, 215
Law on Proscribing Stalking Behavior
　　and Assisting Victims　171
Law for Punishing Acts Related to
　　Child Prostitution and Child
　　Pornography and for Protecting
　　Children　170
layoffs　240, 241
LDP　*see* Liberal Democratic Party

legalization of the contraceptive
  pill 165
Liberal Democratic Party (LDP)
  92, 102
liberalization 199
  Japanese computer market 12
licensing requirements 9
life-cycle 118, 132
lifetime employment 110, 111, 131,
  132, 137
Long-term Bank of Japan 187
long-term employment 110, 111,
  231, 240, 244
LSD (lysergic acid diethylamide) 71

Maedayama (Master Takasago) 148
main bank 229
Mainichi Art Award 20
Makuuchi championship 144, 146
male workers 108
male–female wage differential 119
Malta 82
management 6
  labour committees 138
  skills 11
mandatory retirement 134, 135
'Marginal interested parties' (MIPs)
  211, 212, 213
  hypothesis 211
market access 230
market economy 24
market mechanism 205, 217, 218
market value 253
marketization 203, 212
marijuana 71–2
Mazda 249
mass media 49, 65
Master Takasago 148
Meiji Constitution 29, 33
Meiji Restoration 1, 9, 19, 21,
  220, 221
Meiji values 17–18, 34, 37
mental health 55, 74, 74–5
mergers and acquisitions
  (M&As) 185, 187
mid-career
  hiring 116
  workers 240
Midori Cross Pharmaceutical
  Company 43–4
migrant workers 168, 169, 174
military
  bases 5
  government 109

Minamata 254
  Bay 42
  city 41
  disease 49
Ministry of Agriculture, Forestry and
  Fisheries (MAFF) 47
Ministry of Economy, Trade, and
  Industry (METI) 197, 201
Ministry of Education, Culture, Sports,
  Science and Technology 11, 51
Ministry of Finance 12, 37, 255
Ministry of Foreign Affairs 12
Ministry of General Affairs of
  Japan 218
Ministry of Health and Welfare 42–3
Ministry of International Trade and
  Industry (MITI) 12, 42
minority women 158
minority workers
Mitsubishi 228
  Motor Company 249; scandal
    45, 47
  Motor Manufacturing of America
    (MMMA) 122
  Trust Bank 245
Mitsui 228
  Bank 228, 247
Mizuho Financial Group 228, 256
modern civilization 24
Mondale, Walter 91
Mongolian 144, 149, 152
  sumo wrestler (*bufu*) 146, 147
Monsanto 236
multinational enterprises
  (MNEs) 185, 186, 188,
    190, 191, 192, 193, 194,
    234, 254
multiple discrimination against
  minority women in Japan 158
multi-task
  capabilities 252
  skills 110
Murayama, Tomiichi 42
Musashimaru 150, 153

Naoki Prize 19
Nago City 93, 95, 98, 101
Nagoya 66
Nakamura, Masanao 34
Nara 30
negative feedback 43, 51
nenko (seniority-based) 110, 131
neo-colonialism xi
Netherlands, the 12, 28, 30

Network for the Convention on
the Elimination of All Forms of
Discrimination Against Women
(CEDAW)   8
New York City   198
New Zealand   62, 73
Nikko Toshogu Shrine   47
Niigata Prefecture   42
Nippon Keidanren   13
Nippon Steel   247
Nippon Telegraph and Telephone
Public Corporation (NTT)   217
Nisei (second-generation Americans
of Japanese descent)   146
Nissan   109, 186, 243, 244, 255–6
non-economic values   50
non-government organizations (NGOs)
5, 8, 166, 168, 169, 172, 175
non-performing loans
Normal, Illinois   122
North America   55–56, 69, 71, 74,
112, 117, 119, 226
North American Free Trade
Agreement (NAFTA)   114
wage system   133
nuclear criticality   44
Nuclear Safety Committee of
the Science and Technology
Agency   45
Nye Report   83

Obuchi, Keizo   35, 38, 97, 203
Oceania   12
Office of Gender Equality   170
office (white-collar) workers   225
oil crises   137
Okinawa
Prefecture   4, 12, 77–104
City   81
Okinawans   163, 166, 167, 169,
174, 175
on-the-job training   110, 225
Oops!   66
Optional Protocol to CEDAW   172
see also CEDAW
Order of Culture (*Bunka kunsho*)   20
Osaka   66
Osaka Gaigo Gakko   18
Osaka University of Foreign
Studies   18
Ota, Masahide   89, 90, 91, 95, 96
overtime   112
Oxfam International   103
Ozumo (Grand Sumo)   154

Pacific Asia   4
participatory management   249
part-timers   112, 121
Peer Net   60
penal laws   21
Person of Cultural Merits (*Bunka
korosha*)   20
personnel management system   134
Philippines   83
Plaza Accord (1986)   222
Port of Nagasaki   12
positive feedback   51
post-bubble
Japanese business   183
period   223
recession   223
post-Second World War
107, 114, 123, 132, 136,
162, 199, 220, 221, 223,
224, 232
Prefectural Governor   89, 95
Prime Minister   10
prior cost   207, 208–10
intensive system   209, 210
privatization   188, 214
problem-solving   40–1, 47, 48
product liability rules   3
production system   224
just-in-time (JIT) (*kanban*)   224, 235
production (blue-collar) workers   225
professional sumo   7
public decision-making   3
public disclosure   3
public interest   11
public ownership   28

Ramseyer, J. M.   211, 213
ranking order of all sumo wrestlers
(*Banzuke*)   149
Ranks for Grand Sumo wrestlers   145
'rape incident'   80, 83, 99
regulation of foreign sumo
wrestlers   147
Renault   186, 243, 244, 249
research and development
(R&D)   115, 193, 195, 240
revision of Alien Registration Law
(1999)   213
Ripplewood   187
ritsuryo system   21–2
Round Table on the Municipalities
of Okinawa Accommodating
US Military Bases   92, 93
Russo–Japanese War   51

Secondary labor markets 248
Sakamoto, Ryoma 19
Sakigake New Harbinger Party 102
Sakura Bank 245, 247
salary system 155
samurai 32
  class 25
  values 25, 31–2
San Francisco Peace Treaty
    (1952) 167
Sangyo Hokoku Kai (Wartime
    Association of Industry) 109
Sankei Shinbun 19
Sanwa 228
Sasakibara, Eisuke 37
Sato, Eisaku 12
Satsuma domain 36
Shiba, Ryotaro 2, 17–39
second-generation Americans of
    Japanese descent (Nisei) 146
Second World War 1, 5, 51, 146,
    185, 240
secondary labor markets 226
Seibu Group of companies 123
seniority-based wage system
    7, 110, 131
seppuku (self-immolation) 32
sex commodification 161
shareholders 231, 232,
    233, 238–9, 245,
    247, 248
Shinto 51
Shojiki 32–3
Showa Denko 42
shunto (annual wage round) 136
Singapore 28, 30
Sino–Japanese war 51
social cohesion vii, ix-xi
Social Democratic Party (SDP) 102
social disorder ix-x
social safety-net 138
social security 214
sojourners 55–75
Sony 206
Spain 140
Special Action Committee for
    Okinawa (SACO) 86, 87–91,
    93–4, 98
Spirit of the Edoites (*Edokko
    kokoroiki*) 25
Sri Lanka vii
stable shareholding practices 247
stable-masters 153
standardization 9

statistical discrimination 13
student visa 58
Sumimoto 228
  Bank 228, 229, 245
sumo
  wrestlers 144; foreign 144,
    146–54, 156; human capital
    of 155
  wrestling 6–7
suppliers 11, 109, 114, 242–3

Taiheiki (Record of the Great
    Peace) 28
tainted blood incident 43, 49
Taiwan 90, 146
Taiyo Kobe Bank 247
Takahanada 153
'Takahanada boom' 153
Takamiyama, Daigoro 146, 148,
    150, 152
technology vii
Thailand 140
Tokugawa 19, 28, 30, 31, 33, 36
  Shogunate 250
Tokyo 66, 85, 99, 100
  District Court 43
  War Tribunal 51
Tonari Gumi 75
Toyota 109, 139, 226,227,
    237, 238, 243, 249,
    253, 256
  Prius 236
  production system 139, 224
Toys Я Us 196, 197
trade in services ('GATS
    Agreement') viii
trade-related intellectual property
    ('TRIPs Agreement') viii
trade-related investment measures
    ('TRIMs Agreement') viii
transaction cost 205, 208
TRIPs (Trade-Related Aspects of
    Intellectual Property Rights)
    Agreement viii
TRIMs (Trade-Related Investment
    Measures) Agreement viii
twentieth century 7
twenty-first century 7

UK 23, 125, 127
unemployed 108, 138
unemployment 107, 115,
    129, 130, 139, 218,
    223, 252

United Nations   159, 164, 171, 174,
    176, 201
  CEDAW Convention   8
  Convention Against Transnational
    Organized Crime   171
  Convention on Contracts for the
    International Sale of Goods
    (CISG)   viii
  Convention on the Rights of the
    Child (CRC)   164
universality of civilization   21
University of British Columbia
    (UBC)   59
US   3, 4–5, 10, 13, 23–4,113,
    122, 127, 221, 226,
    233, 254
  Ambassador to Japan
  Defense Secretary   82, 83
  government   44
  military bases   77, 78, 79, 80–93,
    97–101
  policies   109
  -style law schools   114
US Center for Disease
    Control   43
US–Soviet Summit   82

value system   vii
values, Meiji   17

Vancouver   55–63, 65–8, 71–5
  Vancouver Shinpo   65–6
  Vancouver Tonight   66
Violence Against Women in War
    Network Japan   163

wage adjustments   111
Wakanohana   153
'WakaTaka boom'   153
Wartime Association of Industry   109
Weber, Max   29
Western
  civilization   33
  feminism   160
women   5, 117, 119, 225
  career   13
  equal opportunities for   7
work permit   59
working holiday visa   12, 55, 57
World Conference Against Racism
    (WCAR)   159, 166, 168, 176
World Trade Organization
    (WTO)   viii, 49

Yasukuni Shrine   40, 51
Yokozuna rank   145, 146, 149

zaibatsu families   220, 250
Zhejiang University   52